ALONG AMSTERDAM'S WATERFRONT

Compiled and written by: Sabine Lebesque

With contributions by: Daphna Beerdsen, Yttje Feddes,
Aart Hiemstra, Maarten Kloos, Ernest Kurpershoek,
Merel Ligtelijn, Marinus Oostenbrink, Ingrid Oosterheerd,
Evert Verhagen

Photography: Lard Buurman, Johan Olsthoorn

Valiz, Amsterdam
Amsterdam Development Corporation
ProjectManagementBureau Amsterdam

ALONG AMSTER- DAM'S WATER- FRONT

Exploring the architecture of
Amsterdam's Southern IJ Bank

Foreword

For centuries the South Bank of the IJ was
characterised by activities connected with the
harbour. Amsterdam owes its existence to them.
But during the twentieth century the docklands
area increasingly became an industrial zone
that no longer really belonged to the city. The
harbour began to move westwards in the 1970s,
leaving the bank of the IJ deserted.
During the last thirty years, however, a radical
change has taken place in thinking about the
waterline. And that is not all. Within a relatively
short period of time, the South Bank has been
transformed into a mixed zone of housing,
commercial activities and recreation, and the
North Bank is following in its wake to undergo
the same metamorphosis. The spatial qualities
of the IJ are utilised to the full. The city has
given the water a new meaning which has an
economic, social and cultural influence.
The local authority has cooperated intensively
with residents, users and market parties to get
the development of the IJ Banks under way in
a manner that is appropriate to Amsterdam. It
was a process of exploration, doggedness and
determination, but in the end we have chosen
a course that has strengthened the peculiar
quality of Amsterdam.
Together with the ProjectManagementBureau
(PMB) and Port of Amsterdam, the Amsterdam
Development Corporation (OGA) has taken the
initiative of visually charting the areas and projects on the South Bank of the IJ. Thematic texts
by several authors and a special photographic
assignment provide background information
about the IJ and its significance for the city. In
addition, an interview with the former project
managers of the South Bank Project Group
provides insight into the deliberations and activities of the local authority which have determined the implementation of the development.
As official placer of assignments of the South
Bank project, for the last six years I have been

intensively involved with many of the projects for buildings, both those that have been realised and those that are still awaiting completion. But what is more, as a citizen of Amsterdam I am fascinated by the way in which the IJ has gradually become the centre of the city again. I hope that everyone who follows these routes on foot or by bicycle will be as enthusiastic as I am about all the buildings, bridges, works of art and other locations that determine the aspect of the South Bank.

Edo Arnoldussen
Director* Amsterdam Development Corporation
(OGA)

*director until October 2006

ANCHORS IN THE IJ

Interview with two former project managers of the South Bank of the IJ

Ingrid Oosterheerd

The banks of the IJ in Amsterdam are undergoing a profound metamorphosis. Where the waterfront and related activities once determined the character of the banks, a new waterfront is slowly but surely emerging. It is the site of a new urban environment built as an extension and reinforcement of the historic heart of the city. It is characterised by high building densities and a large degree of combined functions. By 2006 building activity is going ahead at full pace on the quays and banks of the IJ. The South Bank has taken the lead, where large residential, commercial and cultural buildings have been completed with great regularity since the late 1990s. The developments on the North Bank got under way later: the first building activities on this bank commenced at the start of 2006.

Kees van Ruyven and Pierre van Rossum have both been project managers of the South Bank of the IJ. Van Ruyven, who is now project manager for the Hembrug area, was project manager from 1994 to 2001. Van Rossum, who is now deputy director of the ProjectManagementBureau (PMB), was project manager from 2001 to the end of 2005. It was partly under their inspiring leadership that the plans were formulated and implemented. Van Rossum: 'As project managers of the South Bank of the IJ, within the history of the development we were part of a larger whole. The South Bank has a long history and many of those involved played a leading role. Councillors like Jeroen Saris and Duco Stadig, as well as Edo Arnoldussen and Hans Gerson in their capacity as directors, were of great importance in this history, as were the supervisors Tjeerd Dijkstra, Kees Rijnboutt and Michael van Gessel. And I have not yet mentioned all the other parties involved, such as the urban planners, the architects, and the various developers. Intensive cooperation and consultation at every level, a typically Amsterdam process.'

The formulation of plans for this large-scale transformation began dozens of years ago. A major stimulus was the definitive decision of the local authority in the mid-1970s to transfer all harbour activities to the western side of Amsterdam. A large 'empty' area was the result. In spite of the opening of the North Sea Canal in 1876, the Eastern Harbour Area was still in use in the mid-1970s, and many ocean-going vessels had to pass from IJmuiden past the inner city of Amsterdam on their way to the Eastern Harbour Area. This situation had become inconvenient because of the increase of scale in industry, the steady growth of harbour activities and other factors. After the Second World War operations began to develop a real Amsterdam Harbour region on the banks of the North Sea Canal. From the 1960s, the Eastern Harbour Area gradually fell into disuse, and the decision taken in 1975 to transfer all harbour activities once and for all to the West was the final straw. In the ensuing years the Eastern Harbour Area and the areas that flanked them were slowly but surely abandoned. The moment had come for the city to think seriously about what that meant for the future.

In 1978 a new city council took office. The economy was slowing down at the time and there were plenty of business locations available, but the housing market was under strong pressure. Urban renewal called for new land for housing and relocated businesses. The land in the Eastern Docklands passed from the hands of the Port of Amsterdam to those of the Development department (Grondbedrijf) of the Amsterdam Local Authority, and in the municipal programme agreement for 1978-1982 this archipelago of dockland islands was designated as a new residential district. The existing qualities of the Java Island, KNSM Island and Borneo-Sporenburg – the enormous stretches of quayside, incorporated in the large-scale infrastructure of waterways and situated on the outskirts of the inner city –

made this area a potentially highly attractive residential district.

The character that the dockland architecture imposed turned out to be a great asset. Several characteristic warehouses have been deliberately preserved, while the new architecture refers to them. The elaboration of the first urban development plans got under way in the late 1980s, and between 1985 and 2001 an entirely new city district was built in the former Eastern Harbour Area.

But Amsterdam set its sights further afield: other areas on the South Bank were interesting for urban expansion. In 1986 the Economic Affairs department initiated a successive IJ Banks study. The winners were Alle Hosper and Henk de Boer. It is interesting to note that the municipal initiative came not from the Spatial Planning department (dRO) but from that of Economic Affairs. This initiative was taken primarily to revive the economic life of the inner city and to strengthen the business climate. It was also a reaction to the international Zeitgeist. One waterfront after another sprang up in large cities abroad, such as in Baltimore and Seattle, but also in the United Kingdom and Germany. The new waterfronts in the United States were a particular source of inspiration.

In 1986 the councillor for Economic Affairs held a competition for the Oosterdok, where the Oosterdokseiland is being redeveloped in 2006. Urban planners, artists and well-known architects submitted ambitious plans and ideas. This was a signal for the Spatial Planning department to take over the initiative.

That department issued a 'Memorandum with Premises for the IJ Banks' in 1991, and in the same year the urban designer Urhahn, who was employed by the department, developed the so-called Land Abutment Model. This urban development plan contained a design for a waterfront to the East and West of the Central Station with a lot of high-rise buildings and a generous office programme. Some parts of this plan were implemented at the time: the Chamber of Commerce, the Ibis Hotel, and the office tower block next to it. The tower block was part of the Land Abutment Model. High-rise buildings were planned at the ends of the island on which the Central Station stands, above the underground passages running beneath the rail viaduct, on both the IJ side and the side facing the city.

The economy started to pick up and the time was ripe for ambitious plans. Private initiatives received a lot of elbow-room and support from the local authority. The public/private enterprise Amsterdam Water Front (AWF) was set up in 1991. It developed a very ambitious business plan for the South Bank. 'In retrospect you can say that the Amsterdam Water Front was a reaction to the failure of the Spatial Planning department's plans to materialise. It was thus the result of frustration', says Kees van Ruyven. He continues: 'But at the time there was also a strong conviction that a Public Private Partnership (PPP) was the solution for the development of the South Bank, and Amsterdam Water Front was given a lot of elbow-room and support, stimulated by national government.'
The starting capital of the enterprise was 30 million guilders (more than 13.6 million euros). The Amsterdam local authority as public partner had a 50% share in the whole and provided half of the starting capital. The private partners (15% for the Nationale Nederlanden insurance company and 35% for NMB Postbank) provided the other half. 'An unusual feature was the fact that the director of the Amsterdam Water Front, Jaap van Rijs, came from the private sector. In other words, the private party directed the design team led by Rem Koolhaas and thus largely determined the direction and content of the business plan. The local authority was more or less left out and was only

entrusted with the zoning plan. This zoning plan was the only way that the local authority could exercise influence, try to keep the market under control, and guarantee the quality.'

In spite of all the effort and ambitious plans, the Amsterdam Water Front was a flop. There were various reasons for this. The business plan of the Amsterdam Water Front had a considerable programme and proposed important changes at the political and financial levels that were financially and politically out of the question in the short term. Koolhaas came up with a proposal for several islands beside the river bank (the archipelago concept). An IJ boulevard was introduced to make the area easily accessible. This two-lane boulevard ran both in front of and behind the Central Station. This turned out to be a highly sensitive political issue. And that was not all. Proposals followed for a North-South metro link, an IJ metro to IJburg, and the closure of the small circle line. The Central Station was to become the big central junction for all this. The programme was pumped up to make the plan financially feasible. The logic behind this was that a modified (office) programme was supposed to contribute to covering the financial side of the plan. This turned out to be a mistake, because the office market collapsed again at that very moment, so that the basis of the whole plan crumbled.

But there other reasons too. The plan won less and less political support and the councillor responsible, Saris, could no longer count on backing. Clutching at straws to get the plan through, the Amsterdam Water Front asked for another planned top location for the office market in the city, the Zuidas (South Axis), to be frozen because of competition. This demand fell on deaf ears, because by then the Zuidas already had a dynamic of its own. Pierre van Rossum: 'At that turbulent moment the Development department issued a booklet on the locations in the city. It stated that the international top location was not the IJ Banks but the Zuidas. In fact, you can say that this statement dealt the coup de grâce to the Amsterdam Water Front. The business plan was presented to the cabinet in 1993, with a book that had the format of half a table. That was typical of the plan, that exaggeration. Soon afterwards, less than six months later, the Amsterdam Water Front went under.'

After this débâcle the local authority began to tread water. It was dissatisfied with its role and position within the Amsterdam Water Front. The local authority had relinquished control too much. That had to change. In response to all this, an important management instrument was created in 1994: the official principalship. This meant that from now on the commissions for every metropolitan project would be placed by a duo: the councillor responsible and the official principal. As project director, the latter was ultimately responsible for and organised the entire project. Another important change was that a project budget was now introduced for each project. To achieve the objective, the official principal could now decide which (municipal) services or disciplines would be brought in to fulfil that purpose, whereas in the past those services had been able to determine whether they took part in projects or not. Finally, the directive mechanism, the political decision and the plan formation system acquired more status.

In 1994 the local authority defined the South Bank as an individual metropolitan project with Hans Gerson, director of the municipal Development department, as its official principal. Kees van Ruyven, who at that time was still project manager of the Eastern Harbour Area for the Spatial Planning department, was invited by the official principal to become manager of the project. His brief was to issue a proposal on how the local authority could regain control of the project. Three months later he came up with the strategy memorandum 'Anchors in the IJ'. His proposal was to begin not with an urban development plan, but with a development strategy, so that urban development could then be directed in the light of that strategy.

In 1995 the memorandum 'Anchors in the IJ' was accepted by the council. The memorandum is conceived in terms of the process as a strategy for conquering the area. The basic idea was: chop the South Bank up into pieces, and take over the archipelago concept formulated by Koolhaas. Each island is given an identity of its own, and as many of the existing buildings as possible are preserved. The relation with the existing city is brought about by the deliberate placing of a number of 'Anchors': public attractions such as a building or a square. Breaking the plan down into sections enables development per area, while the water and infrastructure guarantee the links. An important point was that this separate development of each area was independent of the development of the structure. A separate urban development theme could be formulated for each island, and several developers would work on it. Van Ruyven: 'The anchoring was to proceed through existing corridors, such as the Kattenburgerstraat and the Damrak, in other words, take advantage of those links in order to reach the IJ from the city centre at all. Accept the railway embankment, accept the existing passageways beneath the viaduct, but invest in them and invest in the public space to make it more accessible.'

Van Rossum adds: 'On the South Bank we deliberately sought public buildings that would attract people to the area. Not just the library and the conservatory on the Oosterdokseiland, but also buildings on the Oostelijke Handelskade such as Panama and Warehouse De Zwijger. De Zwijger was really intended as an anchor, and that is what it has become. But you also have the Central Station, the Muziekgebouw, the Passenger Terminal, NEMO, the Maritime Museum, and ARCAM. A conglomerate that has become a worthy counterpart to the Museumplein.'

Van Ruyven had described in his strategy memorandum how the implementation of urban development and architecture in each separate area was to be organised. First a supervisory team had to be set up that would join in the consultations regarding content and exercise a supervisory function. The architects Tjeerd Dijkstra and Kenneth Green had already been involved in the Amsterdam Water Front as supervisors. Dijkstra came back into the new team, to which were added the landscape architect Alle Hosper and the urban designer Ton Schaap from the Spatial Planning department. The first priority was to take a good look at the existing conditions on each island and to contract out the urban design and architecture research creatively, each time anew, via a multiple assignment or a competition. Van Ruyven: 'From the formulation of the assignment it is possible to exercise a strong directive function and to choose from what will provide the best content. That embroidered on the procedure followed for the development of the Eastern Harbour Area, but the South Bank was a different task, especially because of the different programme and different property relations. The Eastern Harbour Area was a council housing assignment, while the South Bank was more of an inner city assignment in which different programmes had to be introduced. Thus the Westerdokseiland has much more of a housing programme, the Stationseiland is above all a logistical assignment, and the Oosterdokseiland has an absolutely urban programme combining housing, work and recreation. Those differences were then elaborated programmatically.'
After seven years of intensive work on the South Bank, Kees van Ruyven resigned in 2001

as project manager. The drama connected with De Zwijger was a signal for him to stop. He had devoted a lot of energy to preserving De Zwijger and giving it a programme. Then while pile-driving was going on for the Jan Schaefer bridge, the construction was in danger of collapsing. At that moment the second developer came up with a financially impossible plan. Councillor Stadig and the official principal Gerson then said: stop and demolish. There was no more political support for him. Van Ruyven: 'De Zwijger was a real turning point for me. I felt absolutely that they had wiped the floor with me, and then I felt that I was not up to it any more and decided to leave.' But Van Ruyven did not go until the negotiations concerning the Oosterdokseiland had been completed.

Pierre van Rossum was his successor. Van Rossum: 'I had been working on the Zuidas for a considerable number of years. We were in the implementation stage there, but the South Bank project still had to cross that bridge. The first thing I did was to see whether the strategy still made sense. No objections could be raised to the urban development concept, the development strategy, it was just very good.' His brief was to simplify it in certain parts, because it had become too complex and too ambitious. Generally speaking, however, it was already too late for that, because the development contracts had already been signed and the zoning plans were in production. Marking time would mean delay, and delay costs money. The stake was to carry out the splendid plan and to arrange the organisation in a way that would make that possible.

From experience he know that a good organisation of the building logistics is crucial on building locations. All the developments were taking place at the same time and, in contrast to the Amsterdam Water Front, not one but forty initiators were active. The management of the public space was also an important focus of attention. Van Rossum: 'When I took over as project manager, the Oostelijke Handelskade was a dump. Sawn down trees, street lighting that did not work, and no fences around the building sites. I had learnt on the Zuidas: that is not on. If you are presently going to ask the developers to invest a lot of money in good architecture, the local authority has to make sure that the public space is in order.'

A lot of investments were also required to settle a number of unresolved issues once and for all. Several zoning plans had not yet been completed, and the building and demolition permits still had to be arranged. A good legal apparatus was set up to get it all done. Another crucial point was directing the programme. Public attractions were essential to get the area moving and a number of very important initiatives for public investments were not yet complete. The economy was entering another bad period, so it was important for the local authority to liquidify unresolved initiatives. Enthusiastically, Van Rossum continues: 'A few words about ambition. The Zuidas was once regarded as a competitor and the Amsterdam Water Front wanted it to be frozen. That did not happen. Later the functions for the South Bank and the Zuidas were separated so that there was theoretically no competition any longer. Both projects are a great success. In practice (healthy) tension can arise from time to time. If the Ahold concern has to decide where to relocate, it considers the Zuidas and it considers the South Bank. Or if the magistrate's court beside the Prinsengracht has to find new premises, it considers both the Zuidas and the South Bank. The stakes for the South Bank are very ambitious. On the Oosterdokseiland we started with foreign architects like Chipperfield, Ito, and Cruz & Ortiz. In the course of the process these architects dropped out of the running. And on the Westerdokseiland the originally strong position of a fantastic firm like MVRDV collapsed. Practice shows that not everything is possible, nor is everything necessary.'

Both of them are very satisfied with what has already been built. Many of their ambitions have been achieved, not only because the time was on their side, but also because a climate could be created for them. They are particularly proud of the addition of many functions to the inner city. Van Ruyven: 'The tip of the Oostelijke Handelskade already works, and that is just the start of the route. And soon, with the completion of the various functions on the Oosterdokseiland and Westerdokseiland, it will be a revelation to the people of Amsterdam.' Van Ruyven and Van Rossum view the current developments with interest, such as the design of the public space and the taking over of the area by the new users. Erna Hollander is the new project manager for the South Bank. It is her task to round the project off successfully. Van Ruyven and Van Rossum have their reservations about the plan of the newly appointed council to build a bridge over the IJ. The link with North Amsterdam is by means of the ferries, the water taxis and water buses over the IJ, not with a bridge.

Van Rossum:' If we have to wind up the interview by telling what the most successful building or event was, I can cite a splendid moment. Kees and I were both at a course when we were asked: "What is your most fantastic project, and what is your most terrible project?" We both replied: "Warehouse Wilhelmina" – the most terrible project in my eyes, the most fantastic project for Kees.' They laugh. Pierre van Rossum: 'Kees contested the plan and I had to see how we were going to get it implemented... and now we are both proud that it has worked!'

Along Amsterdam's Waterfront

Ferries behind the Central Station

1.

MINERVA-HAVEN, HOUT-HAVENS

The Minervahaven and Houthaven area has been traditionally characterised by 'wet' industry: businesses that receive and supply deliveries by water, such as timber firms. When these companies increasingly switched to road transport, the Houthaven was filled in in 1945. The Minervahaven remained a genuine harbour area, but is now in need of attention: it no longer satisfies today's requirements, despite the proximity of the A10 ring road access is becoming increasingly a problem, and it is very untidy. Amsterdam Harbour has drawn up a development vision based on the principle that the area should gradually be transformed into an urban business estate. Through intensive use of the space and the addition of more land it will be possible to offer more space to a variety of small-scale enterprises, with an emphasis on the creative industry, such as advertising agencies and firms of architects. The Minervahaven cannot be used for housing as long as the industrial activities west of the Mercuriushaven with their specific environmental requirements continue to exist.

In the Houthavens, on the other hand, the water is being reintroduced because of the popularity of waterfront housing. According to the urban development plan drawn up by Vera Yanovshtchinsky, the area can accommodate around 1,700 homes (30% of which are rented council homes), about 54,000 m² of office and business space, a hotel, a primary school, a water sports centre, the studio building De Bonte Zwaan, and moorings for houseboats and retired skippers. Seven islands are planned with a lot of water, greenery and recreational facilities. The transition from the existing prewar Spaarndammer neighbourhood to the new neighbourhood will be effected by means of a wide green recreational strip for residents from both parts of the district, with a tunnel underneath for through traffic. Building is expected to commence at the beginning of 2008. Until then, the abandoned sites are being used as temporary accommodation for students.

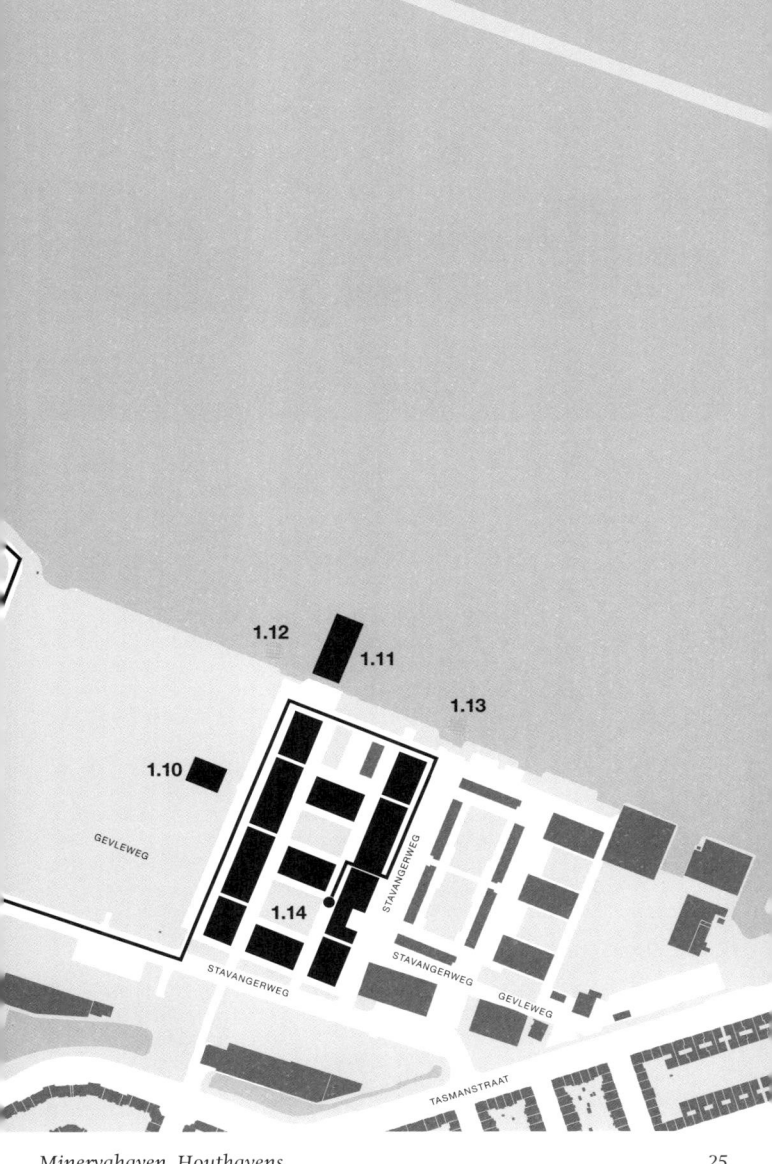

1.12

1.11

1.13

1.10

GEVLEWEG

STAVANGERWEG

1.14

STAVANGERWEG

STAVANGERWEG

GEVLEWEG

TASMANSTRAAT

Minervahaven, Houthavens

1.1 **Danzigerbocht 'Breeding Ground'**
(2002)
Danziger Bocht 35

Commissioned by
Broedplaats
Amsterdam

The Amsterdam local authority's 'breeding ground' policy is an indirect consequence of the development of the banks of the IJ, where many refuges for artists arose in old (squatted) premises over the years. When these were increasingly cleared out to make room for new projects, the artists united and, in cooperation with the artists' union (FNV), submitted a request to the city council for 'a constructive settlement policy for this target group of young cultural economic growth', in other words, for new studios. In 2000 the local authority voted to earmark funds for this purpose and even to set up a separate project group for it. At least 539 places had been found on 24 locations by 2004, many of them on the banks of the IJ.
This policy enabled the TransformArt group of artists to find a collective studio in this warehouse, which is inconspicuously located at the back of a sawmill. There are five temporary studios here.

| **Business complex** (2006) Danzigerkade 2 | **Architect** Peter Capelle | **Commissioned by** Houthaven BV | 1.2 |

The building at Danzigerkade 2, which continues to the Danzigerbocht, is a multifunctional premises built for the flat-bottom rental and towing company De Houthaven BV. This firm is part of the Scheepswerf Koning William on the Hoogte Kadijk, where Coen Kerkelaan and his sons have been providing invaluable services in the Amsterdam harbour for donkey's years. The company in the Houthaven rents flat bottoms and provides towing services to and for everyone who is active in the harbour.

The ground flour is a maintenance workshop, while above it are offices for administration, a captain's room, and accommodation for the skippers. The architecture is as down-to-earth as the company: a concrete skeleton with a no-nonsense finish. The architectural idiom is very similar to the Dedato projects and is thereby in harmony with the new look of the area around the Minervahaven.

| **Dedato designers and architects office** (2007) Danzigerkade 9-10 | **Architect** Dedato ontwerpers en architecten | **Commissioned by** Danzig Projects | 1.3 |

This new business premises on a broad but shallow plot is entirely orientated towards the IJ. Most of the front façade has therefore been kept as open as possible with a lot of glass in wooden frames. The second floor, where the multidisciplinary design agency is housed, is impressive thanks to the double floor height in the front façade and a mezzanine inside against the back wall.

A semi-closed wooden screen has been used to fence off the parking facility on the ground floor. These kinds of lattice structures are typical of the storage depots in the Houthavens. They used to be used to dry wood before it could be processed.

1.4	**Barts head office** (2006) Danzigerkade 11	**Architect** Dedato ontwerpers en architecten	**Commissioned by** Nemaco

Many businesses dependent on water have settled on the Danzigerkade, such as a company that repairs the sides of the canals. This is also the location of the depository of the Department of Inland Water Management, the 'detention centre' for all confiscated vessels and houseboats. Behind the quay is a harbour for flatbottom craft.

Because of its function as a distribution centre, this building has a closed ground floor, with large concrete entrances on the quay for the goods transport. A striking wooden door is the main entrance. Daylight enters via a continuous strip of windows and glass building bricks. The second floor, where the design studios are situated, has a wooden façade inspired by the rough beams that were unloaded and processed in the Houthavens. The dimensions and details of the wooden construction are a continuation of the concrete building, resulting in a sturdy façade. While the base of the building has a solid look about it, the smaller construction on top of the roof, crowned with a generous overhang, is light and transparent.

1.5	**Business complex** (2002) Danzigerkade 17	**Architect** Dedato ontwerpers en architecten	**Commissioned by** Danzigerkade Beheer

This business complex for small-scale creative enterprises is the first new building of the quality that is being aimed for in the planning zone. The fifty-metre deep complex with a front and a rear building looks fresh and businesslike with its simple prefab concrete structure and large casement doors with terraces, but above all uncomplicated. The design is based on the idea that every part of the interior must offer a view of the IJ and the Minervahaven. This has been achieved by means of the transparent front and rear façades and by keeping the area below the high ceiling on each floor open. The concrete façade elements, columns and beams have been deliberately left in view, which accentuates the functional character of the building. The introduction of a central light shaft, seen as an interruption in the side wall, ensures that the middle of the floor receives enough daylight.

Hot ITem bv	**Architect**	**Commissioned by**	1.6
(2007)	Dedato	Nemaco	
Danzigerkade 18	ontwerpers en		
	architecten		

Like the building next to it, this one was designed by the house architects of the Minervahaven. The office has a character of its own, partly because a third dimension of transparency has been added with the open/closed roof surface, with the possibility of a large roof terrace. The user (an ICT design bureau) had already seen the potential of this site and moved from an old business premises on the Danzigerkade to this customised building.

At the end of the Minervahaven pier are the wooden warehouses of a wood transshipment company. Big Russian vessels often still moor at the quay and many pallets with timber are unloaded. This company will disappear in the near future to make room for new buildings. The plans are still in the development stage.

1.7 Coasters and barges for living and working
Minervahavenweg

There are a number of moorings for freight vessels without a motor beside the Minervahavenweg. These vessels are used as flexible storage depots for the Igma company, which produces dry bulk (including fodder) on the north side of the IJ. Every now and then the boats cross to the other side to be loaded or unloaded, after which they return to their moorings. The skippers live on them.

Enormous coasters regularly moor at the pier on the north side of the quay. The pier is a place where ships from all over the world pass the time between arriving on the IJ and loading and/or unloading dry bulk on the other side. When one of these ships arrives in the Minervahaven, a message is passed on to De Koperen Ploeg, a cooperative of steersmen and other dockhands who help the ocean-going vessels to moor and drop anchor safely.

The Hilt (2006)
Minervahavenweg 3-5

Architect
Dedato ontwerpers en architecten

Commissioned by 1.8
Nemaco

This building was specially built for a company that designs and distributes clothing for children. It has a look of its own in black and white, while at the same time the design is in keeping with the other buildings. The idea was to give individual buildings a character of their own, while achieving a balance among the new buildings as a whole in the zone.

The front façade with a glazed open structure is entirely orientated towards the Minervahaven, but the rear is also partly transparent and affords a view of the city. The basis of the design and arrangement was to allow daylight to enter as far as possible into the premises. The construction and functions are clearly legible, such as the entrance and the staircase on the corner, and the closed concrete plinth behind which the distribution area is located.

Houtpark (2006)
Archangelkade, Haparandaweg

Architect
Penning Architectuur en Stedenbouw

Commissioned by 1.9
Houtpark Ontwikkeling

This businesses complex comprises 21 units, divided among three two-storey buildings which enclose a car park. They are in anthracite-coloured brick with a yellow wooden façade sheeting, which is intended as a playful allusion to the historic function of the Houthavens. At the end of the complex is a small office that functions as a beacon for the whole. The main load-bearing structure and the roof are made of concrete.

1.10	**Strand West**	**Architect**	**Commissioned by**
	(2005)	Total-X	Strand West
	Stavangerweg 900		

Strand West is one of the temporary city beaches which have been introduced in Amsterdam in the last few years. The best-known is Blijburg Beach on IJburg. The temporary beaches owe their success to two factors. On the one hand, they make it possible to enjoy sun and sand without leaving the city, and on the other, they offer a perfect opportunity to promote a particular location. West Beach puts the Houthavens on the map, to the benefit of their further development. All kinds of recreation are possible on the layer of sand. Children can go for a spin in the whirligig or enjoy the view from the miniature Ferris wheel. There are also child-free areas for sunbathers who do not want to be disturbed. When it is really warm, the barbecue and the paella pan make their appearance. Besides the large beach, there are seven volleyball and two footvolley courts. But you cannot cool down in the water, because the IJ is too polluted for that here.

Along Amsterdam's Waterfront

De Bonte Zwaan
'Breeding
Ground'
(2005)
Stavangerweg 890

Architect
CASA architecten

Commissioned by 1.11
Woonstichting
De Key

Within the framework of the Amsterdam 'breeding ground' policy, this boat was converted into
22 studios, four group studios, four business
units and an exhibition space with catering facilities. Originally built as a floating office, it was
turned into a shipping fair in 1980: a place with
all kinds of facilities for skippers, such as freight
offices, shops and bank, as well as welfare officers
and a room for films and parties. The shipping
fair had to close down in 2003, after which De
Key Woonstichting bought the ship.
During the conversion the upper half was finished with corrugated sheeting, while the lower
half was left unfinished so that the side of the
ship with all its repairs is still visible.

1.12 Pont 13
(1927/2005)
Stavangerweg 891

Architect
Scheepsreparatie
R. Langendijk

Commissioned by
R. Langendijk

There is an old ferryboat moored behind the student accommodation at the end of the quay. It is now in use as a café-restaurant. The restaurant entrepreneur bought the ferryboat, which dates from 1927, for 'the price of scrap metal', after it had loyally served the municipal transport corporation for a long time crossing to and fro between the banks of the IJ, and had more recently been used to carry freight to IJburg. An authentic landing stage leads on board the industrial monument, which has been fitted out with rough wooden ship's tables in the main area, and steel tables hanging from the side of the ship in the aisles, with old school chairs. Heating is by an enormous wood stove. It is an unusual setting for a restaurant, to say the least, and according to gourmet Johannes van Dam, the mainly French dishes are excellent.

Rochdale One
(2004)
Stavangerweg
42100-42420

Commisioned by   **1.13**
Rochdale, AWV,
DUWO

Various creative solutions have been devised
in the course of the last few years to tackle the
shortage of student accommodation. This ship,
which was constructed in France and launched
under the name of Ayvazovsky in 1977, is one
example. After transporting tourists over the
oceans for years, it was purchased in 2004 by a
number of housing corporations to be converted into a student boat in North Amsterdam. It
has almost 200 rooms, each approx. 13 m², most
with their own sanitary facilities.
The project did not proceed immediately as
planned; within a month there was an outbreak
of legionnaire's disease on board, which caused a
good deal of commotion. The ship did not satisfy
the fire safety requirements either, and a number of extra measures had to be taken. The cabins
are not large, but then the rent of around 200
euros a month is not particularly high either.

1.14 **Qubic Houthavens**
(2004)
Stavangerweg
10-877, Gevleweg
20-91, 100-115

Architect
hvdn
architecten

Commisioned by
De Principaal,
Woonstichting
De Key

After the fire in the complex of cells at Schiphol Airport, there was a brief upsurge of concern about the fire safety of such container homes, but after extra investigation by the fire brigade, the units have been given a new certificate of approval.

On the other side of Tasmanstraat is the Spaarndammerbuurt, built for dock workers at the end of the nineteenth century. The blocks of flats in the style of the Amsterdam School (1913–1920) by Michel de Klerk are famous. The neighbourhood has been thoroughly renovated during the last few years. The Tasmanstraat is being partly tunnelled to ensure good connections between the future buildings in the Houthavens and the old Spaarndammerbuurt.

What was the site of firms related to the timber industry until recently is now a student campus, which can stay here until the construction of a new commercial and residential estate gets under way on the site.

The hvdn firm of architects was given the unconventional assignment by Woonstichting De Key to design 715 student housing units in a very short space of time: there were twelve months between design and completion. Standard 3 x 9 metre containers were used with built-in prefab electric twin hot plates with sink and toilet/shower unit. The blocks of containers stacked in twos and threes have white profiled prefab façade panels which are partly fitted with coloured Plexiglas. A plinth of pavement slabs forms the base on which these separate containers stand. An overhanging roof edge, supported by slender columns, forms a long veranda. The complex has acquired a surrealist look about it and when seen from a distance it looks a bit like Le Corbusier's Nôtre-Dame du Haut in Ronchamp, the white church with the recessed horizontal stained glass windows from 1955. Three shared courtyards have been reserved between the complexes. Two of these have been provided with greenery for sport and relaxation, while a student café-restaurant, Paviljoen Aan 't IJ, has been built in the third. The rent of a single unit is slightly more than 300 euros incl. per month for 24 m² of self-contained accommodation, which is not expensive by Amsterdam standards, although the students have to be able to put up with a lot from one another and they need good ear-plugs, because there is a lot of noise.

Minervahaven, Houthavens

Along Amsterdam's Waterfront

The IJ towards the North Bank

FOCUS ON WATER

Maarten Kloos

Along Amsterdam's Waterfront

Vital artery

Historically, the IJ inlet and the River Amstel are Amsterdam's vital arteries. For centuries, the Amstel was crucial to the supply of food and drinking water and it remains an important link with the hinterland; the IJ was the time-honoured opening to the sea via the Zuiderzee (now the IJsselmeer), a source of fish and, from the early 16th century, of exotic goods from the Far East. Unsurprisingly, Amsterdam developed into a city focused on the harbour.

Relocation of port activities

Things started to change in the late 19th century with the construction of the Oranjesluizen (1871) and the North Sea Canal (1876). Following the closure of the Zuiderzee, Amsterdammers had to get used to the idea that the sea had suddenly moved westwards. In response to the new possibilities opened up by the railway, port capacity to the east of the centre was increased by building finger wharves and running rail tracks along the quays. At the same time, the construction of the Central Station in 1889 severed all connections between the old waterfront and the city. As a result, the IJ disappeared from the consciousness of Amsterdam's inhabitants and this feeling was so strong that when many port activities were actually relocated from the centre to the west, the area 'behind the tracks' became both a physical and psychological void.

The IJ rediscovered

This changed again with the earliest redevelopment plans for the Eastern Harbour Area. In the late 1980s, when people started to move into the first new dwellings in the former docklands, the IJ, and by extension Amsterdam's waterways in general, were rediscovered. Since then the city and its people have benefited handsomely from the enormously long shoreline of old port. Nowadays no development plan is made in which the relationship with the water does not play a role. After the Eastern Harbour Area, the Oostelijke Handelskade and Oosterdok, Westerdok and Houthavens on the other side of the Central Station are now about to be 'returned to the fold' as it were. Most recently, the development of the northern IJ shoreline has given rise to a situation without historical precedent.

Link with North Amsterdam

Until the construction of the station, the situation was clear: the waterfront (Prins Hendrikkade) constituted the northern limit of the city. To the north of this was another world, and the things that occurred there were not the kinds of things people wanted to see happening in the city. The first genuine port activities on the North Bank date from the last decade of the 19th century, the first workers' dwellings from just before the First World War. The 1935 General Extension Plan incorporated the development of Amsterdam-North, but for a long time it was unclear whether or not a canal embracing the north would be built. Amsterdam-North was eventually linked to the city in 1968 (via the IJ Tunnel), and embraced with the completion of the A10 ring road in 1990, but it didn't really prosper until the North/South line became a certainty.

City on both banks of the IJ

This infrastructural project supports current thinking about the North Bank and so, with redevelopments on the old Shell site, in Buiksloterham, on and around the NDSM shipbuilding site, and – in a somewhat more distant future – further to the east, the urban perception of the IJ will for the first time in history be almost symmetrical. This will be

most apparent when the ring of development
around the Central Station – public library,
Sweelinck Conservatorium, Muziekgebouw, film
museum, law courts and a lot of new housing –
is finally complete. This, in combination
with an enlarged Central Station, which now
also engages with Amsterdam-North, and a
redesigned public space (including water), will
give Amsterdammers the sense of an enlarged,
perhaps even a new, city centre.

Along Amsterdam's Waterfront

Recreation on Strand West

2.
WESTE-LIJKE EILANDEN

At the beginning of the Golden Age, the centre of Amsterdam was bursting at the seams: ship production stood at about one vessel a day, and all the shipbuilding yards, warehouses and timber firms could no longer be accommodated on the existing built-up area. It was therefore decided to create Prinseneiland, Realeneiland and Bickerseiland. The function of the district can be read off from the street names: the Nieuwe Teertuinen were the new domain of the tar industry, the names of the Zeilstraat and Ketelmakersstraat refer to the sail-making and boiler-making industries.

For centuries industries of this kind continued to determine the character of the Western Islands, but when city formation was put on the agenda, the local authority decided to start building big office complexes here in the 1960s. The idea behind this was a separation of functions: working in the centre, living outside it. But the residents put up a fight. Although it proved impossible to block the construction of colossal blocks like de Walvis (the whale) and de Narwal (the narwhal – now demolished), they did manage to bring about a U-turn in policy. From then on more space was created for housing and small-scale business activities in a more gradual development. The result can be seen today: the islands have become a popular housing area on which every scarce empty space is being carefully filled. A striking feature of these adaptations is that, without lapsing into retro-architecture, they merge seamlessly with the old, renovated buildings.

Because the islands are situated behind the railway track, they became self-enclosed worlds. The development of the Westerdok and the Silodam has given the islands a central position without the loss of the old village-like atmosphere.

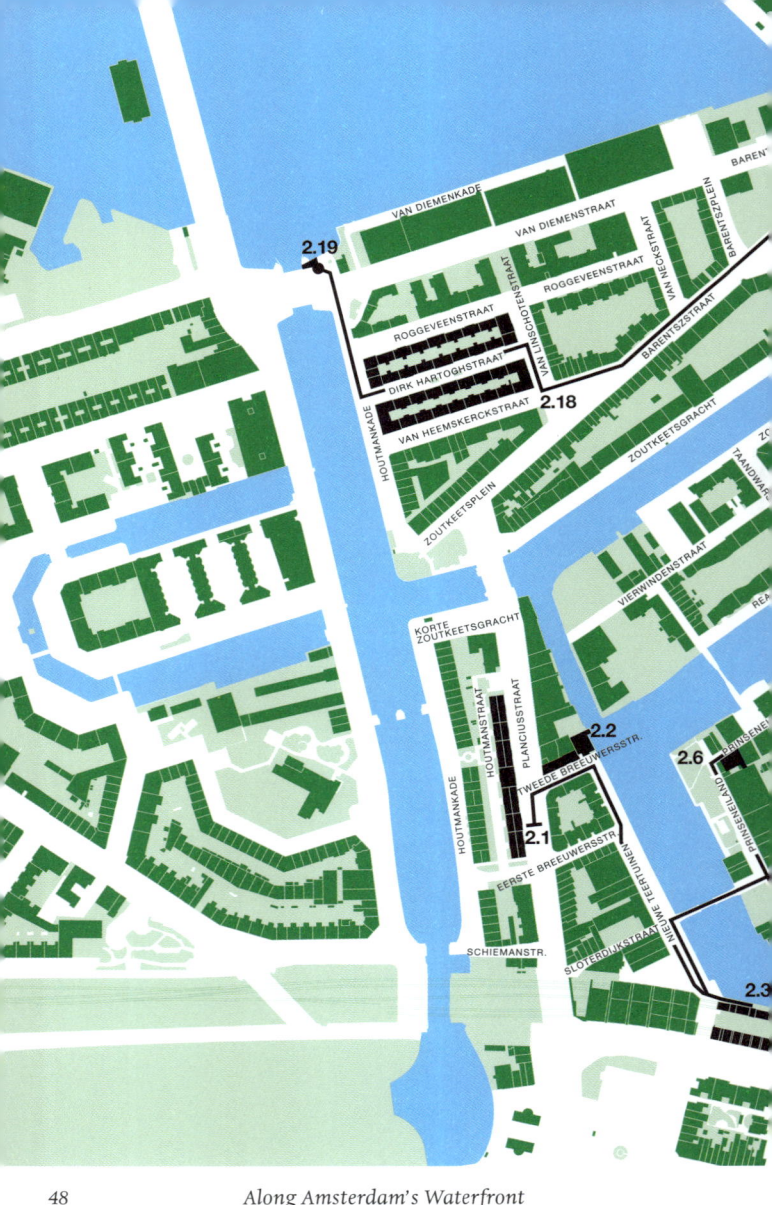

Along Amsterdam's Waterfront

2.17

BARENTSZPLEIN

BOKKINGHANGEN

MEDIANVANGER

GRACHT

TAANSTRAAT

ZANDHOEK

HT

2.15

2.16

2.14

2.13

2.12

2.11

KL. BICKERSGRACHT

GROTE BICKERSSTRAAT

KL. BICKERSSTR.

BICKERSWERF

2.5

2.11

NSTRAAT

TOUWSLAGERSTRAAT

HOLLANDSE TUIN

2.4

PRINSENEILAND

ZEILMAKERSTRAAT

2.10

2.9

BICKERSGRACHT

GROTE BICKERSSTRAAT

ZEILMAKERSTRAAT

2.10

MINNEMOERSST.

PRINSENEILAND

2.8

BLOKMAKERSTRAAT

KETELMAKERSTRAAT

HENDRIK JONKERPLEIN

2.1 **Houtman Plancius** **Architect** **Commisioned by**
(1856/2006) P.J. Hamer/ Ymere
Planciusstraat 8-18, area architekten
Houtmanstraat
1-93

This earliest example of rented council housing with the typical back-to-back typology has been entirely renovated in cooperation with the local authority Historic Buildings and Archaeology Department. The particular properties of the monumental building have been left intact as far as possible. That the corporation has worked with great care bears witness to a growing tendency among the parties who place commissions to deal with cultural heritage in a more serious way.

Architect Hamer, who also designed other housing complexes in the city, was commissioned by the Association for the Working Class to design a block with sober decoration containing more than a hundred housing units, most of them displaying the back-to-back typology. Although the first Law on Housing of 1901 banned housing of this kind because of the inadequate light and air supply, these back-to-back homes with running water, primitive toilet and a separate bedroom were still regarded as quite a luxury by many people at the time. The rents were therefore too high for the really poor.

The original grey of the frames and the green of the doors and windows have been restored during the renovation, making the complex less sombre than it was.

A vegetation plan for the surroundings has been drawn up by landscape architect Paul van Beek in consultation with the neighbourhood. Magnolias, and ornamental apple and pear trees decorate the pavements, while creepers are allowed on the outer walls.

26 owner-occupied housing units and 5 working units
(1994) Plancius-straat 23-25, Tweede Breeuwerstraat 2-32

Architect
Van der Waals, Zeinstra Architecten

Commisioned by
De Nijs

2.2

This project illustrates the volte-face which took place in local authority council housing policy in the early 1990s. While the preceding period had been characterised primarily by urban renewal projects in the social sector, this complex was initiated as a combination of housing and work functions and private sector owner-occupied housing units. The building of the project had to be postponed in mid-1992 because of procedural errors in the consultations with the residents. They put up a lot of resistance to the plan: they called for a green area instead of more buildings, and had serious objections to a building 25 metres tall. In the end, the local authority decided to let the plan go ahead without any modifications. The complex consists of three volumes on top of a shared underground car park. The most striking is the tower overlooking the Prinseneilandsgracht. The topmost of the eight and a half storeys is a penthouse of 150 m², which had an asking price of half a million guilders at the time. The units on the bottom floor have a 'water room' situated just above the water line.

| 2.3 | **Business complex Tussen de Bogen** (1997) Tussen de Bogen 4-113 | **Architect** Van der Waals, Zeinstra Architecten in collaboration with Tijmen Ploeg | **Commisioned by** Woningbouwvereniging Het Oosten, Woningbedrijf Amsterdam |

Efficient use has been made of this space beneath the arches of the first rail link between Amsterdam and Haarlem. These tunnel areas had already been taken over informally by music studios and small businesses. When an extra railway line was needed on the north side, the whole area had to be cleaned up, but – partly in response to a request from the residents – the initiative of small-scale businesses underneath the tracks remained. The old railway bridge arches on the city side, beneath the track on the south, have been maintained and contain workshops and studios. New work spaces for cultural institutions have been created back-to-back under the three tracks on the north (Bickerseiland) side, as well as a car park. The artist Guido Geelen placed 35 gilt bronze statues of recognisable tools against the brick wall and between the arches to refer to the varied business activities.

You do not forget that you are underneath the railway for long: the shaking of the furniture and a buzzing noise in the background every couple of minutes are a free extra.

De Nieuwe Prins
(2007)
Galgenstraat 3-17,
Prinseneiland
549-583

Architect
Studio Y

Commisioned by
Zaanse Ontwikke-
lings Maatschappij

2.4

The construction of the complex of apartments
on this high-density location met with a good
deal of opposition. This had originally been
the site of a steam-driven coffee bean husker.

Though not an officially recognised protected
historic building, it was characteristic of the
atmosphere of the Prinseneiland, which was
rapidly spoilt by all the new buildings that were
going up. Although a demolition licence was
granted in 2000, the project developer did not
start on demolition until 2005, after the appeal
procedures. It was not until February 2006 that an
agreement was eventually reached.

The character of the façade is determined by the
floor-to-ceiling double doors that can be opened
inwards. The horizontal laminated timber beams
are a characteristic reference to the former
shipbuilding activities on the island. The roof
contour is formed by the sloping roof structure.

*The characteristic black,
wooden shipyard De
Walvis [The Whale],
originally from the seventeenth century, is located
at the corner where the
Prinseneiland meets the
Realengracht and the Bic-
kersgracht. A little further
on, at Prinseneiland 6, is
the 'head office'.*

**House with pho-
tographic studio**
(2004) Prinsen-
eiland 10

Architect
BBVH architecten

Commissioned by
private party

2.5

In a typically historic part of the city like the
Prinseneiland, architects are expected to pay extra
attention to the way in which their designs blends
with the existing buildings. That this does not
necessarily have to result in historicising architecture can be seen from this house cum studio,
which was commissioned by a private party.
The moveable wooden panels on the outer walls
have been specially designed for the function of
photographic and kitchen studio. The owners
wanted a maximum of daylight to enter, but also
to be able to control that light as they chose. On
the canal side the panels have been incorporated
in sliding shutters.

2.6	**De Prins** (2003) Prinseneiland 55-57	**Architect** Architectenbureau ir. Henri Leloup	**Commisioned by** Novavast Holding

Unlike other projects, this design met with little opposition from the residents. De Prins does its best to blend in with its surroundings. The original plan, made when the economy was in a healthier state, envisaged one apartment per storey. Because of the width of the volume, the apartments would be very light and would have a splendid view of the street and the Realen- gracht. But the price was to match: around one million guilders. It was not long before three of the four storeys were split, so that in the end seven apartments were built.

2.7	**Three apartments** (1995) Prinseneiland 91	**Architect** Tijmen Ploeg	**Commisioned by** Friso Broeksma and Benno Premsela

In spite of the modern, Spartan-looking façade, this new construction makes no attempt to stand out in the row of houses. Upon closer inspection, it is noteworthy that the rectangular horizontal frames have exactly the same dimensions as the three vertical windows of the neighbouring house from the nineteenth century.

That behind this façade lies a 33-metre deep building cannot be seen from the outside. It was precisely the length of the plot that was the starting point for the design of the ground plans. Next to the diagonally situated staircase in the middle of the building is a void with skylight so that daylight can reach the bedrooms in the rear.

The project was originally designed for a housing corporation, but was sold before it had been built to the architect Friso Broeksma and the designer Benno Premsela. Together with the same architect Tijmen Ploeg, they altered the design from five to three apartments, with a special focus on spaciousness and light.

Prinsenwerf
(2002)
Prinseneiland 36

Architect
Studio Y

Commisioned by
E. Gerritsen and
P. Stoutenbeek

2.8

All that can be seen from the street is a dark
brick wall with three doors that lead to a kind
of front patio, but from the other side of the
Bickersgracht this new housing project with
three semi-detached houses can be clearly seen.
A striking feature is the robust wooden roof
truss, a direct allusion to the shipyards nearby.
The roof is covered with a sedum moss, a type of
succulent that changes colour with the seasons.
Although this cannot be seen from outside,
these housing and work units have a floor
surface of no less than 160 m², divided into
a mezzanine, a ground floor, and a spacious
basement with patio built in a concrete basin
in the water. A garden with a large wooden pier
has been built on top of the basement facing
the water.

*The warehouse that has
been converted into apartments at Prinseneiland 443
is named after the three
princes Willem, Maurits
and Frederik Hendrik of
Orange. They were Stadhol-
ders of the province of Holland in the sixteenth and
seventeenth centuries. It
must have been one of the
most important buildings
in the area, and this is
probably how the Prinsen-
eiland got its name.*

| **2.9** One-family hous-
ing unit (2004)
Minnemoers-
straat 2 | **Architect**
PERMETA
architecten | **Commisioned by**
Neuteboom family |

The Prinseneiland has many small-scale
private building projects. This one is a
housing unit with a bicycle repair shop on
the ground floor on an extremely small plot
of land (4 x 6 metres). The apartment rooms
are all stacked. The staircase is the hub of the
building. It winds its way upwards along the
outside walls and ends in the kitchen on the
fourth floor.
The façade is in an inconspicuous, ordinary
brick. The details of the frames give
expression to the façade: the lowest part of
the frames has a deep recess, while the part
above the apron wall is flush to the masonry.

| **2.10** Hollandse Tuin
(1982)
Hollandse Tuin
2-14, Grote Bickers-
straat 12-36 | **Architect**
Paul de Ley | **Commisioned by**
Woonstichting
Lieven de Key |

On the location between the Grote Bickersstraat and the Hollandse Tuin were there used to be a steel factory, there are now two closed blocks with 171 housing units and studios. The corners give access to the public inner courtyards. The gas concrete blocks from which the outer walls are made were later painted grey and now look rather dated. Still, the cubic shapes and the human scale that can be found in the dimensions make the complex an icon of an era when urban renewal went hand in hand with the political engagement of the residents.

Squash City, the large fitness complex with squash courts between the Ketelmakerstraat and the railway line, has been in this former factory shop since 1986. The brick walls have been clad with corrugated materials.

| **Nieuwveld/ Narwal** (2003) Bickerswerf 1-84 | **Architect** HM Architecten | **Commisioned by** Hemavan | 2.11 |

This housing project consists of two volumes overlooking the water. The Narwal block stands on part of the site of the office complex of the same name that has been demolished. This was one of the last remains of the city-formation of the 1960s and 1970s. The Nieuwveld block is on the former site of the shipyard of Wouter Nieuwveld, which has now moved to Bickersstraat 1.

The building has been constructed 'on the run': it leans forwards on both sides. The façades are made of prefab brick elements. The flats are 26 metres deep, which is why they have open areas to introduce daylight. The living rooms all face the Westerdok. The Narwal block stands with its façade in the water; the Nieuwveld block, on the other hand, is slightly further away from the water and has terraces on the water side with closed parapets for privacy. A boardwalk follows the same route, part of the public route from the new bridge to the Westerdok and the Hollandse Tuin.

2.12	**4 Stadse stegen** (2003) Grote Bickers- straat 54-70, Bickerswerf 86-96	**Architect** FARO Architecten	**Commisioned by** De Principaal

The developer's brief was not to put too many students in one building for the sake of manageability. Five separate buildings were therefore built, with a total of 88 student flats. Most of them have their own services. Those on the top floors are shared: the students who occupy four separate rooms share a kitchen-diner and a roof terrace.

The five buildings are separated from one another by narrow alleys. As a result, each unit has the dimensions of an Amsterdam house and therefore fits in better with the surroundings, unlike the office giant that stood on the site before. The architects describe the project as 'simple quintuplets with a wink at the past'.

2.13	**Urban renewal** **Grote Bickersstraat** (1977) Grote Bickersstraat 305-319, Bickers- gracht 242-254	**Architect** Paul de Ley, Jouke van den Bout	**Commisioned by** Woonstichting Lieven de Key

The Bickerseiland was once the most densely populated part of the islands in the western area of the docklands. The district went rapidly downhill in the first half of the twentieth century, and in the report *Slum Demolition and Clearance* (1960) the Bickerseiland occupied second place (after Kattenburg) as the worst residential area in the city. The process of city-formation took hold of the district after that. But the office blocks De Narwal and De Walvis on the Bickerseiland provoked a revolt on the part of the residents of the Western Islands. Paul de Ley was one of the first architects to sympathise with this movement. Like his partner Jouke van den Bout, at the time the architects looked more like pop singers, with long hair, tight black leather jackets and stirring stories. They motivated the residents to act. More and more administrators and civil servants joined in the movement. This movement was of great importance for the future of Amsterdam. It was stated in the programme agreement of 1978 that from now on urban renewal would be tackled in a more gradual way. The motto was 'street by street', without large traffic arteries and with a lot of attention for the context of the new projects.

De Walvis office block (1964) Grote Bickersstraat 74-78	Architect W.F. Lughthart	Commisioned by Mr. Gaus	2.14

De Walvis, one of the three colossal office blocks in the Grote Bickersstraat, was not demolished in the 1990s. The architect is W.F. Lugthart, who was mainly engaged in hospital

The Dierencapel children's farm (the name comes from Mr. Capel, who runs it), an initiative of action committees in the neighbourhood, has been in existence on the quay of the Bickersgracht since the 1970s. It regularly organises activities on Saturdays. One of the highlights is the annual sheep shearing at Easter. It is now an oasis of calm in the neighbourhood, where the goats and chickens can walk around undisturbed.

design and worked on the BovenIJ Hospital in Amsterdam. The no-nonsense modernist façade is in itself beautifully proportioned. The solid concrete frieze along the roof and the solid concrete gutter along the first floor contrast with the light, flat lower window construction in between. This contrast was toned down during a renovation of the façade in the late 1990s.

The roof contains not only the usual utilities but also a caretaker's house, slightly raised in order to be able to look over the top of the frieze and thereby forming an expressive, less businesslike element.

De Walvis was initially the first part of a development plan along the Westerdok, but only part of it was implemented. As far as its design is concerned, the building has absolutely nothing in common with its surroundings. This was typical of the office buildings that were built in the city in the 1960s within the framework of city-formation. The recently constructed apartment complexes around it and the new building on the Westerdok are so large that De Walvis no longer seems as oversized as it was at the time it was built.

All that is left of the former De Walvis shipyard is a wooden sign with a relief of a large grey whale. It has been nicely restored and now graces the entrance to the office.

| 2.15 | **Montessorischool De Eilanden** (2002) Grote Bickersstraat 102 | **Architect** Architectuurstudio Hertzberger | **Commisioned by** Stadsdeel Centrum |

A rather strange combination of functions has been implemented on this unusual waterside site: a primary school with flats on the upper floors, designed by different architects. The original idea was to build a shipyard here for Wouter Nieuwveld, who ran the Westerdok shipyard here, but residents did not want the new school on the Hendrik Jonkerplein, so the shipyard and the school exchanged places. The flats on top have remained.

The Montessori School has a composite volume in brickwork with glass lower window fronts. Architect Herman Hertzberger designs his schools on the principle that a school is a place where children should feel at home, instead of a place where they spend the day. Every detail has been designed seen through the eyes of a child. Coat-hooks have been made so that a bag can be placed above them. The main hall has a stepped structure and can be used as a playroom or for school performances.

The building received an honourable mention for the School Architecture Award 2002.

Bickershoek	Architect	Commisioned by	2.16
(2003)	HM Architecten	Hemavan	
Grote Bickersstraat 86-100			

As a contrast with the variety of forms of the school and to introduce calm into the design, HM Architecten have conceived the apartments as solid, closed volumes that open themselves fully on the water side. The wooden side walls are fitted with shutters that can be opened vertically or horizontally, depending on the storey. Because the larch rebates are one centimetre apart, daylight enters the apartments in an attractive way. The project was nominated for the Wood Architecture Award 2003.

2.17 Renovation Westerdokshuis (1996) Barentszplein 7	Architect de architecten-groep (Bjarne Mastenbroek)	Commisioned by de architecten-groep

Along Amsterdam's Waterfront

The area of the Barentszplein, the Zoutkeetsgracht and the Westerdoksdijk was wholly devoted to bread production in the nineteenth century. The Westerdokshuis was built in 1915 as a silo for the flour transshipment; this building supplied the Amsterdam bakeries. Previous renovations had completely eradicated the original character of the building. In 1996 de architectengroep subjected the premises to a new renovation to install their offices there. The solid wooden floor on the south side of the Westerdokshuis looks like a patchwork cloak because at the time it was usual to transport flour vertically as much as possible, and to adjust the openings to that. This is where the drawing rooms are situated today. The silos stood on the north side of the building. They were demolished in the 1950s and replaced by concrete floors. Large voids on the sites of the silos create openness between the floors and allow daylight to reach the lower levels. The new entrance, robustly designed in wood and glass, is a striking feature in the façade.

Nineteenth-century homes (1883) Van Heemskerck-straat 2-86, Dirk Hartoghstraat 1-85 en 2-78, Roggeveen-straat 103-169	Architect B. de Greef	Commisioned by Vereeniging tot het bouwen van Arbei-derswoningen	2.18

These two elongated, almost identical blocks were built at the end of the nineteenth century for the Association for the Building of Workers' Homes, which was closely associated with the local authority. It developed projects on local authority land with money borrowed from the authority after designs by the municipal architect Bas de Greef. When a housing complex of a workers' association or philanthropic institution occupied an entire block, it was often designed as if it were a

single building. These blocks too consist of a symmetrical composition with an accent on the central part.

The staircases are clearly recognisable because they jut out slightly from the façade and have stepped gables. The masonry pilasters provide a further vertical accent. For a long time neighbourhoods with rented council homes of this kind looked rather dingy. But in spite of the synthetic frames, which were probably implemented in the 1980s and which do little for the whole, the sober but carefully designed brickwork façades now create a fresh impression. This is partly because the public space has been cleaned up. The Dirk Hartoghstraat was redesigned in 2005 as a green pedestrian area. Residents and pupils from the Brede School help with the upkeep of the gardens.

Both complexes have been selected by the Historic Buildings and Archaeology Department to be designated as local authority monuments.

At the moment there are plans to widen the Van Diemenstraat. This would mean that the backs of the homes on the north side of the Roggeveen-straat would have to be demolished, as well as the outbuildings of the school, dating from 1891, to be replaced by a new entrance.

| 2.19 | Westerkeer Sluice Operating Post (2004) Van Diemenstraat | **Architect** ZILT Architecten | **Commisioned by** Dienst Infrastruc-tuur Verkeer en Vervoer Amsterdam |

This light green building next to the bridge leading to the Tasmanstraat is the new operating post of the Westerkeer sluice. Its design had to comply with strict regulations, but these limiting conditions were the starting point for the architects. The extension of the floor space has been done at the back with a floor that juts out a long way above the water. The building had to be able to offer an unobstructed view, which is why the umbrella construction was chosen. This consists of a steel functional core which supports a roof that juts out in all directions. This leaves the glass façade around the building clear of any obstruction. The top and bottom of this open strip are held in place by a floor with parapet wall and a roof with a frame of varying height, clad with a rubbery polyurethane coating. The light green is an allusion to shipping, where this colour coating is used on steel decks. The walls of the conference room are printed with a seventeenth-century maritime scene to obtain the requisite sun protection.

Along Amsterdam's Waterfront

Harbour activities in the Western Harbour Area

PORT ON THE MOVE

Ernest Kurpershoek

Nomadic port activities

The port of Amsterdam has never been very firmly anchored in one spot. Over the centuries since its establishment early in the 14th century, at the mouth of the River Amstel (now Damrak) and along today's Prins Hendrikkade, the port has moved 360 degrees around the IJ inlet to its present location to the west of the city. The port and accompanying industry followed the urban periphery and thus every urban expansion resulted in a major relocation.

Heyday of the Eastern Harbour Area

In the 16th century, the focus of port activities started to shift in the direction of the Lastage (Nieuwmarkt district). From there it moved to the Eastern Islands, first to Uilenburg, Marken, Rapenburg, and around 1660 to Kattenburg, Wittenburg and Oostenburg. And there it remained for a long time. In 1830, shortly after the construction of the Noordhollands Kanaal, two new docks, Oosterdok and Westerdok, were built. But the bulk of port activity was still concentrated in the Oostelijk Havengebied (Eastern Harbour Area). This did not even change when the North Sea Canal between Amsterdam and IJmuiden was opened in 1876 and shipping traffic moved westwards. The opening of the North Sea Canal turned the entire port, including infrastructure, on its head, but the Eastern Harbour Area blossomed as never before. It was as if people could not get used to the idea that the centuries-old Zuiderzee connection with the open sea had had its day. Of course, some activities took place in the Westelijk Havengebied (Western Harbour Area), and new docks were built there: Houthavens (timber) and Petroleumhaven (oil). But the amount of investment was nowhere near the development costs of the Oostelijke Handelskade, IJ Island, the Levant and Suriname wharves and, finally, Amsterdam-North where the shipbuilding industry was based.

Space for the construction of harbours

It was several decades before the realisation dawned that a major mistake had been made. This was confirmed by the Amsterdam General Extension Plan (AUP) which was published in 1935: 'Nowhere in the world,' it concluded, 'is there a port city that cargo vessels must first sail past in order to discharge their cargo, which must then be transported back to the city on barges.' The AUP also drew attention to the costs involved in deepening and maintaining new harbours and the channel leading to them in order to service the ever-growing cargo ships. The future of the port lay in the west, in the IJ polders along the North Sea Canal, where there was space for the construction of harbours and associated large-scale industry.

New functions for the Eastern Harbour Area

After the Second World War the port did indeed develop along the North Sea Canal ('Zeehavens Amsterdam', which includes the harbours of Zaanstad, Beverwijk and Velsen-IJmuiden). The port disappeared from the cityscape around the IJ inlet. But it did not vanish without a trace. The banks of the IJ are thronged with reminders of the past: the names of streets and quays, and more tangible monuments like the Havengebouw (harbour master's office), the NDSM shed, the Scheepvaarthuis, Scheepvaartmuseum, the VOC (Dutch East India Company) warehouses and the well-known emigrant hostel, the Lloyd Hotel. Urban planners are only too happy to link into port history. Gigantic warehouses have been converted to other uses while the large-scale new buildings seem intent on emulating the look and feel of the sturdy transit sheds and other old port installations. The street pattern, even the paving, betrays the influence of the port. On KNSM Island, for example, the original paving was partially retained, while the north quay was laid with rust-coloured steel-reinforced concrete paving slabs (Stelcon) and grey cobblestones. So the historic link between the port and the city would appear to be guaranteed for the rest of the century.

Along Amsterdam's Waterfront

Industry on the North Bank of the IJ

3.
SILODAM, WESTER-DOKS-EILAND

Along Amsterdam's Waterfront

The Westerdokseiland is one of the spearheads in the development of the South Bank of the IJ. The former shunting yard with old customs sheds was until recently a non-man's land beside the IJ. The transformation into a housing and commercial district with metropolitan functions, including the magistrate's court, is in full swing.

In 1999 the local authority drew up the urban development plan that was based on the design by the architect and urban designer Peter Defesche from the bureau OD205. The premise was to match the density and diversity of functions and lifestyles that are so typical of the inner city of Amsterdam. The main plan was for very dense, varied buildings around inner courtyards (called cours) on the side facing the city, with a more uniform and monolithic style of buildings on the waterfront.

Westerdokseiland will come to accommodate 900 homes and about 80,000 m² of non-housing functions. The apartments are mainly situated in three blocks (Westerkaap I and II, VOC Cour, and La Grande Cour). Reasonably uniform seven-storey buildings are envisaged on the north side, implemented as a shell of dark kinds of brick. Behind the building line the limit is eleven storeys. Sixty mooring places for houseboats have been replaced along the quay of the Westerdok, by which some of the original atmosphere has been preserved.

Non-housing functions are mainly concentrated in the IJdok. This is a large volume, part of which will stand on new land in the IJ, and in which various different buildings will be incorporated. The different parts of the zone have been developed by several firms, with one of them acting as coordinating architect each time.

The nearby Silodam traditionally had an industrial character. By now the silos have been converted into apartments and the container-like building designed by MVRDV has given Amsterdam a new landmark.

3.3

3.

3.6

SILODAM

3.2

3.1   VAN DIEMENKADE   BARE

VAN DIEMENSTRAAT

Along Amsterdam's Waterfront

Silodam, Westerdokseiland

3.1 Het Veem (1887)
Van Diemenstraat
410-412

Architect
Roelof and
Foeke Kuipers

Commisioned by
Het Nederland-
sche Veem

Het Veem warehouse was one of the first disued industrial buildings beside the IJ to be given a new function. The new users have become trendsetters for the present informal and varied atmosphere beside the river. The Oranje Nassauveem warehouse, dating from the late nineteenth century, was given this name because it was built in the year of the coronation of Queen Wilhelmina. It was one of the first 'modern' warehouses in the Western Harbour Area, with electrically driven cranes and lifts, flat, large floors supported by cast-iron columns, and a large carrying capacity. The brothers Roelof and Foeke Kuipers from the Dutch province of Friesland used predominantly Neo-Romanesque elements in the details of the yellow brick façades (arched windows, symmetrical composition), while the side facing the quay is in the more traditional idiom of the Amsterdam warehouse façade.

The building was used to store luxury items from the Dutch colonies, such as coffee, tea, tobacco and cocoa. The building fell into disuse in the 1970s. In 1981 a group of cultural entrepreneurs squatted the warehouse, which was in a very dilapidated state by then, and ten years later the users purchased it. In the meantime the old warehouse has been gradually renovated by the users themselves, who have respected its special character, and now contains more than seventy units for artists and small enterprises. Solidarity within the community is still important; the 'newcomers committee' decides on the renting of vacant space. Downstairs is a large exhibition space (De Veemvloer), while the room where consignments of tobacco used to be inspected, right at the top of the building, now houses a theatre. There is also a café-restaurant with a fantastic view of the IJ.

In the wake of the reuse of Het Veem, the two neighbouring warehouses have been converted into business complexes, though run on a commercial basis. Next to Het Veem is the former Deli Maatschappij, designed by W. Hamer in 1913, which is now called Y-point and stands out because of the semicircular dark-red bays on the street side. Next to that is the former Koningin Emma, designed by G. van Arkel in 1914, which has been renamed Y-tech because of the high-tech style of the renovation.

| **Kop van Diemenstraat** (2007) Van Diemenstraat | **Architect** Tekton Architekten | **Commisioned by** Woningbouw-vereniging Eigen Haard, Rabo Vast-goed, Giesbers-Eemland Bouw | 3.2 |

The new building forms a link between the old warehouses in the Van Diemenstraat and the Grain Silos. The volume has been partly raised to maintain the important lines of sight between Houthavens and the city. Beneath it is a sunken and roofed square, where the entrances to the apartments are also situated. The business units in the plinth have doors opening onto the street. The studio apartments can be reached from the water by means of a landing stage running from the quay. Beneath the building is an underground car park with lifts and staircases to the different floors. All of the units are arranged around two patios. One of the patios is open on the side facing the square so that the public space receives enough daylight. The height of the storeys and the broad grid dimensions enable a large diversity of flexible apartments and business premises. The exterior is made of robust Cor-Ten-steel-coloured concrete panels with a facet-shaped relief and refers to the harbour. The interior is clad with wood and has less of an industrial look.

3.3 **Silodam** (2002)
Silodam 303-459

Architect
MVRDV

Commisioned by
De Principaal,
Rabo Vastgoed

This striking new complex is one of the major landmarks on the South Bank of the IJ. Not just the volume, which has been conceived in this way for urban design reasons because of the relation to the two other existing silos, but the architecture and programme too display a new dynamism in the field of housing that has been implemented on the river bank.

The complex consists of 142 owner-occupied apartments, 15 rented apartments in the social sector (including a 'commune' of senior citizens), 600 m² of business space, and 105 underground parking lots. The apartments are divided into 'mini neighbourhoods' of four to eight similar typologies each, which are recognisable inside the building from the different colours of the corridors and access balconies. There are studios, workshops, maisonettes and lofts. The neighbourhoods can be recognised from the outside by the different materials and colours in the façade. The variegated composition of the

façades refers to the big and colourful container ships that pass by every day.
A terrace has been built on the waterside that can be reached by non-residents as well by means of a broad wooden staircase. An anemometer on the roof automatically closes the windows of the terrace when the wind rises above force six to prevent the visitors from being swept away. To stop large vessels from entering, a dyke marked with buoys has been created underwater in the IJ.

Stone grain silo (1896/2001) Silodam 100-256	Architect Jacob F. Klink-hamer, A.L. van Gendt/ Architecten-bureau J. van Stigt	Commisioned by Rabo Vastgoed	3.4

This brick silo was built in 1896 after a design by Klinkhamer and Van Gendt and commissioned by the trader Korthals Altes. Entirely in the spirit of its day, it was an industrial palace that expressed the importance of the grain trade at the time. The building had a classical composition with the storage space in the wings and weighing machinery, cleaning and office functions in the middle. In 1996 the building became not only a local authority protected historic building but also a national one. When the architect André van Stigt devised plans for the building in the late 1990s he was not allowed to change much on the outside. The apartment windows cut out of the stone façade fit naturally into its structure. The reinforced masonry support columns continue without interruption. However, elements have been built on the roof and on the sides which have somewhat obscured the contours of the original building. The 92 apartments, in 37 different typologies, are owner-occupied in the private sector. There are also business units.

3.5	Concrete grain silo (1952/1999) Silodam 1-96	Architect Architectenbureau J. van Stigt	Commisioned by De Principaal, Rabo Vastgoed

When the stone grain silo was no longer adequate, a new one was built alongside it in 1952. A large part of this building consisted of square silos (3.6 x 3.6 metres). They fell into disuse in the late 1980s and were soon afterwards squatted and used for accommodation and as work spaces. The silos were originally due for demolition so that tall tower blocks could be built on the site, but vigorous actions on the part of the squatters, locals and interested parties saved the silos from the wrecking ball. The renovation plans left the volume of both silos intact. In 1990 they were declared protected historic buildings. The Van Stigt firm, which had carried out the renovation of the stone silo, implemented this one too. The industrial building was transformed into a ten-storey block of flats, with 89 apartments, most of them council property. The apartments on the lowest floors still follow the dimensions of the grain silos. Larger rooms were obtained by breaking down the concrete walls between the shafts, which were sometimes as much as a metre thick. Each of these flats is thus composed of four silos. The design for the reuse of the silos won the Durable Building Award from the Amsterdam local authority in 1997.

3.6	Car park Silodam (2001) Silodam	Architect Ecosafe Parking	Commisioned by Rabo Vastgoed

A fully automatic car park has been installed underneath the Silodam on the basis of a slide puzzle system. You drive from the quay into the glass lift and onto a pallet of a good 5 x 2 metres. You leave the lift shaft and when you press the button your car is taken down to the underground car park (12 x 135 metres). There are always at least two lots free in that car park. When the car is summoned again, empty and loaded pallets are moved around until the right car reaches the lift. The car parks can be very large because individual modules can be interlocked. The car park beneath the Silodam has space for 210 cars.

Het Stenen Hoofd
(1905)
Westerdoksdijk

This unused site is a short pier that was built in 1905. Together with the storage facility that used to be here, it was used for harbour transshipment until 1968. Foreign warships that docked in Amsterdam also used this pier as a mooring place.

Many plans have been made for this plot of land since 1968, from a rehabilitation centre for drug addicts to a location for luxurious tower blocks of flats, from a prison to a heliport. Partly thanks to the dedication of the Stichting Het Stenen Hoofd, consisting of residents who feel involved with the future of this harbour monument, it is now the site of many events and summer activities. Amsterdam Beach has been putting out its beanbags here for a number of seasons, there is herring tasting, there is live music, and there is open air cinema.

For the time being no definitive destiny has been found for it. The possibility of a small catering pavilion has been raised, but there are also many in support of leaving it empty as a 'place of abstinence'.

| 3.8 | **Goedkoop building** (1961/2002) Westerdoksdijk 40 | **Architect** Dekeukeleire and Grolle/Gunnar Daan | **Commisioned by** Reederij Voorheen Gebr. GoedKoop/ LeMarque |

This striking example of functionalism from 1961 has managed to retain its position amid the developments around the Westerdok. It was built as an office for the Goedkoop shipping company. This waterside location was chosen because of its central position and because the company tugs could moor in front of it. The company left in 1994, and the building was temporarily let to various firms of architects and graphic designers. They appreciated the design of the building, in spite of the no-man's-land in which it was situated at the time. The building was later incorporated in the redevelopment of the Westerdokseiland and has by now been thoroughly renovated.

Café-restaurant Onassis on the ground floor keeps up the tradition of the building in being named after a shipowner, though a Greek one in this case. Above it are an advertising agency and a legal practice.

| 3.9 | **Westerkaap I** (2008) Westerdokseiland | **Architect** awg architecten, Concrete Architectural Associates | **Commisioned by** Hofmakerij VOF (Amvest and Ymere) |

The tip of the most westerly part of the plan for the Westerdokseiland, Westerkaap I, has a block of eleven storeys designed by awg and a lower one of six storeys designed by DKV. A large part of the whole complex is clad with brick. The windows are distributed evenly and some types of apartments have balconies. There are eight different typologies, the most unusual of which are the Panorama apartments at the tip, the Penthouses with roof terrace on the eleventh floor, the Concrete Architectural Associates apartments on the seventh floor, and the Dual View apartments in the middle of the block.

Some of the apartments in the lower block are
intended for senior citizens and those with a
handicap, and are linked with a care concept.
The apartments in the tip are almost entirely
made of glass and offer a view of both the
IJ and the Westerdok, so that the name
Panorama apartments is justified. On the
seventh floor of the taller block the uniform
appearance of the façade is broken by the
strip of de luxe design apartments which
Concrete Architectural Associates, whose
designs include the Supper Clubs, have
designed for different lifestyles. The buyer
buys not only the apartment but also the

Silodam, Westerdokseiland

interior design. These lifestyle apartments consist of two floors interrupted by voids so that at some points the ceiling is twice as high. There is the pied-à-terre, with a large and luxurious living room but a relatively small kitchen. There is the family apartment for a family with young children; the wallpaper and plants have already been chosen. And there is an artist's apartment which is delivered as empty as possible, although the occupier is recommended to buy Marcel Breuer chairs for it.

| 3.10 | **Westerkaap II**
(2007)
Westerdokseiland | **Architect**
DKV, baneke,
van der hoeven
architekten | **Commisioned by**
Hofmakerij VOF
(Amvest and
Ymere) |

Within the framework of the 'breeding ground' policy, new studio space on the ground level of both Westerkaap II (1,000 m²) and La Grande Cour has been reserved for the group of artists who used the customs sheds before they were demolished.

The Westerkaap II part of the project is due to be completed in the summer of 2007. The buildings on the Westerdok side consist of three six-storey tower blocks on a tall plinth, alternating with low-level buildings. In the two side streets are two high-rise blocks of eleven storeys with a large overhanging roof. There are three seven-storey blocks on the enclosed area, while on the side facing the IJ the buildings consist of separate five-storey blocks on a high plinth. The materials chosen for the façades is maily in red

Along Amsterdam's Waterfront

and brown tints. A variety of materials in grey, green and dark brown have been applied to the façades facing the courtyards to create a contrast between the dark exterior and the light interior. Amid this interaction of different building blocks, three of the courtyards have been left open and each has a character of its own. Warm hardwood is predominant in one, chic natural stone in another, and in the third all the walls are covered with ivy and the centre is planted with bamboo. In the evening the courtyards are only open to the residents. Westerkaap II contains apartments in every price category, from rented council housing to expensive private sector owner-occupied apartments. Because the apartments in the first stage of the Westerkaap plan came onto the market at a time when the housing market was at an ebb, the developer has given them very competitive prices.

VOC Cour (2007) Westerdokseiland	Architect MVRDV, Jeroen Schipper Architecten, Bosch Architects, Art Zaaijer	Commisioned by Wodan CV (De Dageraad, Volker Wessels, Nijhuis Rijssen, OMA Hoek van Holland)	3.11

The central part of the new building in the Westerdok is about 100 metres square. It consists of 382 housing units, a sports school, a local supermarket, and a childcare centre and is built around a large courtyard, the 'cour', which provides access to all the apartments. Unlike the neighbouring Westerkaap and Grande Cour blocks, the 'cour' is a large open space. There are five entrances and an underground car park. The 'cour' has the atmosphere of a square, with a greenhouse for the so-called VOC café, a meeting place for residents. The idea is to build the greenhouse from replicas of the cast-iron supporting elements of the demolished warehouses on the Westerdok. A green recreational area is also

The new side streets on the Westerdokseiland are named after historic sailing vessels: the Coffijboomstraat, the Leliëndaalstraat, and the Winthorststraat. The Green Left political party on the district council for the centre of the city submitted a motion – which has been rejected – against those street names because they might have been ships on which slaves were carried.

planned with three large trees, whose roots will be at the level of the car park. Large terraces and roof gardens are situated on the rooftops.

Four firms of architects are working on the elaboration of the different buildings, each with its own character. The block facing the IJ is continuous and has six storeys, like the neighbouring blocks. The principle has been applied to the Westerdok of four building volumes that consist of seven storeys on the building line and rise to eleven storeys when they stand further back from that line. The gate houses with bells and letter boxes have been located in the lower links between these blocks as well as a number of ground-level villas.

Art Zaaijer opted for dark brown brick for the façades. MVRDV alternates a glass façade with layers of concrete. Almost the whole surface of the façades of this block is covered with balconies, which is an essential and un-Dutch aspect of this design. Jeroen Schipper applies a liver-coloured hand-formed brick in alternating horizontal and vertical bond.

John Bosch finishes his block in industrial rough stone.

The prices of the apartments vary considerably within a single block: two buildings consist entirely of rented council flats, while others boast penthouses costing up to 1,150,000 euros. There is also a lot of variation in terms of housing types: there are large and small apartments with balconies, villas, and luxury apartments. The buildings have been given the names of old VOC ships, such as *Bosschenhoven*, *Pallas*, *Morgenster*, *Barbesteyn*, and *Duyfken*.

La Grande Cour (2007)	Architect Meyer en Van	Commisioned by City Cour Com-	3.12
Westerdokseiland	Schooten Architec-ten, Heren 5, de Architekten Cie.	bination (Bouw-fonds MAB, Smits Bouwbedrijf)	

For the density study for the southernmost part of the area, La Grande Cour, Meyer en Van Schooten have placed building programme as far as possible on the sides to ensure that, in spite of the high density, a maximal number of homes with a view could be created. With this aim in view, the higher volumes, which are only allowed in the central part, have been bent to extend over the buildings on the edge. These periscopes bend halfway over the three 'cours' and determine the impact of the design. The blocks combine business units with apartments. Almost all of the apartments have a generous balcony, and there are common roof terraces.

The design of the block has been given to three firms of architects. Each part of the plan has its own 'cour' and periscope. All three firms have chosen the same purple-brown stone for the street façades, but their individual signature can be seen in the design and composition of the façades. The differences between the firms are more pronounced in the 'cours'. Heren 5 has opted for a gradually sloping 'cour' with adjacent wooden terraces and trees in tubs, surrounded by azure façades. In the 'cour'

by de Architekten Cie., the difference in
level is resolved with a grand staircase. The
inner façades are finished with upright
aluminium panels. The frames are edged with
a pronounced white border. The 'cour' by
Meyer en Van Schooten is on a gradual slope. It
includes a tub with a mature tree. The façades
are finished with light grey fibre-reinforced
plates on a cement basis. The periscope tower is
distinguished by cladding of dark grey panels
with deep grooves.
There is a car park for residents underneath La
Grande Cour.

3.13 Landing stages and facilities for houseboats in the Westerdok (2006)	Architect Bureau B+B Stedebouw en landschaps-architectuur	Commisioned by Spatial Planning Department, Royal Haskoning

For decades there were houseboats moored
on the city side of the Westerdokseiland.
Some were legal, others illegal or temporary,
but taken together they formed a tight-knit
group of amphibians with private gardens on
the quays. In developing the area, it has been

Along Amsterdam's Waterfront

decided to leave the quay as a part of the public space. A large number of the houseboats have been given a place on the new landing stages with hardwood finish, specially suited to the type of boat. The boats now lie at right angles to the quay and have direct access to the landing stage and to their own metre cupboard.

| **Han Lammers-bridge** (2003) | **Architect** Meyer & Van Schooten Architecten | **Commisioned by** Amsterdam Development Corporation (OGA) | **3.14** |

The new moveable bridge for cyclists and pedestrians over the Westerdok sluice is a link between the west of the city centre and the Westerdok. In view of the large number of different environmental elements (the railway line and the various different types of buildings), the architects designed the bridge as a sober, tranquil element. The bridge is 48 metres long and 5 metres wide, and has two supports in the water. Because of the height that the bridge has to span, it is the steepest bridge in Amsterdam with a gradient of 20 per cent.

The bridge is entirely constructed and clad in a light material: aluminium. The part that opens hangs just above the water level when it is vertical. This eliminates the need for a bascule cellar. The counterweight and the hydraulic

pumps are small in size because of the light
material used for the moveable part, and could
therefore be concealed beneath the road surface.
The lighting is placed beneath the balustrade
and shines through the perforated sheets. Like
the Jan Schaefer bridge, the bridge is named
after a representative of the Partij van de
Arbeid on the local council. Han Lammers was
councillor for Urban Development from 1970 to
1976 and was a proponent of large-scale urban
renewal, including the construction of the
metro line to South-East Amsterdam. His motto
was: 'Necessary things always happen'.

3.15 Wester IJdock (2010)	**Architect** de architecten-groep (Dick van Gameren, coordinating architect, Bjarne Mastenbroek), Koers, Zeinstra van Gelderen, Jan Bakers Architecten, and Ben Loerakker, Claus en Kaan Architecten	**Commisioned by** Amsterdam Local Authority, Ministry of Housing and Construction, Wester IJdock cv (William Properties, Woonveste)

A new pier is being constructed as a counterpart
to Het Stenen Hoofd, but on a larger scale also
as the pendant to the end of the Oostelijke
Handelskade with the Muziekgebouw. A large
volume of 70,000 m² is to be built here with
commercial functions, a public car park,
a hotel, apartments, a new station for the
national police force, and a new magistrate's
court. In addition, a passengers harbour is
to be built on the station side between the
Westerdoksdijk and the pier to make the IJ
more accessible for water tourism.
The design has been produced by an initial
stage of throwing all the parts of the
programme together in one pile. Subsequently
the maximal contour of the volume that could
be built on this site was determined,

and this resulted in a size that was twice as large as the space required for the programme. Sections have been cut out of this volume to keep the lines of vision from the centre to the IJ as open as possible., such as those from the Bickerseiland to the IJ and from the Central Station to the Westerdoksdijk, but on a larger scale to the Keizersgracht as well. This creates a relationship between Bickerseiland and the IJ and between Central Station and Westerdoksdijk and, on a larger scale, with the Keizersgracht as well. In this way the new volume fits tidily into the existing city. The volume with the prescribed empty areas was then broken down into five separate buildings, each of which is to be elaborated by different architects.

This 'City in the IJ' is intersected longitudinally by an inner street. The quay beside the IJ continues in this central public area with catering establishments, shops and access to the apartments and offices. A covered terrace facing south will be built at the end of the inner street. Cars drive straight into the car park as soon as they enter the island.

The functions within the complex have been determined in terms of level: commercial functions at ground level, offices in the intermediate levels, and apartments on the top storeys. According to the master plan, the

The Koloniaal Etablissement facing the Westerdoksdijk, which accommodates the river police at the moment, is an unusual building that leaves its mark on the surroundings. During the planning stage, attempts were made to integrate it in the urban development plan. The Gouden Reael community centre also tried to get it put on the list of protected historic buildings, but was unsuccessful because of its poor condition and the fact that the interior no longer contains any original parts. In the end it was decided to demolish the complex in view of the development of the IJdock. The idea was to wait until 2010 to do this, but given the dilapidated state of the building, it will have to be demolished earlier than that for safety reasons.

outer façades of all the internal blocks must be as transparent as possible.

The design for the northwest part by Koers, Zeinstra van Gelderen contains apartment and office space for the river police. The exterior is in a blue, glasslike material. The corridors make a turn on each floor and end in the façade: on the outside 'holes' can be seen in the façade, each with a different colour.

The southwest part, designed by Jan Bakers and Ben Loerakker, will accommodate a hotel with three hundred rooms. The transparent façade with a steel supporting construction has internal balconies on the south side.

The east is intended for the new magistrate's court and is designed by the Claus and Kaan firm of architects. Arising from the architectural brief, the Public Prosecutor has been accommodated separately on the north side, while the magistrates are accommodated in the part on the south side. Many elements are brought together on the ground floor: there is a public entrance with facilities, a separate entrance for employees, and an entrance to the bicycle park. The construction of the south part is based on four enormous supporting walls, between which different chambers are suspended, connected by bridges. The interior of the court will be primarily determined by a finish of broken natural stone. Like the rest of IJdock, the exterior will be treated like a transparent membrane, in so far as the function of a magistrate's court permits.

| 3.16 | Railway bridge 19S/ Open (2007) Westerdoksplein | Architect de Architekten Cie. (Pi de Bruijn) | Commisioned by Gerry Mekes, Floriaan Hackmann, Tristan Brinckman |

There are only three rotating railway bridges in the Netherlands, and the bridge between the Westelijk Stationeiland and the Westerdokseiland is one of them. Because the bridge lost its function when the shunting area on the Westerdokseiland was closed, the local authority decided to give it a special catering function in line with the developments of the South IJ Bank project. A competition was organised, which was won by the design of de Architekten Cie. The jury chose this design because of the open character, the 'elegant open window area for fine weather', and the fact that the restaurant does not overshadow the bridge itself.

The volume fits exactly on top of the existing bridge. It consists of a floor, a roof and a glass façade, entirely formed by pivot windows that can all be opened. Isolated elements have been used in the space to give the separate functions, such as the kitchen, toilets and bar, a place of their own without disturbing the experience of the total space.

The construction consists of steel columns and girders. Because the floor joists at the ends of the bridge can slide, unwanted tensions in the old bridge caused by changes of temperature can be accommodated.

Silodam, Westerdokseiland

Along Amsterdam's Waterfront

IJ harbour

ARCHI-TECTURAL DIVERSITY

Sabine Lebesque

Development of new waterfront

Almost twenty years ago a group of us
– architects and architectural historians –
were in the habit of cycling through the derelict
harbour zone, along the broken-up quays of
Java Island, to the Houthavens or even further
afield. We waxed sentimental about the faded
glory of the old utilitarian structures, because
we knew that it was all going to change. New
architecture would colonise the waterfront with
glitzy buildings, just as in London, Copenhagen,
Hamburg and Barcelona.

New metropolitan spirit

Atelier Pro's serpentine Entrepotbrug
apartment complex had taken the lead
in 'the big building in vast surroundings'
phenomenon without much ado. But the
Piraeus superblock by Berlin architect Hans
Kollhoff caused an uproar. The dark brick
was massive and heavy, the façade was tautly
detailed. Although the architecture world was
captivated by the grand gesture – after all, it
testified to a new metropolitan spirit that was
certainly warranted here on the waterfront –
the average Amsterdammer was distinctly
unimpressed. In the prize for the most
beautiful building, organised by the Parool
newspaper, they voted for its neighbour, the
neo-traditional Barcelonaplein block by Belgian
architect Bruno Albert.

Sea of houses

On Java Island, where a reiteration of
different apartment blocks interspersed with
narrow canals was deployed in an attempt
to reintroduce the diversity of the historic
Amsterdam canal zone, the various elements,
however differently and colourfully designed,
played a subordinate role in the overall concept.
In the 'sea of houses' on Borneo and

Sporenburg architectural expression was a square millimetre affair. Apart from the private development plots on Scheepstimmerman-straat, which is a showcase of twentieth-century fin-de-siècle architectural chic, the design constraints laid down by the supervisor were so tight that variation had to be sought within very narrow margins. Only a few architects were able to cut loose with 'meteorites' like The Whale by Frits van Dongen, a photogenic building with its aluminium cladding and pronounced forms.

Contours take shape

MVRDV's Silodam had at least as much impact on the architectural taste of the city as Piraeus a few years earlier. The container style was robust, arrogant and trendy and it was either loved or loathed. The complex and the renovated concrete and grain silos that gave it its name, stood a little apart from the IJ Banks project. With construction on Westerdok now proceeding apace, it too falls within the new contours of the IJ.

New horizon

On Oosterdok, Jo Coenen's public library is currently under construction. The façade will have large, coffer-like windows and a sculptural roof edge. Once the island has been fully developed, the library will be less dominant than it now appears. The artist's impression promises a cluster of buildings that together form a hill beside Central Station.
From the end of Wittenburgereiland there is an invigorating view of the new horizon of the Oostelijke Handelskade. The warehouses, old and new, do indeed look like a long train with carriages, as intended by the masterplan.

Locomotive

The Muziekgebouw is the locomotive. The projecting roof edge above the glazed façade is spectacular, from all sides of the IJ. Yet it is not a showy building, which it might easily have been on that location. As a whole it is modest, and the materialisation of the base is even shared with its three neighbours. Perhaps this is what makes it an especially Amsterdam building, even though it was designed by 3xN, a Danish practice that is active around the world.

New urban centre

Just as the canals of Amsterdam were laid down as a template before the merchants were able to build their own houses, now a structure of strong urban design plans and strict supervision are giving rise to a new urban centre along the banks of the IJ. Each building has its own place in the whole, without detracting from the others. Is this perhaps the characteristic strength of Amsterdam's building culture? Nowadays, when I cycle from the Minervahaven to the Cruquiusterrein, alone or with Japanese architecture tourists, I realise that the nostalgia of twenty years ago has been replaced by a sense of confidence: without Gehry, Nouvel, Foster or Koolhaas, the IJ has won back the city.

Along Amsterdam's Waterfront

The Stenen Hoofd and the Silodam

4.
STATIONS-
EILAND

The Central Station is sometimes called 'the biggest urban planning mistake ever made in Amsterdam'. The plan for a station on the present site was already criticised from all sides in the 1860s. There were fears that the inner city would lose its prosperity if it were both physically and visually cut off from its main source of wealth, the harbour. The Leidseplein and the Reguliersgracht were suggested as alternative sites. In the event national government took the decision for Amsterdam and opted in 1869 for the construction of the island on which the station stands in front of and at right angles to the Damrak. The building designed by Cuypers was completed twenty years later.

In economic terms this construction, like that of the Western and Eastern Islands, was not a bad idea. With the arrival of the station, the area around it underwent a metropolitan development with an enormous leap in scale: imposing buildings like the Mercurius building, the Victoria Hotel and the St Nicholas' Church rose amid the small-scale warehouses and trading houses that had originally been situated on the open waterfront of the harbour.

The South Bank project is restoring the waterfront to the city, with the Central Station as the main public transport junction operating as a protagonist. The IJ side is becoming more important, a 'second face', a 'gateway to the city'. The surrounding area is being given back the old island character that had gradually disappeared in the course of the last hundred years, clearing the way for slow traffic and more water on all sides. The quay beside the river is being turned into a pedestrian promenade, while motorised traffic is led underground or handled at a higher level. As a result, the inner city once again comes to lie beside the IJ and the connection between the old and the new districts is strengthened.

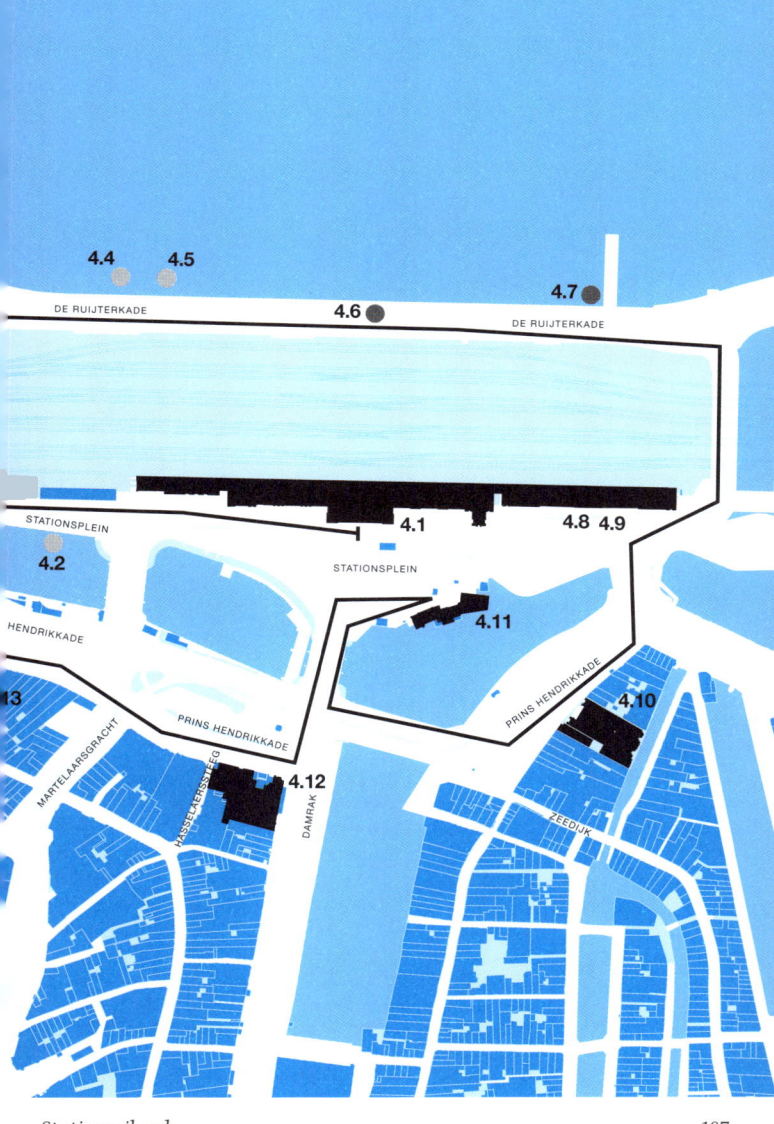

DE RUIJTERKADE

4.4 **4.5**

4.6

4.7

DE RUIJTERKADE

STATIONSPLEIN

4.2

4.1

4.8 **4.9**

STATIONSPLEIN

HENDRIKKADE

4.11

3

4.10

MARTELAARSGRACHT

PRINS HENDRIKKADE

PRINS HENDRIKKADE

4.12

DAMRAK

HASSELAERSSTEEG

ZEEDIJK

4.1 Cuypershal, Stationsplein (1889/2012) Stationsplein

Architect
P.J.H. Cuypers in collaboration with A.L. van Gendt/ Benthem Crouwel Architekten

Commisioned by
Amsterdam Local Authority, NS Vastgoed, Prorail

The Central Station is no doubt the most widely discussed building in Amsterdam because of its location. After it had been built, the inner city no longer enjoyed a view of the IJ.
At first there was still some uncertainty as to where the station should be built. The local authority favoured a site on the Leidseplein, while central government preferred the present location. The decision was eventually taken in 1876 to go ahead with the government proposal. Building work began, and the station was opened in 1889. It was the first station in the Netherlands to be designed by an architect; previously these buildings had been designed by engineers. Cuypers was commissiond to design the building in the 'Old Dutch' style which was very fashionable at the time.

In the meantime plans have been made to restore the Cuypers building to its original state and to bring the wealth of decoration of his plan back into view again. The central reception hall will be made visual by removing the floors with offices that were added later, so that the hall will afford a view of the original monumental roof. The functions accommodated there will also be attuned to the present-day use of the station. The catering functions wll remain, and there will be congress facilities too.

On the right-hand side of the eastern entrance is the Queen's Pavilion, an extension building with a royal waiting room with richly decorated walls and a special toilet for the queen. The outside doors are very wide to allow coaches (and nowadays cars) to enter.

Today the Central Station is an intersection for all kinds of public transport: besides a station for trains to every point of the compass, there is a stop for three metro lines (four when the North/South Line is completed), eleven tram lines, more than thirty bus routes, and five ferries. With the development of the areas on both sides and the extension on the side facing the IJ, the building will acquire a very different position in relation to the one that it has occupied for the last hundred years.

The renovation is under way and will take several years. The west concourse has been completely renewed, after which the central section will be tackled. Further to the west a new subway for cyclists will be constructed, and the one to the east will be renovated and widened.

The square in front of the station will become the exclusive preserve of pedestrians and trams. All the obstacles that stand there at the moment will be removed, and apart from the entrances to the metro, the square will be entirely empty. The paving will be cut granite. Because buses and cars will pass on the IJ side, the volume of motorised traffic on the Prins Hendrikkade can be reduced. Red cobbles will

There is a characteristic signal house on platform five. The plan is to give it a special function. Among the possibilities are a bar or lunchroom with a view of the plat- forms and tracks.

be laid here to match the inner city.
To emphasise the insular character of the area and to create space for canal boats, the water of the historic open harbour front will be expanded. Facilities for the canal boat companies will be accommodated in a group of ticket booths on the lower quays. The bridges connect the land with the station island. Like the square, they will be paved with large sheets of granite. The quays are of masoned basalt.

4.2	**Bike flat** (2001) opposite Stations- plein 49	**Architect** VMX Architects	**Commisioned by** Dienst Infrastruc- tuur, Verkeer en Vervoer

The bike flat was designed for purely functional and practical purposes and has quickly become one of the tourist attractions of the city. More than 2,500 bicycles can be parked in this guarded facility seven days a week, twenty-four hours a day. The steel construction is 100 metres long, 14 metres wide, three levels high, roofed, and built on piles above the water. A system of ramps on the water side provides access to the different levels. The lowest of the ramps is 6 metres above water level so that the canal boats can manoeuvre properly to reach their landing stage. The bike flat was constructed in Friesland and transported to Amsterdam by water.

Although the bike flat is very popular, there are also complaints: a lot of cyclists cannot find their bike among the hundreds of others. The bike flat has become the victim of its own success.

When the bike flat was built in 2001, it was supposed to be a temporary structure for three years. In view of the building activites

on and around the Central Station, it has been
decided to leave it in place until the new bike
sheds are ready.
The design won VMX Architects a nomination
for the AM NAi Award.

Ibis-hotel/	Architect	Commisioned by	4.3
Zilverentoren	Benthem Crouwel	NS Vastgoed	
(1992/2007)	Architekten/		
Stationsplein 49	Ruland + Partner		
	Architekten		

The present Ibis-hotel and the Zilverentoren
were completed in 1992 and soon appeared
on lists of the ugliest buildings in Amsterdam.
The unusual oval shape, the contemporary
materials and the high tech look on a site
where old and new buildings rub shoulders did
not find many supporters. Demolition of the
Ibis hotel was considered, but it has now been
decided to expand the hotel from 187 to 370
rooms. The six-floor extension will hang over
the rails on columns that rest on platforms 1
and 2-3. The new annex will be connected with
the rest of the hotel by glass walkways.
A method has been adopted for building above
the tracks by which the building activity takes
place on a crash deck that hangs above the rails.
Once the first two floors are ready, the object is
jacked onto its supports.
Special safety regulations are in force during
the building activities, and it will not be
possible to use the rails for a while.

4.4   Ferry
Pontplein C.S.

Architect
Scheepswerf
Grave

Commisioned by
Gemeentelijk
Vervoersbedrijf

Plans for bridges over the IJ are nothing new. The Amsterdam sub-contractor Galman made no less than 36 designs for such a bridge in the second half of the nine-teenth century, but none of them was implemented because of the limited economic significance of North Holland at the time and the fear of sediment-ation around the columns. The first long-term solu-tion was the IJ Tunnel in 1960, and the North/South Line will also contribute to improving connections between North Amster-dam and the rest of the city. All the same, specula-tions about a permanent bridge over the IJ do pop up now and then. For in-stance, there are ideas for extending the Jan Schaefer bridge over the IJ. More-over, in its agreement for the period 2006–2010, the city council has included a proposal to carry out a study on a bridge between the Houthavens and the NDSM wharf. This is a dif-ficult assignment, because the IJ is relatively narrow, carries heavy traffic, and must be able to offer a passage to vessels with a height of up to 70 metres above water level.

Until the North/South Line is opened, the ferry is the main means of transport to carry cyclists and pedestrians to North Amsterdam. The local authority has been operating a ferry over the IJ since 1897. The first ferry landed at the Toll House in North Amsterdam, and this is still the main connection, but there are also links with the NDSM wharf, de Meeuwenlaan, and the Java Island. The Tasmanstraat-Distelweg link, which also carries cars, is situated slightly further to the west. In the nineteenth century the price of a passage by chain ferry was between 5 and 15 cents per person. A calf, donkey or pig cost a further 15 cents, and an ox, bull or cow 30 cents. Civil servants travelled free of charge. So not everything goes up in price every year, because the ferry is free of charge today.

A new generation of ferries, the 50 series, was introduced in 2002. The main innovation is the roll-on-roll-off construction with front and rear access. The new ferries are half roofed and half open to meet the demands of many passengers. A ferry can carry 240 passengers. The old ferries have been converted to the model of the 50 series. Now that the ferries are all of the same type and new mooring constructions have been made, the ferries are all multi-purpose.

The construction and renovation of the ferries is done by the shipyard in Grave.

Pier 10 (1932) **Architect** **Commisioned by** 4.5
De Ruijterkade 50A J. de Meijer West-Frieslandlijn

With the construction of the Eastern Harbour Area and the North Sea Canal the banks of the IJ became a hive of activity. The big international shipping companies set out from the eastern docklands. The smaller vessels with local traffic set out from behind the Central Station. Eighteen piers, each with its own office, were constructed for that purpose. This building, commissioned by the West-Frieslandlijn, was constructed in 1932 and is a good example of the New Building style.

The wide facing the water is almost entirely glass so that the management could have a good view of what was going on on the IJ. Originally a periscope was planned to offer a view of the quay as well, but in the end that turned out to be too expensive. In spite of what one might think at first sight, the building is not made of concrete but of brick, which was plastered, sanded and painted afterwards. Within the framework of the expansion of the Central Sation, the quay has been widened, the building has been placed 17.5 metres further in the IJ on a large floating trestle, and has been shifted about 30 centimetres to the east. Restaurant 10 has been serving a French-style cuisine for years.

4.6 IJ hall
(2012)
De Ruijterkade

Architect
Benthem Crouwel
Architekten

Commisioned by
Amsterdam
Development Cor-
poration (OGA)

Some hundred buses stop at Amsterdam Central Station each hour. The new bus station will break with the system in which each bus route has its own stop. The 24 dynamic bus stops will be allocated to different bus numbers depending on how busy they are.

To improve the situation on the side of the station facing the city, it was necessary to devise an alternative for the bus and car traffic. A natural solution has been found on the side of the Central Station facing the IJ. By putting the buses literally and metaphorically on the same level as the trains, a more compact public transport junction can be created. Moreover, with the completion of the North/South Line a direct transfer between bus and metro can be made. To make the bus station on level +1 easily accessible to passengers and to add a minimal extra surface area to the island on which the station is situated at the expense of the IJ, it has been decided to lead car traffic coming from the De Ruijterkade on the IJ side of the Central Station underground. New station entrances will be created as an extension of the passenger corridors in the Central Station. Water traffic on the IJ side can now also form a more direct part of the public

transport junction. The result will be a unique public transport junction in Amsterdam where almost all forms of transport are represented. The side of the Central Station facing the water will be roofed by the IJ Hall, a new hall that forms a counterpart to the Cuypers Hall on the city side. This building will provide shelter not only for the passengers waiting for buses, but also for the forecourts of the new station hall, the tunnel exits, and a part of the waterfront. Because the roof extends to the waterfront, passengers can easily transfer from the station to a ferry. The covered area also accommodates large shops and catering establishments which are also directly accessible from outside. The view over the water makes the site a special location. The IJ Hall strengthens the relation between the city centre, the IJ and North Amsterdam.
The fourth station roof is largely covered with glass and its shape is a continuation of the existing roofs. The roof is 360 metres long and has a span of 60 metres. The glass sheets are each more than 1 by 3 metres large and only 1 centimetre thick. The curved form nevertheless makes them strong enough to walk on. A total of around 4,500 glass sheets will be used, a large number of which will be coated with a transparent red and orange foil to spell the name AMSTERDAM. The letters of 28 by 21 metres will make this the largest place name sign in the Netherlands. The station roof will be a landmark on the banks of the IJ and will form a new, grand entrance to the city for all kinds of passengers.

| Naco build-ing and Stolp (1919/2008) De Ruijterkade | Architect G.F. Lacroix/Zwarts & Jansma with Kentie en Partners | Commisioned by Noordhollandse Auto Car Onder-neming | 4.7 |

The Naco building, which is now temporarily accommodated in the harbour of Zaandam, was built, like Pier 10, for a small shipping company, in this case the Noordhollandse

Auto Car Onderneming. But the style in which it was built is completely different: Amsterdam School combined with a time-hallowed Indonesian style, as typified in the tilting roof. The building is one of two hundred new protected national monuments. It has been moved because of the expansion of the station. It is planned to be replaced on the waterfront square east of the IJboulevard as a catering establishment with waiting room. To create more space and to protect the fragile building, a severe modern glass cover has been designed by Zwarts & Jansma, like a showcase for a museum piece. However, the heirs of the initiator and financier of the project, who recently died, have pulled out and the search is going on for a new party to participate in the venture.

| 4.8 | **Post Office parcels building** (1924/2007) Stationsplein 5-7 | **Architect** J. Cuypers |

The former Post Office parcels building has always been overshadowed by the main building of the Central Station. It was designed around 1924 by Jos Cuypers, a son of the great architect. In the 1960s it lost its function as a parcels handling facility and was taken over by Dutch Rail. The top floor, for instance, was used by the Amsterdam Rail Sports Association. It had an archery room, a billiard room, changing room and canteen.
The building is now being renovated and given a new function. The cellar will house cycle racks, the ground floor is earmarked for a public function, and the first, second and top floors will be converted into offices. The top floor has an unusual construction of riveted steel roof trusses.
The façade has been cleaned and the original multicoloured masonry has reappeared from behind the layer of soot that had been

Along Amsterdam's Waterfront

deposited in the course of eighty years. The building is still modest beside the large building of the Central Station, but some of its former glory has been restored.

North/South Line (2012)	Architect Benthem Crouwel Architekten	Commisioned by Dienst Infrastructuur Verkeer en Vervoer, Amsterdam Local Authority, Projectbureau Noord/ Zuidlijn	4.9

The North/South Line will go right under the Central Station for a length of 130 metres. The design of all the public space has been integrated in the total design for the station and the area in front of it on the city side. Glass and steel are the dominant materials. The construction of the underground line is technically very demanding and has therefore already been delayed several times. The work is expected to be completed around 2012. When the North/South Line is finished, it will be possible to travel from the Buikslotermeerplein in North Amsterdam to the WTC Station in South Amsterdam in sixteen minutes. In the long term there are plans to continue the metro line to Schiphol, Zaandam and Purmerend.

Although the North/South Line has been on the agenda since the 1960s, it took a long time for it to gain sufficient political support. A referendum in 1997, which was won by the opponents but declared invalid because of the low level of participation, tipped the balance in favour of implementation. During the construction of the metro to South-East Amsterdam a lot had to be demolished, leading to much protest from residents. Nowadays it is possible to work below ground level with a minimal interference with the buildings above. Moreover, this new technique has speeded up the process: the drill covers between ten and fifteen metres a day.

There is an information centre about the new constructions in the Post Office parcels building. The construction of the metro line is shown in a variety of interactive formats. For instance, it is possible to see not only the route but also the depth of the tunnel for the whole trajectory.

4.10 St Nicholas' Church (1887) Prins Hendrik-kade 75	**Architect** A.C. Bleijs

Long before the St Nicholas' Church was built there was already a church with this name in Amsterdam: the present-day Oude Kerk. After the decision of Amsterdam to become Protestant in 1578, the Catholics lost this church to the Protestants and were forced to practise their religious in clandestine churches for the next two centuries, until an official separation between Church and State was instituted in 1795. The Catholics did not start to build their own churches again until late in the nineteenth century.

The church, which now has a very dirty façade, stands on a prominent spot opposite the station and towers high above the surrounding buildings. The architect chose a Neo-Renaissance style combined with Neo-Baroque features, in clear opposition to the predominance of Neo-

Gothic architecture for Catholic churches at the time. The building has a tall octagonal dome above the point where the nave and the transept intersect, and two towers on the front façade. At the top, in the middle of the façade, is a sandstone statue of St Nicholas, the patron saint not only of this church but also of the city of Amsterdam. Every year the saint voyages in his steamship from Spain to Amsterdam and moors in front of the church.

Noord-Zuid Hollandsch Koffiehuis (1911/2007) Stationsplein 10	**Architect** J.H.W. Leliman/ Kentie en Partners Architekten	**Commisioned by** Noord-Zuidhollandsche Tramweg Maatschappij	4.11

The Noord-Zuid Hollandsch Koffiehuis (North-South Dutch Coffee House), which houses a café and the tourist information office, was originally the waiting room for the Noord-Zuidhollandsche Tramweg Maatschappij. Passengers were taken by boat from here to North Amsterdam, where they could change to the tram to Purmerend and Edam-Volendam. The wooden building dating from 1911 is a beautiful example of a combination of styles. The architect J.H.W. Leliman drew his inspiration from the sixteenth-century Paalhuis (House on Stilts) that stood in the Damrak and functioned as an office for the collection of mooring and harbour dues. That was the source of inspiration for the row of Doric columns, the little stair tower, the upper façades and the waterside terrace. The coffee house was enlarged in 1930; in 1971 it was dismantled for the construction of the metro, and more than ten years later it was rebuilt on practically the same site. The premises were recently extended even further and the paving around the building was also renewed. It also serves as a test for the future paving of the whole area in front of the station.

4.12 Victoria Hotel
(1890)
Damrak 1-5

Architect
J.F. Henkenhaf

Commisioned by
Victoria Hotel

The opposition of a private owner to the demolition of his house to build a large hotel is beautifully described by Thomas Rosenboom in his Publieke Werken [Public Works]. The Amsterdam violin maker Walter Vedder puts up a fierce fight against the building of this hotel, in spite of the considerable sums that he is offered to leave. In actual fact there were two owners who turned down offers to buy them out. Time was running out for the developer of the hotel because the Central Station was almost finished. It was therefore eventually decided to build the hotel around the two seventeenth-century buildings, even though this meant a rather striking break in the style of the richly decorated building. Above all the entrance on the corner with Corinthian half-columns and the dome on the roof make it abundantly clear that a luxury hotel is established here. The scale and the international style of the building are an early example of the attempt to turn Amsterdam into a real city. The architect Henkenhaf also worked on the Kurhaus in Scheveningen.

Mercury Building (1883) Prins Hendrik-kade 20-21	**Architect** H.P. Berlage, Th. Sanders, B. van Hove	**Commisioned by** firma Focke & Meltzer	**4.13**

The tympanum of this building showed Mercury, the god of commerce, flanked by allegorical figures of the River Amstel and the River IJ. It is a direct reference to the function for which it was built in the nineteenth century. Following the example of other European cities, a hotel was built here with a shopping arcade leading to the Nieuwendijk. The idea was to profit from the 1883 World Exhibition, but the project was not a success. Three years later it was converted into an office building and has housed a variety of companies since then.

The 'Department Store of the New Age', Oibibio, moved in in the 1990s, but this New Age centre was unprofitable. Even after a new start had been made under the name 'Oininio', the rent arrears piled up astronomically and the housing corporation Het Oosten decided to terminate the contract. At the moment a restaurant owner who targets the tourists is trying to live up to the symbolic value of the monumental building.

The point where the Singel used to flow into the IJ was once the site of the Haringpakkerstoren. The name refers to the place where herring was salted and put into barrels. Like the Montelbaanstoren and the Schreierstoren, it was originally a part of the medieval defences. It was given an elegant spire, probably designed by Hendrick de Keyser, in 1607 with a gilt herring as a weather vane.

The tower was demolished in 1829 because it was considered too expensive to maintain, but all of the parts were measured and put into storage. There are now plans to rebuild this historic tower. Stadsherstel would like to celebrate its fiftieth anniversary by donating it to the city.

4.14 Former School for Skippers' Children
(1925)
Droogbak 1c-1d

Architect
P.L. Marnette

This building was completed in 1925 as a school for skippers' children. The original function of the building is easy to see from the outside. On the south side the nine classrooms are clearly visible next to the large windows. The north side, which is somewhat higher, is adjacent to the railway track. That is why the outside wall on that side is more closed and has smaller windows. The building is in typical Amsterdam School style by the architect P.L. Marnette, who worked for the Public Works Department. The rounded corners give the impression that the façade has been folded around the actual building.

The building has been used as a shelter for the homeless for some years. Under the name Blaka Watra ('black water'), it offers them food, day care and a user's place.

4.15 State Administration Building
(1884)
Droogbak 1a

Architect
C.B. Posthumus Meyjes/ Architectenbureau J. van Stigt

Commisioned by
Hollandse IJzeren Spoorweg Maatschappij

This colossal office building, remarkably situated between the tracks and the old façades of the Haarlemmerbuurt, must have made a strong impact on its surroundings in the late nineteenth century. It was completed while the Central Station was still under construction. Even today, the square complex, built for the Hollandse IJzeren Spoorweg Maatschappij, heralds the increase of scale that takes place in the transition from the ring of canals to the buildings connected with the railway and harbour. The richly decorated, symmetrical composition of the sandstone façade in Dutch Renaissance style was recently completely cleaned, which makes it look so fresh and striking. The building is now on the list of state preserved historic monuments. The Van Stigt firm of architects, which is responsible for the renovation, has converted the building into offices that satisfy current demands. The inner courtyard – which cannot be seen from outside – has now been given a glass roof, supported by steel stay wires. By putting the reception and library here, this atrium has become the central part of the building.

Droogbak housing (1989) Nieuwe Westerdokstraat 10-200	**Architect** Rudy Uytenhaak	**Commisioned by** Stichting Lieven de Key	**4.16**

Because of the noise from trains, the busy traffic artery and the harbour behind, innovative solutions had to be devised to make housing possible on this site. The building is situated on a narrow strip between the tracks and the old houses and warehouses of the former seventeenth-century waterfront. The side of the building facing the tracks operates as a noise barrier, fitted with soundproofing glass screens. The topmost strip rises above the roof, thereby catching light from the south side. The details are accentuated above all in a horizontal direction, following the large dimensions of the adjacent infrastructure. The side of the project facing the south and the city has a very different character. Not only the playground that was designed along with the building, but also the balconies within the concrete framework of the façade turn it all into a sheltered spot.

The interiors of the apartments have been adapted to the situation: the main bedroom and the living room are on the south side, while the kitchen and other rooms are on the side facing the tracks.

4.17 VLTC building
(1996) Traffic
Management and
Transport Control
Centre
De Ruijterkade 1-4

Architect
Rob Steenhuis

Commisioned by
NS Vastgoed

Trains around Amsterdam are controlled from
this building. Until 1975 this was still done by
hand: there were mechanical signal houses
besides the tracks that operated the points.
Later an operating table was introduced, and
since 2003 all stations in the Netherlands have
been using computer-operated systems.
The building was designed at a time when
there was no clear vision of the future of
the IJ Banks, so Dutch Rail followed its own
course. The architect Rob Steenhuis, who
later became the official architect of the
company, devised a flying saucer in the
Postmodernist architectural jargon of the
1990s, characterised by expressive forms and
the use of different materials.

**4.18 Chamber of
Commerce/SNS
Bank** (1989)
De Ruijterkade 5

Architect
W. van Oostrum

Commisioned by
Mabon

This shiny building was completed before there
was a clear vision of the future of the South
Bank of the IJ. The colossal office block, divided
into two blocks with a surface area of 11,700
m², is located on the Ruijterkade parallel to the
railway line, with a raised terrace in front of
the entrance to the Chamber of Commerce. The
building has a curious history: the architect was
commissioned in the early 1980s to design an
office immediately next to the Harbour Building
for the N.O.G. (a predecessor of the current user,
SNS Reaal Bank), and next to it a block with
105 rented council flats. The land, however, was
enormously contaminated; it was the former
site of a Dutch Rail gas works to provide the
lighting for the Central Station. The delays

involved in cleaning the ground were such that by the time the building application had been submitted, the grants for rented council housing had run out. The local authority did not waste any time in finding another user: the Chamber of Commerce was prepared to move to this location overlooking the IJ and the project could be completed without any further delay. The architect deliberately chose to make the outer walls as glassy and reflecting as possible. The alternation of reflecting glass and blue panels, framed between black profiles, enables the surroundings to be reflected in the façade. The plinth is of white brick interrupted by red plates. The reference to Mondrian and De Stijl seems evident.

4.19 Harbour Building (1965)
De Ruijterkade 7

Architect
W.M. Dudok,
R.M.H. Magnée

Commisioned by
Scheepvaart
Vereniging Noord

This design by the architect Willem Marinus
Dudok is no longer very conspicuous because
there are now so many new buildings along the
IJ, but it is still a good example of the postwar
style, with its emphasis on no-nonsense, prefab
construction.

Dudok owes his fame mainly to the Hilversum
City Hall (1927) and the Bijenkorf department
store in Rotterdam (1930). When he was
commissioned by the Scheepvaart Vereniging
Noord in 1951 to design a 'new Shipping
Authority', he already had a lot of practical
experience and a measure of arrogance. He
designed not only a thirteen-storey complex
but also a number of subsidiary buildings, a
post building and a hotel, which he submitted

together with a quotation for almost 17,000 guilders, an enormous sum at the time. The plan was reduced to the original assignment. The local authority expressed the expectation that this plan would lead to a great improvement in the appearance of this part of the city, and that this part of the riverside would thereby become an attractive point in the harbour. The building was thus the starting point for the developments along the banks of the IJ.

The innovative feature of the building is that the composite skeleton is not concealed by the tiled outer walls, but has been deliberately left in view. The façade on the top two floors, which house a restaurant and a canteen, is slightly recessed, which creates the space for a terrace and leaves the steel construction in full view.

Supperclub Cruise (2004) De Ruijterkade, pier 14	**Architect** Concrete Architectural Associates	**Commisioned by** Supperclub Cruise	**4.20**

The *Supperclub Cruise* moors now and then at Pier 14. This is a floating restaurant and night club where the hip in-crowd can recline to eat. The concept already existed on a location behind the Kalverstraat, and by now there are also branches in Rome, San Francisco and Istambul. The successful formula has here been extended to the water, for which the *Pieter Caland/Comtesse* was bought, which had been sailing through the harbour of Rotterdam since the 1960s. Queen Juliana liked to take her guests on board the *Pieter Caland* and had her own royal cabin on it.

Design agency Concrete, the house architect of the Supperclubs, has turned the interior into a *salle neige* (completely in white) and a *bar noir* (completely in black). Passengers can recline to enjoy a five-course dinner or a club evening. The interior architecture received the Lensvelt de Architect Interior Award.

Along Amsterdam's Waterfront

Construction of the North/ South Line

CHAN-GING INFRA-STRUC-TURE

Merel Ligtelijn

Traffic junction

Traffic jams, construction pits, the thud of tunnel-boring machines and pile-drivers, traffic directors, chaos, bemused tourists. The radical reconstruction taking place on Stationseiland (Central Station and its environs) should eventually result in an efficient, effective, calm and attractive transport node. The construction of the IJ tram route, the North/South rail line, and a bus station, cycle/pedestrian route and car tunnel along the IJ inlet are all aimed at improving public transport and infrastructure. The starting point of the design by Benthem Crouwel Architekten is a station complex that combines just about all public transport functions, thus delivering greater convenience and more transfer possibilities to travellers.

North/ South rail line

The new Stationseiland, part of the redevelopment of the South Bank of the IJ, is scheduled to be completed in 2012. That year will also see the completion of the first 10 kilometres (from Buikslotermeerplein to Zuid/WTC) of the regional North/South rail link, which will eventually connect the city of Purmerend with Schiphol Airport via the heart of Amsterdam. The North/South Line will have eight stations, five of them underground along a length of 7.1 km. The stations are vertebrae within which the infrastructural marrow will give direction to a new metropolitan economic, social, cultural and morphological organisation. The main vertebra is the metro station under Amsterdam's Central Station (CS), through which 550 trains are expected to run every day in 2012. As a whole, the CS, which is the link between the city centre and the IJ, will process 300,000 train travellers and 1000 trains daily. In 1890, just after the station opened, the figures were 15,000 travellers and 185 trains.

Travellers' Palace

The architects of the station, P.J.H. Cuypers and A.L. van Gendt, characterised their creation on man-made islands in the IJ as The New City Gate and the Travellers' Palace. Their symbol for an economically expanding Amsterdam continues to defy time, even though 1200 of the 3000 pinewood piles on which it is built will make way for a new foundation and a construction pit 18 metres below ground into which the sections of the metro tunnel will be floated and sunk in place.

Transformation of the IJ side of CS

The IJ side of the CS has long been a chaotic and cheerless residual zone: a strip of land neglected by town planners where everyone gets in everyone else's way. That is set to change. The vehicular traffic currently tearing along De Ruijterkade behind the station, will eventually be moved underground. Its place will be taken by two glazed hangars in the style of the original arched station roof by L.J. Eijmer. A similar roof was added in 1922, now another two are under construction, parallel to the new IJ cycle/pedestrian boulevard and the two water plazas where boats tie up and the ferries to IJmuiden, Amsterdam-North and Java Island dock. One hall is earmarked for the new terminal for city and regional buses, the other for shops, cafes, lounges, conference and other facilities. The little Naco building, a former shipping agency built in a mix of Amsterdam School and East India styles in 1919, will be placed inside a protective glazed shell and contain food outlets and waiting rooms for the Amsterdam-IJmuiden hydrofoil. A little further along, Pier 10 restaurant is back in place and open for business again.

CS on an island

Radical transformations are not confined to the IJ side of Stationseiland. A new stretch of water between CS and Damrak will form a fluid transition between the historical city centre and the IJ. The Open Havenfront will be enlarged, thereby reinforcing the island character of Stationseiland. There will be new quays and landing stages with facilities for the canal tour boats and other water transport, in the style of the Noord-Zuid Hollandsch Koffiehuis. The unsightly multi-storey bicycle shed in front of the station will be demolished and bicycle storage facilities inside CS increased accordingly. Through traffic will also be rerouted over a new bridge. The forecourt of the Travellers' Palace will become the domain of the pedestrian, 'well-organised, safe and free of obstacles'.

Along Amsterdam's Waterfront

Bike flat

5.
OOSTER-DOK, OOSTER-DOKS-EILAND

With its many shipyards, the Oosterdok was a hive of activity in the seventeenth century, serving as a base for the naval vessels and the merchant ships of the VOC (United Dutch East India Company). As the IJ silted up, however, it became more and more difficult for large vessels to enter the harbour. The 'canal king' Willem I ordered the construction of the Oosterdoksdijk in 1832, which guaranteed sufficiently deep mooring places for the city.

All the same, in the succeeding decades the harbour moved its activities towards the east and the Oosterdok came to deal with other activities. The Central Station and a shunting yard were built, the Oosterdokseiland was created to house the PTT postal handling building, and the IJtunnel was built. Only the Maritime Museum and the harbour for historic ships still refer to the maritime past of this site.

In the 1990s the local authority decided to include the area in the city within the context of the development of the South Bank. Erick van Egeraat's master plan keys in with the centre in a contemporary way. The radial structure of the ring of canals is here continued, dividing the island into six plots. The heights of the buildings on these plots rise gradually from the Central Station to the size of the post office tower. The rhythm of the Amsterdam inner city has also been continued by means of guidelines for the choice of windows and materials.

The programme of the Oosterdokseiland is very metropolitan. The main branch of the Public Library is the biggest attraction, but the conservatory and leisure facilities, a hotel with a conference room, shops, catering and offices also play their part. The total of 343 apartments ensures that the area remains lively outside office hours too.

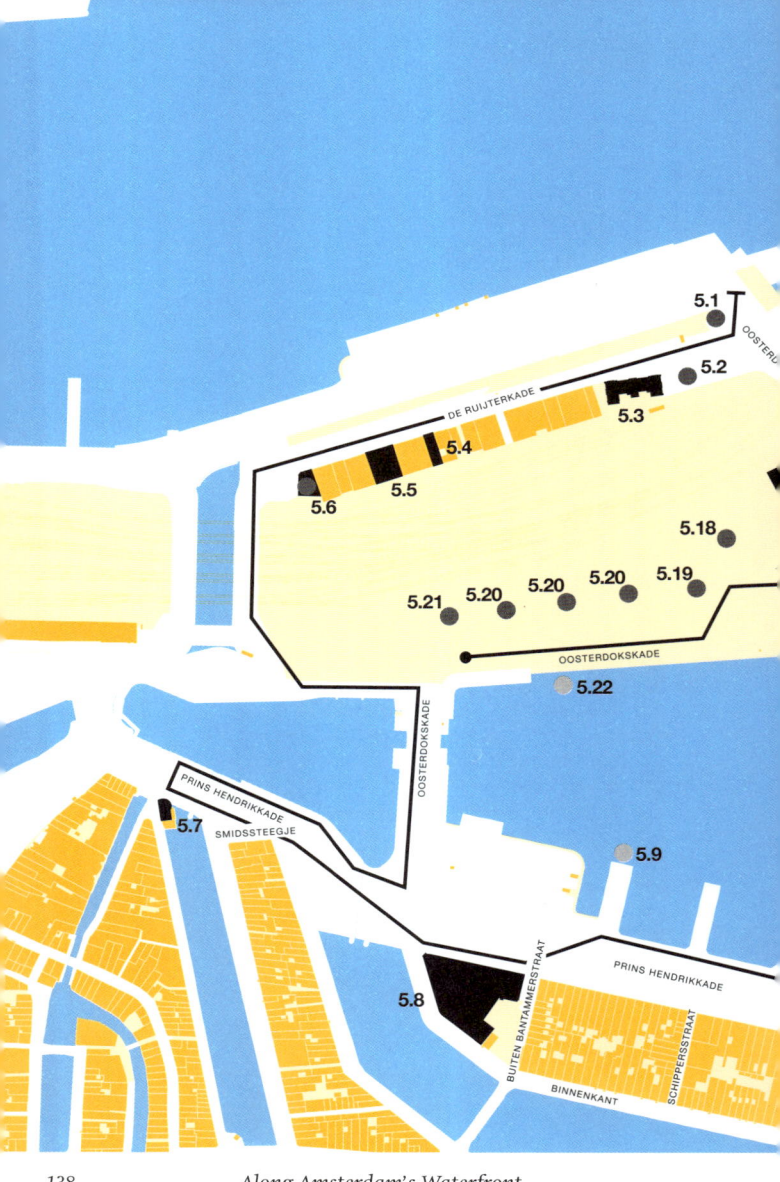

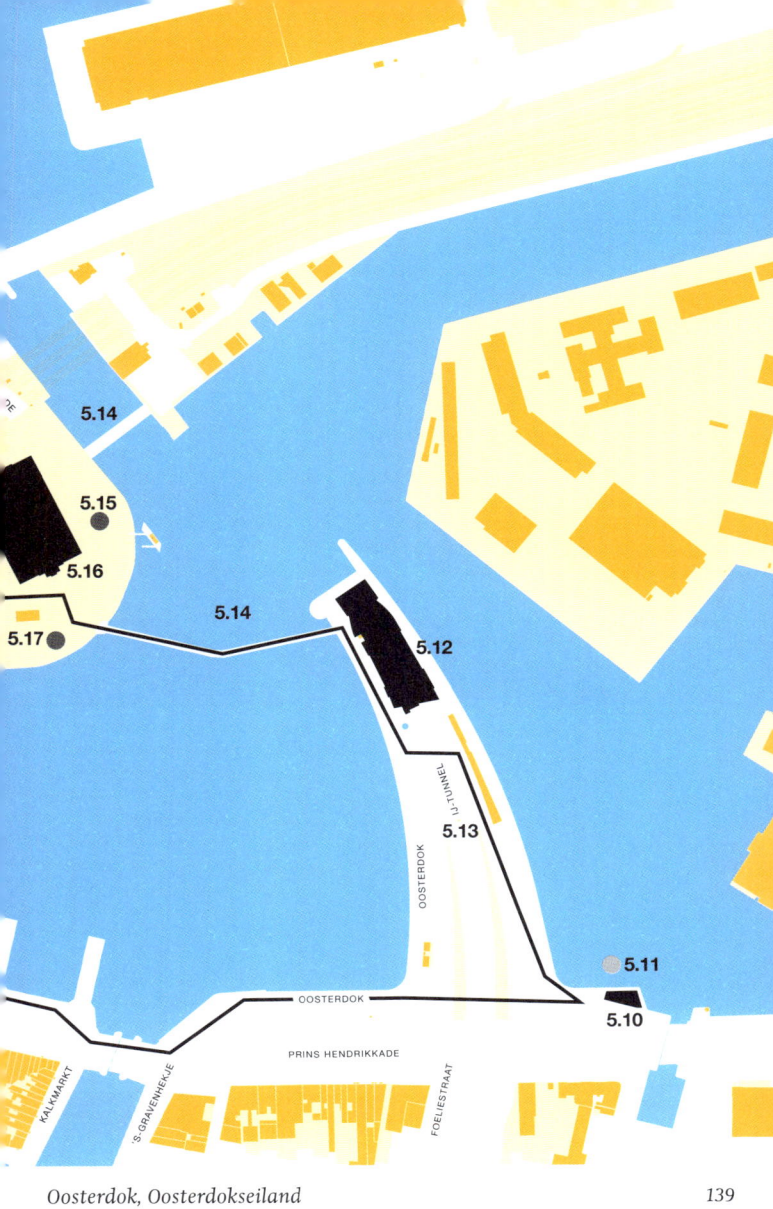

5.14

5.15

5.16

5.14

5.17

5.12

IJ-TUNNEL

5.13

OOSTERDOK

5.11

5.10

OOSTERDOK

PRINS HENDRIKKADE

KALKMARKT

'S-GRAVENHEKJE

FOELIESTRAAT

Oosterdok, Oosterdokseiland 139

5.1 **Business pre-**
mises under-
neath bridge 485
(2007)
De Ruijterkade

Architect
Hans
van Heeswijk

Commisioned by
Ymere, BAM,
Dienst Infrastruc-
tuur, Verkeer en
Vervoer

*Forty-eight speakers
have been concealed in
the walls underneath the
train viaduct at the end
of the Dijksgracht. They
emit music that has been
specially composed for
the location. The work,
Champsonique, is by
the Belgian sound artist
Mo Becha. It is an initi-
ative of the Amsterdam
Fund for Art and the idea
is that a different com-
poser will produce a new
composition each year.*

In 1900 a stall selling pickles was the
main attraction on this location; with the
developments on the east side of the city, bridge
485 has become increasingly busy. The area
underneath the bridge – over which the new
IJ tram passes – has been converted to make it
suitable for business premises, like the project
Tussen de Bogen underneath the railway
line on the west side of the city. By giving the
business units transparent façades and placing
piers along the quayside, the pedestrian zone
between the Muziekgebouw and the city centre
has been brightened up. Tourism-related
activities in particular are expected here (shops,
bars). Music-related businesses, including the
Muziekpakhuis, are also interested in the
location.

The severe modern design that the architect also applied to the route of the IJ tram is continued here. The wall at the northwest corner leading to the area beneath the bridge is entirely of glass, affording a view of the enormous bascule that moves downwards when the bridge is opened.

De Ruyter (2007)	**Architect**	**Commisioned by**	5.2
De Ruijterkade 152-154	Tijmen Ploeg Architecten	Bouwfonds MAB	

This new office block consists of seven floors, each measuring approx. 1,000 m², and an underground car park with 32 places. The transparent entrance on the ground floor has 5.5 metre headroom. On the fifth floor there is a large roof terrace with a panoramic view of the IJ. The front and rear are very transparent because of the use of glass bays. The liver-coloured masonry on the side walls is in alternating rough and smooth brick. This gives the wall a pronounced vertical character, and the atmosphere and colour blend with the surrounding buildings.
This office block completes the façade wall on the De Ruijterkade.

Former fire station (1890/2007)	**Architect**	**Commisioned by**	5.3
De Ruijterkade 145-149	W. Springer	Amsterdam Development Corporation (OGA), Stadsherstel Amsterdam	

When Amsterdam set up a professional fire brigade in 1874, a growing demand for storage and drilling facilities emerged. One of the new fire stations was the 'Old Nico', designed by the assistant city architect W. Springer, which the Amsterdam fire brigade used until 1973.
The building is constructed with different brick colours. The turrets and the classical division into main and subsidiary components give it the appearance of a fortress. Its former function

can still be deduced from the carvings on the keystones above the semicircular arches on the ground floor: fire-fighting attributes and a salamander, a symbol of fire.

After the departure of the firemen – with the exception of two former firemen and an administrative assistant, who have stayed on and live in the station – the premises were taken over by artists. The building is currently being renovated by Stadsherstel [urban renewal] (with support from the local authority). It will then be managed by Broedplaats Amsterdam, an initiative to provide affordable space for workers in the creative industry, and will thus retain its studio function. The building is among the two hundred new national monuments.

5.4	Bestevaer building (1914/1929) De Ruijterkade 115-120	Architect J.J. Kanters /H.A.J. and J. Baanders	Commisioned by N.V. Maatschappij tot exploitatie van het pand Bestevaer

This merchant's office consists mainly of a concrete skeleton that has been clad with bricks in traditional style. The ground floor is unusually high and was intended for wine storage. The building that is due to rise west of the fire station, the De Ruyter office block, is named after the same naval hero: Bestevaer was a nickname of admiral Michiel de Ruyter and meant something like 'granddad'. He fought for the Republic of the Netherlands in the Anglo-Dutch War.

A relief has been applied above the entrance with the devices of the Seven Provinces that composed the Republic at that time. The building is among the two hundred new national monuments.

Loftice	**Architect**	**Commisioned by**	
(2002)	Bastiaan	Rami Amsterdam	**5.5**
De Ruijterkade 112	Jongerius	B.V.	

The design of this modern office among the row of old shipping companies is inspired by the undulating water of the IJ and by the view of the inner city and the untidy railway. The 25-metre deep block is divided into a front and a rear building, connected by an overhead bridge above the atrium. The bridge also has a constructional functional: it holds the front and rear buildings together.

The front façade radiates tranquillity and blends smoothly with the nearby buildings. The plinth is in ground blue hardstone. The façade above it is an alternation of wide glass strips and narrow hardstone strips.

The rear building juts out six metres from the fourth floor upwards. The overhang is entirely of glass with a clearly articulated dark border, and faces the inner city.

Oosterdok, Oosterdokseiland

5.6 **De Zeevaart/**
De Chocolade-
fabriek
(1884/2009)
De Ruijterkade
105-108

Architect
Y. Bijvoets Gzn./
architect of
the renovation
unknown

Commisioned by
De Chocolade-
fabriek

Seeing, smelling, tasting and feeling chocolate
and imagining that it is about 1880, the heyday
of the chocolate industry: that is the theme
of the future Chocoladefabriek (Chocolate
Factory). Building is due to commence in
2007, and the doors to open in 2009. The
underground 'secret' tram tunnel next to
the corner building, which was built for
the IJ tram but has never been used, will be
renovated for that purpose.
Visitors to this 'treat park' will be able to find
out everything about chocolate interactively.
According to the originator of the idea, children
will pass through the machines in a small cart
as though they were cocoa beans, and will come
out at the other end like chocolates.
The richly decorated building De Zeevaart
dates from the 1880s. The cellar was originally
used to store ice and as a workshop, and
later as a garage, travel agent and café-
restaurant. There is a relief with children
above the entrance on the corner – an
appropriate subject given the future function
of the building. The new building of the
Chocoladefabriek, in a historicising style that
matches the corner building, will occupy De
Ruijterkade 107 and 108.

5.7 **Schreierstoren**
(1486)
Prins Hendrikkade
94-95

The Schreierstoren was originally part of
the stone wall that was built around the city
between 1481 and 1494. At first the people
of Amsterdam did not intend to build a
fortification like this: the surrounding water

and swamps afforded enough protection. It was not until the end of the fifteenth century, at a time of hostilities with Utrecht, that they began to construct a stronger defence. All residents had to contribute to what was then an astronomically high budget of more than 100,000 guilders. By 1600 the city had grown to such an extent that the wall had become ineffective and had to be demolished. The Schreierstoren is the only defence tower that has been preserved. Other parts of the wall of which ruins still survive are two city gates: the Waag (Sint Antoniespoort) and the Munt (Regulierspoort). Originally the tower was directly on the waterside; part of the Schreierstoren is thus now below ground level. The tower functioned as a lookout post for the harbour master down to the 1950s; it now houses the VOC café.

The name is supposed to come from the cries of the women taking leave of their menfolk as they set out to sea. The plaque on the tower with a woman, a ship sailing away, and sea monsters has contributed to this myth. In early documents, however, the tower is called the Schreyhoeckstoren. This shows that the name is actually derived from the sharp corner that the city walls along the Geldersekade and the Oudezijds Kolk made here.

5.8 **Scheepvaarthuis**
(1916/1928/2007)
Prins Hendrikkade
108-114

Architect
J.M. van der Mey,
J.G. & A.D.N. van
Gendt/ architect
of the renovation
unknown

Hotel
commissioned by
Amrâth Hotels and
Restaurants

The Scheepvaarthuis, which was originally
built as a joint office of six shipping
companies, is generally regarded as the first
building to be designed entirely in the style
of the Amsterdam School, because sculptors
and other artists also made an important
contribution to the exterior and interior of
the building.
The clients wanted a design that would
express the greatness of the Dutch shipping
tradition. The Van Gendt brothers designed
the construction and the young architect
Jo van der Mey was invited to provide the
aesthetic design. He called in the assistance
of his colleagues Piet Kramer and Michel
de Klerk, whose later designs included the
famous Amsterdam School complex in the
Spaarndammerbuurt. It is not possible to see
who was responsible for what. Everything was
specially designed for the building, including
the furniture and upholstery. The use of a
concrete skeleton means that the outside
walls did not have to carry a load, which gave
the sculptors the opportunity to decorate
the outside wall to their heart's content
with ornaments that alluded to the Dutch
maritime past.
After the shipping companies had abandoned
the premises, the city transport company
had its office here for several years. The
Scheepvaarthuis is now being converted into
a 4-star or 5-star hotel. The façade has already
been restored. As far as the renovation of the
interior is concerned, part will be modernised
with a lot of attention to design, while another
part will be entirely restored to its former
glory, including the paternoster lift and the
carved panelling.

Jan van Arkel
Houseboat
Pier 1, opposite
Prins Hendrik-
kade 510

Commisioned by   **5.9**
De Volharding

The *Jan van Arkel* is one of the few monumental
houseboats in Amsterdam. It must have been
built sometime after 1900 as a floating office
with counter and waiting room for the Leidsche
Stoombootmaatschappij De Volharding. A
building was constructed on top of a pontoon in
an exotic chalet style, which was very popular at
the time. The ship used to be moored near the
sluices in the Amstel, but after having changed
hands several times – one of the owners was the
Van Arkel regular line – it came to rest in the
Oosterdok. It fell into disuse and was seriously
neglected, but was eventually sold for a song to
private parties and done up as a houseboat.

| 5.10 **ARCAM** (2002)
Prins Hendrik-
kade 600 | **Architect**
René van Zuuk | **Commisioned by**
Amsterdam Local
Authority |

There are twenty floating monuments in the Nautical Quarter of the Oosterdok. These vessels destined for inland shipping provide a survey of the last 125 years of Dutch shipping. There are signs on the quayside with information about the history of each vessel. The fleet belongs to the members of the Vereniging Museum Haven Amsterdam [Amsterdam Harbour Museum Association] (VMA), which is connected with the Maritime Museum. The Christian Brunnings is noteworthy, a steamship that was built in 1900 as an icebreaker, but

The Amsterdam Architectural Centre is housed in one of the new pearls beside the IJ, which was specially designed for this institute. A pavilion designed by Renzo Piano had stood on this location in the armpit of the NEMO, but was never used. René van Zuuk was asked to design the renovation and extension. He adopted a radical approach: all that is left of Piano's pavilion are five columns on the ground floor and a piece of floor. The rest was demolished to create a building with a floor space four times the size.

There were three important limiting conditions in Van Zuuk's architectural brief. First, the building must not be too conspicuous from the Maritime Museum, which was solved by building one floor underneath the quay. Second, it must be closed on the Prins Hendrikkade side, but have a more open

Along Amsterdam's Waterfront

character on the site overlooking the water. The façade on the street side is now almost completely covered with zinc-clad aluminium (Kalzip), which has been wrapped around the volume like a skin. The façade facing the water consists mainly of glass. Third, the building had to be compact, which has resulted in this blob-like form.

The exhibition area is situated at the level of the Prins Hendrikkade. The first floor is divided by glass partitions into various office spaces in the form of an attic studio, while at the level of the water there is a multifunctional area where meetings and discussions can be held. Because the different floors are connected with one another by means of voids, it feels as though all the spaces form part of one large whole.

was also intended as a vessel for directors, which explains the luxurious saloon with a marble fireplace. Another eye-catcher is the large De Amsterdam, lying by the quay of the Museum. It is a replica of the original East India Company ship. The VMA now has a waiting list of 45 ships, and is therefore looking for new mooring locations, for example in North Amsterdam.

'Amphitrite and Triton' (1956/1987) Oosterdok behind ARCAM	**Sculptor** Albert Termote	5.11

There is a striking sculptural group in the water of the Oostdok: Amphitrite, wife of the god of the sea Poseidon, sits waving on the back of a mythological creature that looks like a rearing horse whose body ends in that of a fish. Amphitrite is accompanied by her son Triton, half-human and half-fish, who is blowing a shell. The group also includes a dolphin and part of an anchor.

The work was made by the sculptor Albert Termote in 1956 and was a present from the employees of the KNSM to celebrate the hundredth anniversary of the firm. When the KNSM moved to the Western Harbour Area in the late 1970s, the sculptural group was transferred to the Amsterdam local authority which decided, in lieu of a suitable location, to put the work in storage. At a certain moment no one knew where it had been kept. A few years later, when the Entrepotdok site was being cleared, some green bronze figures were found. Old photographs made it clear that the four fragments were the missing *Amphitrite and Triton* group. It was reconstructed and given a new home in the Oosterdok. The heavy concrete socle was added to protect it against water tourists.

5.12 **NEMO** (1997) Oosterdok 2	**Architect** Renzo Piano	**Commisioned by** Amsterdam Local Authority, Ministry of Economic Affairs, NEMO Foundation

The biggest roof terrace in the city and the one with the most spectacular view – that is the top deck of the NEMO science museum. This urban square towers above the spot where the traffic of the IJ tunnel goes underground, and makes exactly the same angle with the surface of the water as the tunnel does. In this respect, NEMO and the tunnel mirror one another. The tunnel was the most important source of inspiration for the Italian architect Renzo

Along Amsterdam's Waterfront

Piano, whose works include the Centre Pompidou in Paris and the Kensai Airport Terminal in Osaka. Many people see the volume that emerges from the water as a big ship that has suffered shipwreck in the waters of the Oosterdok.

The curved volume is clad with oxidised copper plates, whose green colour goes a long way to defining the exterior of the building. The ground level façade is almost entirely covered with glass. As a result, the copper volume seems to rise above this imaginary waterline. The walls on the side facing the city have been covered with brick to create a link with the city.

There is a rising line in the interior too. A sequence of open, broad staircases lead visitors from floor to floor to the highest point of the building.

In the summer the NEMO roof terrace, named after Wim T. Schippers, who presents the National Science Quiz, is transformed into a public lounge with a variety of activities.

IJtunnel	Architect	Commisioned by	5.13
(1968)	E. Hartsuyker	Amsterdam Local Authority	

The IJ tunnel has linked the northern district of Amsterdam with the rest of the city via the centre since 1968. The tunnel was a long time in the making. Designs for a bridge over the IJ were already made in the nineteenth century, and later the possibility of a tunnel emerged as well. After decades of debating the merits of a bridge or a tunnel, in 1952 the local authority finally took the plunge and opted for the tunnel. Another sixteen years were to pass before the tunnel could actually be used. Financial factors played a particularly important role in all this: there was a shortage of resources, and the local authority gave priority to the Schellingwouderbrug (1957) and the Coentunnel (completed in 1966). The

completed IJ tunnel, which was opened by Queen Juliana, is a two-lane dual carriageway and is 1,039 metres long.

It is easy to recognise the tunnel on the north and the South Banks by the characteristic double funnel-shaped ventilation shafts designed by Enrico Hartsuyker. On the South Bank they stand next to the bridge between the Stationseiland and the Piet Heinkade. The Italian architect drew his inspiration for the towers from chimneys, bell-towers and other towers that are often seen on Italian public buildings. Beneath the towers are operating posts with direct access to the tunnel. The tunnel elements were renovated in the 1980s, when a further operating post was added. Given the compactness of the programme, it is designed like the saloon of a ship.

5.14 Bridges around the Oosterdoks- eiland (1998/2005)	Architect Kerste-Meijer Architecten	Commisioned by Amsterdam Development Corporation (OGA)

The first new bridge to the Oosterdokseiland was built in 1992. It was primarily intended to establish a good pedestrian route between the Central Station and the NEMO science museum, that was due to open above the IJ tunnel in 1997. A second bridge was constructed in 2005 to connect the island via the Dijksgracht with the new buildings along the Oostelijke Handelskade. Unfortunately this bridge got off to a bad start: within two weeks it was rammed by a canal boat, which caused so much damage that it took months to repair it.

Both bridges were designed by the Kerste-Meijer firm of architects. Their design had to take into account the view from the historic city over the water. In other words, the bridges had to be as unobtrusive as possible when viewed from the side. The choice therefore fell

on light steel constructions and little lighting.
All of the bridges around the Oosterdokseiland
are operated from a new operating post, which
was designed by the same firm of architects.

Underground car park, bicycle shed and leisure centre (2008) Oosterdokseiland	Architect Zwarts & Jansma Architecten	Commisioned by Bouwfonds MAB OOACV	5.15

The Oosterdokseiland is not only undergoing a
complete makeover above ground level; a new
environment is being created below ground
level as well. Level –1 is not accessible to visitors
and is used as a loading, unloading and storage
facility by the buildings on top. Level –2 will be
occupied by an underground car park, bicycle
shed and leisure centre, designed by the Zwarts
& Jansma firm of architects.
The car park will grow at the same pace as the
ground-level project: when the first offices, the
library and the Conservatory open their doors,
a small part of the car park will be opened
up for use. At each following stage a new
part of the car park will be opened, until the
full capacity of 2,500 bicycles and 1,600 cars
has been reached in 2010. Since it is easy to
get lost in a car park that size, the architects
have added different orientation elements to
the design. Originally the idea was to fill the
entire side facing the water with an aquarium.
When this proved to be impractical, it was
eventually decided to project fish and people
onto the wall.

5.16 TPG Building Post CS (1968/2009)

Architect
Piet Elling/ Erick van Egeraat

Renovation commissioned by Bouwfonds MAB OOACV

A large part of the former post office headquarters has been demolished by now, but the eleven-storey office tower that is still standing plays an essential role in the development of the Oosterdokseiland. Thanks to the temporary accommodation of the Stedelijk Museum, under the name SMCS, until the new premises on the Museumplein are ready, to the renting of the office space to all kinds of businesses in the creative sector, and to the panorama restaurant 11 on the top floor, the reputation of the Oosterdokseiland has grown enormously in a short space of time. The present users can stay there at least until the end of 2008.

Together with the Havengebouw by Dudok and the Shellltoren Overhoeks on the other side of the river, the post office headquarters designed by Piet Elling are one of the highlights of late 1960s functionalism. The sand-coloured lime stone façade plates of the office block show how luxurious the modernism of that period could be. The deep recesses in the regularly composed outer wall give the building relief.

The designer of the master plan for the Oosterdokseiland, Erick van Egeraat, has used the transverse position of the post office building in drawing up the urban development plan. Van Egeraat himself will be responsible for renovating the building as a modern office block. All that will be left of the post office building is the old supporting construction. The outer walls will be clad vertically with a highly variegated pattern of panels of glass, steel and natural stone treated in different ways.

The Blub	**Architect**	**Commisioned by**	5.17
(2009)	Future Systems	Bouwfonds MAB	
Cultuurplein		OOACV	

A special catering establishment is planned on the quay of the Cultuurplein which is to be given the form of a blub. Future Systems (London), with a reputation for devising and applying new forms and new materials, has made a preliminary design for it. The organically shaped skin of the building, that looks like a jellyfish on land, is at the same time its construction. Building work can only get under way when the rest of the buildings on the Oosterdokseiland have been almost completed.

5.18 Amsterdam Conservatory (2009)
ODE plot 5

Architect
de Architekten Cie. (Frits van Dongen)

Commisioned by
Amsterdam School of the Arts

The new Conservatory has been designed in accordance with the principles of the Japanese *engawa* model. This means that all corridors are situated outside the building. The rooms, such as the auditoria and classrooms, are indoors and are thus soundproofed against noises from outside by the corridors. By introducing as much transparency as possible into the outer walls and partitions, a lot of light can be allowed to enter the rooms inside.

The transparency of the outer walls not only allows light to enter, but also contributes to the openness of the building: the idea is that passers-by can drop in and listen to concerts and recitals by the conservatory students.

The lower half of the building (from level −2 to the third floor) is 'the performing heart': this is where there are five rooms for performances plus a foyer and canteen. The four floors above are intended for the classrooms, while the two floors above them are for the library, study rooms, a lecture theatre and other facilities. The offices are right at the top of the building on the tenth floor. The façades of the upper half of the building are made of clear, heat-absorbing glass and narrow, dark aluminium profiles. The aluminium façade is shaped like the tooth of a saw; the long parts are made of fixed clear glass, while the short ones can be opened and are coated with a prismatic foil, Radiant Colour Film. This is a multi-coloured foil that, depending on the angle from which it is viewed, reflects diverse colours from the light spectrum, from magenta to cyan-blue, orange and gold. In 'the performing heart' the short side of the toothed façade is formed by wooden façade posts of Siberian larch, which rise from the ground floor to the floor of the fourth storey. Together with the red oak finish of the ceiling in the foyer, this creates a contrast with the heavy concrete volumes of the various rooms.

| Amsterdam Public Library (2007) ODE plot 4 | Architect Jo Coenen & Co Architekten | Commisioned by Amsterdam Local Authority, MAB OOACV | 5.19 |

The new Amsterdam Public Library, built to accommodate 7,000 visitors a day, will be one of the biggest libraries in Europe, with a floor space of 28,000 m² divided over eight floors, 750 internet worksites, conference rooms, and a theatre. Who could have imagined it in 1912 when a member of the First Chamber said that 'there is probably no single institute that contributes so powerfully to confusing the mind as the public reading room'? Fortunately times have changed in that respect. The Amsterdam local authority has come up with a budget of 73.6 million euros (excluding VAT) for the building of the new library. Former State Architect Jo Coenen has been contracted for the design. His built oeuvre includes the library on the Céramique site in Maastricht. He has designed a building that is

to become the number one attraction of the Oosterdokseiland and the first building to be completed (on 07-07-07).

The main theme of the design is the raised entrance level and the way in which it offers a view of the higher and lower levels. Large, tall voids create an enormous feeling of space in the interior. At the same time a lot of attention is devoted to creating intimate spots, so that the users can concentrate on the books and other media.

The plinth is as transparent as possible to emphasise the public nature of the building. It is easy to see from outside what is going on in the children's section on level −1. The form of the building is carefully tailored to match its surroundings, so that the neighbouring buildings can continue to receive enough daylight.

The choice of materials for both exterior and interior has fallen on durable materials that radiate warmness. The exterior and the entrance of the building are in shell lime stone. The floors at ground level, the children's section at level −1, the periodicals department on the first floor, and the catering facilities on the top floor, are in walnut wood. The areas near the lifts and escalators on the other floors, where the most traffic is expected, are in the same wood. The other floor areas are carpeted. The indoor walls are partly clad with light ash veneer, which gives the building a clear but warm atmosphere.

Extra colour is introduced to the building by bringing in several designers, some of them young. For instance, the toilets for the visitors on level –1 have received special attention from Neeltje ten Westenend, while NAT Architecten are designing the partitions on two floors in which a pantry, a reception desk and an office centre are incorporated. Interior architect Ingrid Annokkee is designing cupboards for the CDs and DVDs and other items of furniture on the multimedia floor. Claudy Jongstra is designing a felt and silk tapestry for the entrance wall, breathing new life into an old French knot, the *guimpe*. Letter artist Martijn Sandberg is making a design for the light shaft that can be seen from the lifts via a transparent rear wall. Light artist Peter van Kempen has been brought in for the lighting in the building, and the new house style of the library will be designed by design agency Thonik.

Housing	Architect	Commisioned by	5.20
(2007) ODE plots 2 and 3	hvdn architecten, Maccreanor Lavington architects, Crepain Binst architecten, Meyer en Van Schooten	Bouwfonds MAB OOACV, Het Oosten, NCACV	

The housing on the Oosterdokseiland is situated on two plots. Each consists of two projects designed by different architects. The apartments are grouped around public courtyards that can be reached through openings between the blocks. Architectenbureau hvdn is designing thirty de luxe apartments on the west side of plot 2,

The Central District of the city administration is considering the Oosterdokseiland as the location for its offices. The north side of plot 2 is a possible candidate.

adjacent to the square beside the hotel. The plan envisages one block of two and one block of four bays, separated by an alleyway. The trapezoid shape of the plot recurs in the ground plans. The façade with its tight rhythm is clad with dark grey natural stone, giving the blocks a robust, sturdy appearance. The frames and balcony fences are in copper-coloured steel, and the awnings come in a yellow gold colour. The balconies are internal on the Oosterdok side and jutting out on the Zakenplein side.

The appearance of the apartment block by Gerard Maccreanor on the east side of plot 2 is determined by the horizontal concrete parts and the rectangular upright panels, which are perforated with a foliate motif. All the apartments have wedge-shaped internal balconies facing south. The sliding panels form a sort of veil in front of the balconies, so that the front façade remains filled in the building line.

Plot 3 consists of the blocks by Crepain Binst architecten on the west, and by Meyer en Van Schooten on the east. The project by

Crepain Binst architecten has a wide façade on the Oosterdok side in which a clear vertical structure is introduced which fits in with the other buildings on the Oosterdokseiland. The apartments in the central area are orientated East-West and border the side street between the plots, on one side, and the inner courtyard, on the other. The north side is reserved for offices. The block by Meyer en Van Schooten is elongated and extends from the north to the south of the island. It is adjacent to the library on the east side.

The two ends consist of two bays, each with two apartments per storey. The three supporting disks are clad with grey-green coloured building brick. In between are the large, internal balconies with sliding panels. The central part contains apartments with an East-West orientation with protruding balconies bordering on the inner courtyard. On the east side next to the library a horizontal structure predominates because of the access to the external corridor of some of the apartments.

The public space on the Oosterdokseiland is designed with durable materials with a luxurious air about them, such as Norwegian slate. The design is by landscape architect Henri Bava's Agence Ter agency, with offices in Paris and Karlsruhe.

**5.21 Hotel and confer-
ence centre** (2007)
ODE plot 1

Architect
Rab Bennets

Commisioned by
Bouwfonds MAB
OOACV

The 4-star hotel that is being built here fits in
with the motto of this part of the Oosterdokseiland: Ode to the Good Life. The hotel with
500 rooms and conference facilities is one
of the most important components of the
programme. Top restaurants and exclusive
shops will be situated in and around the hotel.
The complex consists of three volumes, which
follow the radial plot division of the rest of
the new buildings on the Oosterdokseiland.
The most south-westerly part stands partly
on columns, so that a public square, the
Zakenplein, is created beneath the building. It
will facilitate the arrival and departure of hotel
and conference centre guests. The materials are
mainly glass, steel and dark brick. Each block
will have a different colour behind the glass,
so that the façade will produce an enhanced
feeling of depth and each part of the building
will have a character of its own.

Sea Palace (1984)
Oosterdokskade 8

This replica of the Sea Palace restaurant in
Hongkong is richly decorated with oriental
frills. The roof of the boat is made of green
glass, which the owners hope will make the
building glisten like a jewel on the water.
Opened in 1984, this was the first floating
restaurant in Europe, and with 700 places
was immediately the largest in Amsterdam.
Tourists are a main source of income, but
the Chinese community in Amsterdam also
makes considerable use of this restaurant
for weddings and festivities. Opinions are
divided on the Sea Palace, also known as 'the
floating Chinese'; some find it a splendid
setting, others consider it to be over the top.
Nevertheless, the restaurant does a brisk trade
and is able to hold its own within the new
developments on the Oosterdokseiland.

Along Amsterdam's Waterfront

CUL-TURAL DRAW-CARDS

Evert Verhagen

Quiet demolition

Empty quays, old warehouses, water you can't get to. There is still a lingering smell of sisal or cocoa, of tar and oil. Once upon a time a lot of money was made here, but the factories and the ships have long since moved elsewhere. The industry and the port that made Amsterdam great and rich, also brought environmental pollution and poor working conditions. So a lot of what remained after commercial activity had departed was quickly and quietly demolished. But not everything went that way. Some buildings were declared national monuments; others were occupied by squatters and thus temporarily saved from the wrecker's ball.

Counterculture and culture centres

For many years people talked and mused about the future of the IJ banks, about the grand transformation that should take place there. Many plans never went ahead, inadvertently winning time in which a counterculture could emerge. New ideas need old buildings, American journalist Jane Jacobs averred several decades ago. Of course, many squatters were simply looking for somewhere to live. But their presence demonstrated that the former shipyards, factories and warehouses were eminently suitable for a variety of activities. For a long time, however, the cultural elite clung to the idea that Culture belonged in the inner city, on the assumption that this was the way to rescue the city centre from the philistine street culture.

So it was initially the squatters and later on the somewhat more commercially minded cultural businesses that inhabited waterfront leftovers like the Veem and Y-tech warehouses in the Western Harbour Area. Long ago there was a squatters' restaurant, 'The End of the World' in the east; later the Panama club.

Many of the initiatives lapsed over the course of time, the most celebrated example being the artistic breeding ground of the Vrieshuis Amerika warehouse.

Creative city

A lively public space and the presence of cultural attractions seem to be hugely important for the successful development of an area. Economist Richard Florida talked about this at length during his visit to Amsterdam in 2003. The importance of 'the creative city', a concept introduced by planner Charles Landry in the 1990s, took some time to reach Amsterdam. Only at a late stage of the development of the IJ banks was it decided to locate institutions like the main public library, a concert hall and the conservatorium there. Now the film museum is set to relocate to the North Bank of the IJ in order to boost the development of a creative city there as well.

New infrastructure

An efficient infrastructure is essential for any kind of economic development. An area with ambitions to become a lively and creative city, must be readily accessible and passable to pedestrians and cyclists. And there must also be a reason for going there – primarily what goes on inside the buildings, but what people encounter outside those buildings is equally important. What happens on the boundary between buildings and public space is crucial to the perceived attractiveness of an area.

Cultural attraction

A refusal to jettison the past can also give rise to exciting environments: a road driven right through a warehouse, a new apartment block built half over an old warehouse. In the same way, enthusiasm and perseverance can turn an impractical and architecturally unexceptional building into a splendid hotel. And the new Muziekgebouw, thanks in part to the combination of marvellous architecture and a perfect location, is on its way to becoming one the foremost cultural attractions of the city. And that is the story of the transformation of public space in Amsterdam.

Along Amsterdam's Waterfront

Oosterdok

6.
OOSTE-LIJKE EILANDEN, FUNEN

The construction of the Eastern Islands (Kattenburg, Wittenburg and Oostenburg) was a direct consequence of the First Anglo-Dutch War (1652-1654). The Dutch Republic lost this war because of a shortage of good ships. Because they suspected that more wars might well follow, they worked feverishly on building a new fleet. There was no room for this in the centre, but the new islands could accommodate it. Kattenburg became the domain of the Admiralty, Oostenburg that of the VOC (United East India Company), and Wittenburg was reserved for the smaller private shipyards. Industry did not disappear after the heyday of the VOC: Werkspoor (later Stork) took its place. This company produced steel for the railways and was thus one of the biggest employers in Amsterdam. A large part of Oostenburg is still earmarked for industry and commerce. The rest of the island, the Czaar Peter neighbourhood, was used to house workers in the steel industry. It is an excellent example of a nineteenth-century working-class neighbourhood: long streets with narrow, small homes and a high building density. Starting in the 1970s, the neighbourhood has been renovated block by block.

Kattenburg was less successful: without exception, the neighbourhood became a slum. The reconstruction plan of 1953 turned it into one of the earliest examples of urban renewal: every single building on the island was demolished and replaced in one fell swoop. Wittenburg followed in the 1980s, but the renewal here proceeded at a slower pace because of the polluted land and the actions of neighbourhood committees. It was not completed until 2006 with the completion of the Groenland complex.

Funen, which was used for decades by the freight handling company Van Gend & Loos, is the last development location in the area. Frits van Dongen's urban development plan envisages a large building to act as a shield against the noise of the railway. In the Funen Park behind it are situated the hidden delights, residential tower blocks designed by different architects.

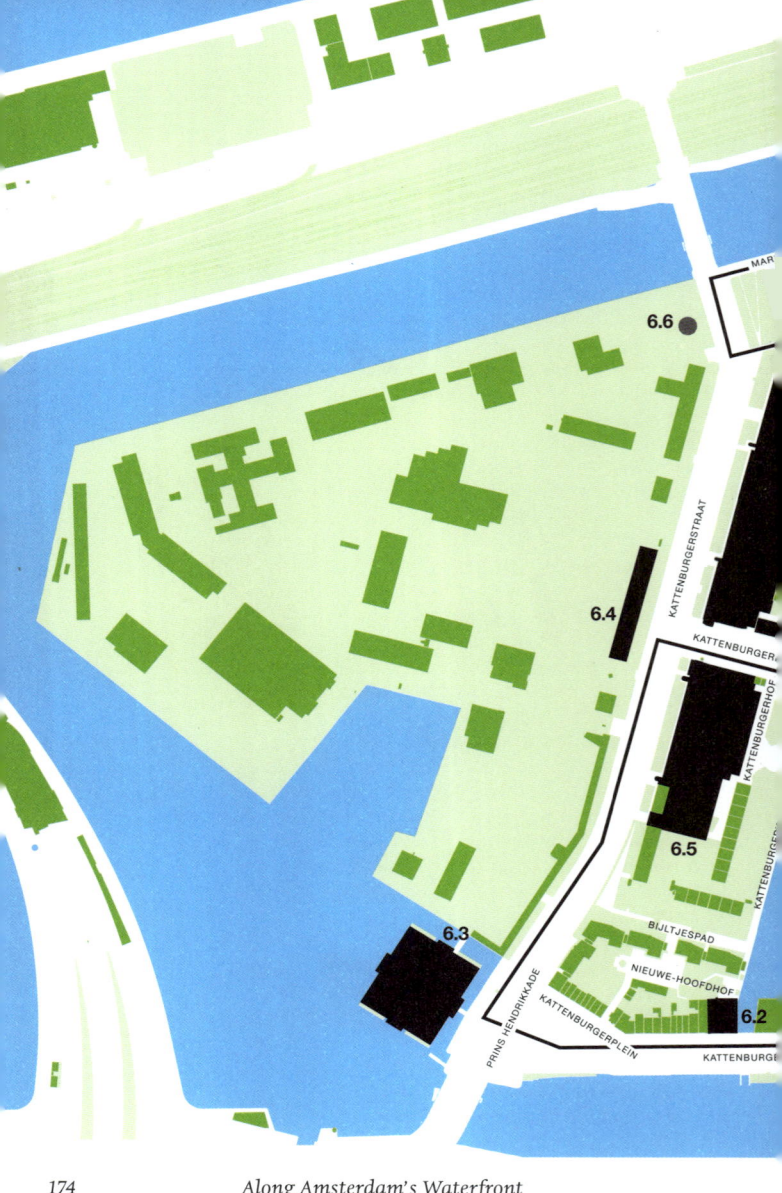

Along Amsterdam's Waterfront

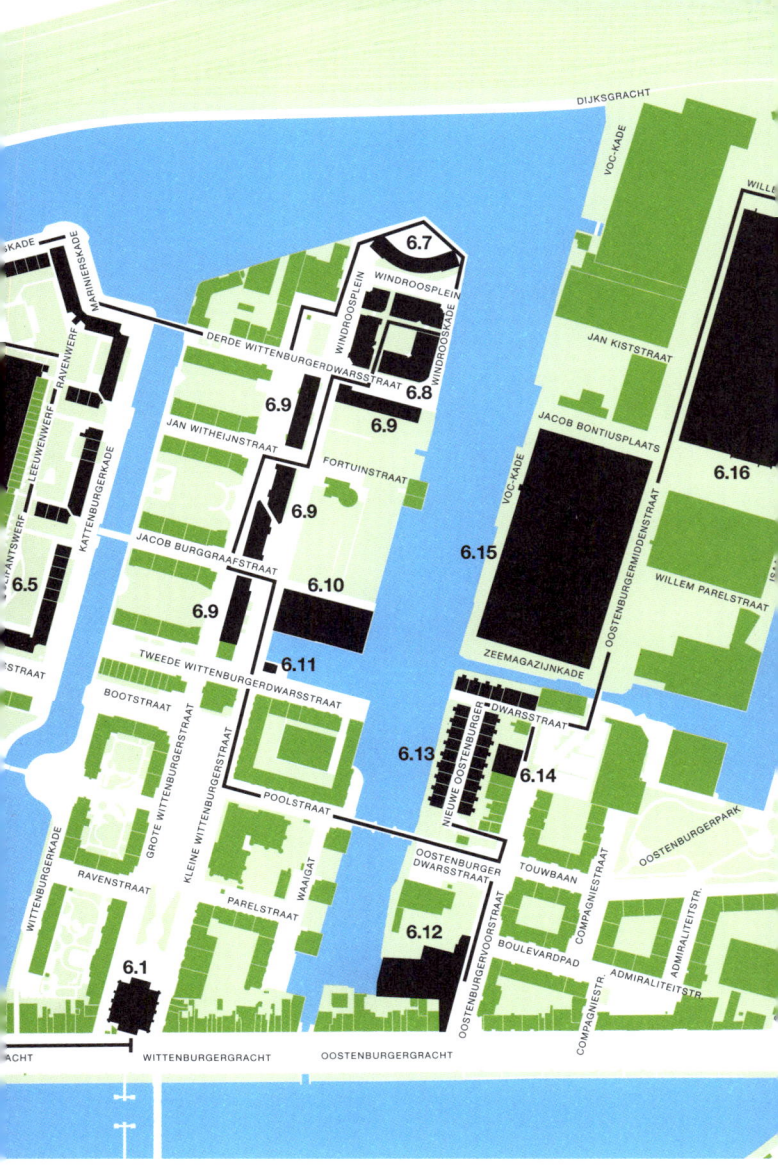

Map labels:

DIJKSGRACHT

VOC-KADE

WILLE

JAN KISTSTRAAT

6.7

WINDROOSPLEIN

WINDROOSPLEIN

WINDROOSKADE

DERDE WITTENBURGERDWARSSTRAAT

6.8

JACOB BONTIUSPLAATS

6.16

-SKADE

MARINIERSKADE

RAVENWERF

LEEUWENWERF

JAN WITHEIJNSTRAAT

6.9

6.9

FORTUINSTRAAT

VOC-KADE

OOSTENBURGERMIDDENSTRAAT

WILLEM PARELSTRAAT

KATTENBURGERKADE

6.9

6.15

JACOB BURGGRAAFSTRAAT

-IANTSWERF

6.5

6.9

6.10

ZEEMAGAZIJNKADE

-STRAAT

TWEEDE WITTENBURGERDWARSSTRAAT

6.11

BOOTSTRAAT

GROTE WITTENBURGERSTRAAT

KLEINE WITTENBURGERSTRAAT

NIEUWE OOSTENBURGERDWARSSTRAAT

6.13

6.14

POOLSTRAAT

OOSTENBURGERPARK

WITTENBURGERKADE

RAVENSTRAAT

WAIGAT

OOSTENBURGER DWARSSTRAAT

TOUWBAAN

COMPAGNIESTRAAT

OOSTENBURGERVOORSTRAAT

ADMIRALITEITSTR.

PARELSTRAAT

6.12

BOULEVARDPAD

ADMIRALITEITSTR.

COMPAGNIESTR

6.1

-ACHT

WITTENBURGERGRACHT

OOSTENBURGERGRACHT

Oostelijke Eilanden, Funen

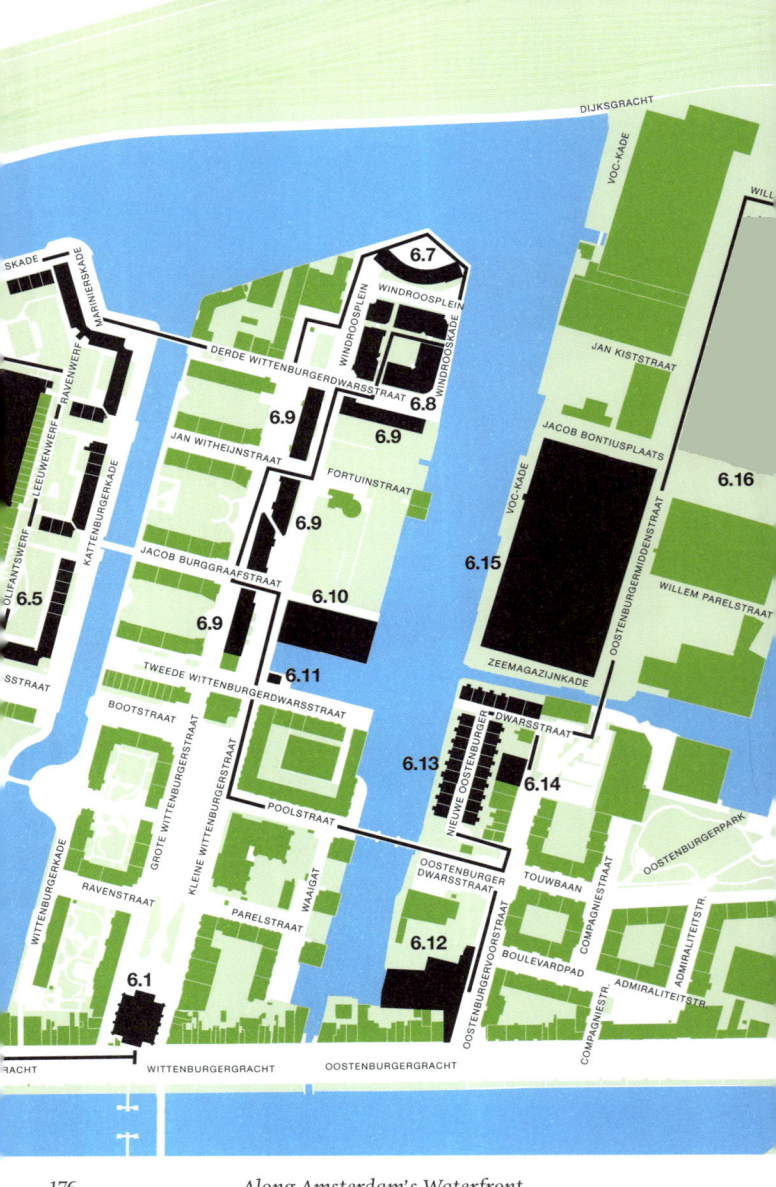

Along Amsterdam's Waterfront

6.1 **Oosterkerk**	**Architect**	**Commisioned by**
(1669)	Daniël Stalpaert,	Vroedschap
Kleine Witten-	Adriaan Dortsman	Amsterdam
burgerstraat 1		

That the Oosterkerk is not properly
aligned with the building line of the
Wittenburgergracht is no accident. The
Oosterkerk formed part of an urban
development plan for the eastern section of
the canals drawn up by Daniël Stalpaert in
1662, in which four churches with squares
were planned for the Kerkstraat, which runs
parallel with the canals. Apart from the
provisional wooden Amstelkerk, which later

had to be replaced by a stone building in the middle of the Amstelveld, only the Oosterkerk was built according to the original design. This was because the development of the eastern section of the canals did not proceed as smoothly as had been hoped, and in the end the Plantage buildings, no longer based on the idea of the canals, rendered it impossible. The Reformed Church is based on the seventeenth-century reconstruction of the Temple in Jerusalem, which is why it is exactly 100 x 100 feet. Both the exterior and the interior are very simple and sober. The church was still in use for religious services until 1969, by which time it had become too derelict to continue. The local authority bought and renovated it under pressure from the residents. It now accommodates various social and community organisations. The nave is used for exhibitions.

Until the 1970s the Neo-Gothic Catholic Sint Annakerk designed by P.J. Dekkers in 1900 stood just west of the Oosterkerk. Remains of the rear façade can still be seen if you pass through the convent gate at Wittenburgergracht 7 and go to the back.

Neptunus en de Parel (2001) Kattenburger-gracht 19-41	Architect CASA architecten	Commisioned by Woningbedrijf Amsterdam	6.2

Ten owner-occupied apartments were built a few years ago in this historic complex with a turbulent history. The characteristic elements have been preserved as far as possible. The apartments with mezzanine at the rear are situated in the old five-metre-tall classrooms. Both buildings date from the seventeenth century. The left-hand one, Neptunus (Neptune), was originally a warehouse that together with the sister premises Ceres was converted into a fire station around 1890. The right-hand building, the Parel (Pearl), used to house the Parelschool (now accommodated in new premises in the Grote Wittenburgerstraat). In 1926 Neptunus and Ceres were transformed into a police station. After the police station had left, the complex was used in the 1990s as the film set for the police series *Baantjer*.

6.3 Maritime Museum (1656/2008) Kattenburgerplein 1	Architect Daniël Stalpaert/ Atelier Zeinstra van der Pol, Rappange & Partners Architecten, Ney & Partners	Commisioned by Government Buildings Department

While many large buildings today require several years for their completion, in the seventeenth century the architect Daniël Stalpaert managed to create 's Lands Zeemagazijn in less than nine months, as is reported on the three entrance arches on the west side. That period does not include the time required for the complex laying of the foundations in the water, but still.

The building was used as a warehouse for the storage of items for the Admiralty vessels, whose task it was to defend the territory and merchant fleet of the Dutch Republic. The items in storage were therefore not confined to shipping equipment, but also included arms and cannon. Every side of the building stands in the water to facilitate loading and unloading. The Zeemagazijn was built in the same time and style – Dutch Classicism – as the Palace on Dam Square, but its decoration is considerably less exuberant given its warehouse function. The openings through which goods were hoisted inside can still be seen. The layer of plaster was only added at the end of the eighteenth century during one of several renovations. The building was used by the navy until the late 1960s, after which it acquired its present function as a Maritime Museum. The building will shortly be restored and the museum has plans to roof the courtyard to enable a new display of the collection. The restoration, which is in the hands of Rappange, is intended to restore the original rugged warehouse atmosphere as much as possible. Liesbeth van der Pol, who designed the museum depot, is working on the redesign of the museum. A thematic approach to the collection will replace a chronological one. It will then be possible to choose one of several routes from the covered courtyard, depending on the target group. The Brussels structural design engineer and designer Laurent Ney devised the transparent glass covering; the shape of the narrow supporting trusses is based on elements from old shipping maps. Given the history of the building and the fact that it is one of the few examples of a seventeenth-century courtyard that are open to the public, the Historic Buildings and Archaeology Department views these plans with scepticism.

Oostelijke Eilanden, Funen

| 6.4 | **Maritime Museum Depot 'Het Behouden Huis'** (2001) Kattenburger-straat | **Architect** Atelier Zeinstra van der Pol | **Commisioned by** North-West Government Buildings Department |

Above the brick walls that surround the former 's Lands Werf can be seen the silvery landscape formed by the contours of the new depot of the Maritime Museum. This is all that can be seen from the road, because the building is situated on land belonging to the Royal Dutch Marines that is not open to the public.

The building had to satisfy strict climatisation criteria because it is used for the storage and restoration of valuable museum items. Liesbeth van der Pol designed a concrete core which contains the storage depots and workshops. It is surrounded by a steel frame containing the cabling, piping and installations. The 90-metre-long building is clad with titanium, which forms an unusual contrast with the brick wall.

Housing (1976)
Kattenburgerhof
1-100, Kattenbur-
gerstraat 32-410,
Kattenburgerkruis-
straat 5-50,
Olifantswerf 1-81,
Leeuwenwerf 1-129,
Ravenwerf 1-58,
Marinierskade 1-44

Architect
ABBT (Dick Apon)

Commisioned by
Onze Woning,
Rochdale

6.5

The homes in Kattenburg formed a slum area after the Second World War. The local authority drew up an urban renewal plan in 1953 and the neighbourhood was the first to undergo this process. It took quite a while because the land was seriously polluted and the old buildings had been occupied by squatters and hippies. The renovation did not really get under way until the 1970s. During the postwar reconstruction period, it had been common practice to erect new buildings in a completely revised allotment of plots, without taking into account the old pattern of streets or the previous use of the area. So 619 rented council homes were built here in a total plan with balcony access maisonettes in short strips and L-shapes that have been laid over the whole area in different directions around public courtyards. The first-floor access balcony was originally intended as a promenade where children could play.

At that time it was already difficult to build council housing because the land so close to the centre was very attractive for investors. A large number of the former residents were able to return to the new flats, although the increased rents caused a lot of unrest. The district still consists exclusively of council-owned rented property, with a very well kept public space. The uniformity of the buildings, with the prefab façade panels with a pebble structure and curved undersides, offers a welcome tranquillity amid the cacophony of forms in the neighbouring districts.

*A number of characteris-
tic seventeenth-century
façades from demolished
homes in Kattenburg
have been recycled in the
façade wall facing the
Kattenburgerplein. The
building is now part of a
student accommodation
complex by De Key with
more than 360 units, that
lies behind it.*

| 6.6 | **Royal Military Police District Building** (2008/2009) Kattenburgerstraat | **Architect** Wansleben- Architekten | **Commisioned by** Dienst Vastgoed Defensie |

The new district building of the Royal Military Police is to be built in the northeast corner of the naval dockyard. The commission, which was placed after a competition had been held, will be implemented very literally by the Cologne architect Norbert Wansleben. The ambiguity of the role of the police in a modern democracy in which there is an interaction between public and secret has been expressed by the architect by combining open and closed explicitly in the building. From outside the square building has the appearance of a fort thanks to the regularly distributed and sunken frames. The façade is made of a rough, crystalline black material consisting of a mixture of concrete with different types of natural stone and Labrador granite. Depending on the season, the surface of the façade changes (thanks to the Labrador granite) as a result of the angle and intensity with which the sun shines on it.

The interior of the building is very friendly with wooden awnings in various colours. It looks out onto a patio with a lot of greenery.

| 6.7 | **Wittenburg North Block F, The Banana** (1989) Windrooskade 2-70 | **Architect** Reynoud Groeneveld | **Commisioned by** Eigen Haard |

This project was developed at the same time as the other urban renewal blocks in Wittenburg. The name of this 35-unit complex speaks for itself: The Banana because of the curved shape and the yellow brick. The design is completely symmetrical. There are hanging semicircular balconies on the first and second floors of the convex wall that are typical of urban renewal. On the concave side the façade is recessed from the second floor upwards, thereby creating room for an access balcony for the maisonettes on top. Following the curve of the banana a small square with radial paving has been created by the waterfront. It offers a view of the new horizon of the Piet Heinkade in full glory.

| House of the Four Winds (1990) Windroosplein 2-220 | Architect Piero Frassinelli | Commisioned by Bouwfonds | 6.8 |

In architectural terms there is nothing particularly special about this building at first sight, but the House of the Four Winds is a block of 89 owner-occupied apartments with a story. The Amsterdam philosopher Fons Elders came up with the ideas, and the Italian architect Frassinelli turned them into stone. The idea was to unite cosmology, social behaviour and architecture in one complex. The design is orientated towards the Pole Star, and the four corners of the square complex are orientated towards the four points of the compass. This is an implicit reference to the Oosterkerk, one of the four churches that indicate the points of the compass in the city. Another important way in which the House of the Four Winds distinguishes itself from the conventional apartment block is the fact that each wing has a common space; the four of them refer to the four primal elements (water, earth, air and fire). Many of the apartments consist of a chain of rooms based on a module of 4.2 by 4.2 metres, which all have access to the terraces that are laid out around the building. Although the genesis of this private initiative project was protracted and difficult, the result is an apartment complex in which the sense of community shared by the residents is a good deal stronger than in the average new apartment block.

6.9 **Wittenburg North, Block A, B, C, D** (1992)
Kleine Wittenburgerstraat 211-365, Grote Wittenburgerstraat 210-358, Windroosplein 3-57

Architect
Van Herk & De Kleijn, Girod & Groeneveld, Paul de Ley

Commisioned by
Eigen Haard

Wittenburg was the last of the Eastern Islands to be tackled in the cleaning up process. Old photographs of the Grote Wittenburgerstraat, for example, evoke a sense of nostalgia for the bygone charm of a genuine working class district. The question arises of whether we should ever allow such a characteristic and authentic neighbourhood to get so run down that everything has to be demolished. The renewal of Wittenburg in the 1980s came about with a great deal of action, support and consultation on the part of the residents. An all-embracing plan was swept from the table to be replaced by a more project-orientated approach in stages. The polluted ground was a cause of delay for many years, but by the end of the 1980s the new buildings started to appear.
The urban development plan was drawn up by Van Herk & De Kleijn together with Girod & Groeneveld, Paul de Ley, and the Environmental Planning Department. It was decided to keep the quays as clear as possible as a reference to the shipyards. The building plan in the strip between Kleine Wittenburgerstraat and the Wittenburgervaart consists of almost 200 rented apartments spread over four blocks, designed by the three firms of architects involved in drawing up the urban development plan. The ends of the blocks are marked with towers accessed by lifts. To avoid making the buildings in the middle strip too elongated, a kink was inserted halfway along with a pedestrian corridor. Typical of the architectural style of the late 1980s are the covered staircases in the block designed by Van Herk & De Kleijn, which were intended to enliven the wall facing the street.

Het Groenland
(2006)
Jacob Burggraaf-
straat 68-224

Architect
awg architecten

Commisioned by
Het Groenland
Amsterdam

6.10

Het Groenland shipyard managed to resist the
first wave of urban renewal of the early 1980s,
but it was later earmarked for new building.
The site was left in disuse for years until the
ground could be cleaned up; like many other
parts of the island, it was heavily polluted by a
wood preservation material that was used a lot
in shipping wharves. Now it is the location of a
complex with 81 owner-occupied apartments.
The references for this building were warehouses, which is not strange on a former East
India Company island, but is still very different
from the urban renewal blocks that were built
earlier around it. It has a fairly calm look: few
different materials or colours, with the windows
and doors arranged in a tight rhythm.
A mooring dock was created from the Wittenburgervaart specially for this block so that the
complex stands with water on both sides. All
residents have access to a waterfront landing
stage, as can clearly be seen from the other

side near the Tweede Wittenburgerdwarsstraat. This new water was also regarded as a welcome expansion of the water storage capacity and could count on a generous state subsidy within the framework of regional flooding policy.

6.11 Marken cottage (1855/2005) Tweede Wittenburgerdwarsstraat 133	**Architect** Lines Bouw- en tekenbureau	**Commisioned by** Stadsherstel Amsterdam with Stadsdeel centrum

This cottage is left over from the last wharf on Wittenburg. In 1855 Gerrit Broerse bought the land from a market gardener and started up Het Groenland shipbuilding company. Gerrit's wife came from Marken, so he had a Marken cottage built for her. Their son Jan laid the first stone on 5 March 1885. At a certain point there were nineteen people living in the cottage. They took turns to sleep in a box bed. It was lived in until 1965, after which it functioned as an office. The Beffers family, who had rented a slipway from Broerse in 1905, took over the shipyard. The company increasingly turned its attention to repairing houseboats and pleasure vessels. As a result of the new environmental legislation as well as other factors, it became clear in 1993 that the company had no chance of survival. It could not make any new investments, and the demolition of Het Groenland could not be stopped any longer. For a long time the Marken cottage stood alone on the sandy waste. In 2001 it was dismantled and put into storage after a request to be put on the list of historic buildings had been turned down. Thanks to the intervention of engaged residents, who could see the historic value of the cottage, it was rebuilt in its original dimensions and using as much of the original building material as possible. The shipyard cottage is now a landmark in an area that could boast twenty shipyards in its heyday, as the plaque on the façade tells. Tasty Portuguese-Mediterranean food is now served inside.

Wiener complex
(1906/1929)
Oostenburgervoor-
straat 1-3

Commisioned by 6.12
Wiener & Co.
Apparatenbouw bv.

Four industrial premises between the Oostenburgervoorstraat and the Oostenburgergracht
that were used as smithies and workshops
have been given the status of municipal
protected building as an example of small-
scale industrial activity. This grew over time to
become the factory complex of Wiener & Co
Apparatenbouw, specialised in the production
of machines for the cocoa and chocolate
industry. Over the years all kinds of additions
were made to the original premises, so that
the protected parts are only visible from the
Waaigat on Wittenburgereiland on the other
side, from where the brick external façades
with typical six-pane windows can be seen. In
the heart of the complex a brick office building
from 1910 is still largely in its original state.
When the company decided to move in 2000,
the site became free for the planners. In

spite of the protected monument status, the developer of the district still managed to obtain permission to demolish the buildings. The developer's ideas have led to a lot of debate in the neighbourhood and planning is at a standstill at the moment. The warehouses have been temporarily let as studios.

6.13 Nineteenth-century homes
(1874)
Nieuwe Oosten-burgerstraat 3-20,
Nieuwe Oostenbur-gerdwarsstraat 1-11

Architect
A.L. van Gendt

Commisioned by
Woning-maatschappij

These rows of old one-room and two-room houses with their sober architecture recall the atmosphere of the nineteenth century when the Eastern Islands were still densely populated working class neighbourhoods. The factory premises behind them were designed by Van

Gendt to harmonise with the homes, which can be easily be seen from the other side of the Wittenburgergracht. That is one of the reasons why the housing complex has been declared a municipal protected monument.

It is remarkable in itself that these houses are still standing, because the pressure to demolish was enormous, especially in the 1950s. In the 1980s the residents managed to get the local authority to buy up the homes, and after a small-scale renovation they can still be used. Unfortunately the renovation was carried out with plastic frames, as was common at the time because they are cheap and low-maintenance. Now that there is more understanding of the historic value of the ensemble, they can be replaced with wooden frames when they are due for renovation again.

| Timber-frame con-struction homes (1992) Oostenbur-gervoorstraat 73-77 | Architect Aad Lambert | Commisioned by Wilma Bouw | 6.14 |

These buildings constructed with a timber frame were developed to fill a plot of land that had become vacant between the nineteenth-century buildings of the Oostenburgervoorstraat. This type of construction has hardly ever been used in the city, with a few exceptions. This complex formed part of an experimental plan to rapidly build up four small locations, scattered over the city.

To make maximal use of the limited façade length and block depth, the staircase has been placed outside the volume against the back wall. This leaves the ground plan open, which has resulted in a combination of two maisonettes and four two-room and three-room homes. The apricot/orange colour of the façade with a mint-green tile in the plinth make the project typical of the period.

| 6.15 | **Van Gendt factory sheds** (1905/2012) Oostenburger-voorstraat 181 | **Architect** A.L. van Gendt/ Jo Coenen & Co Architekten, Rappange & Partners Architecten | **Commisioned by** Nederlandsche Fabriek van Werktuigen en Spoormaterieel/ Het Oosten, Kristal |

From its construction in 1663, the rear part of the Oostenburgereiland, known under the name of the Stork site, was in use by the East India Company as a shipyard. At that time it lay immediately beside the open IJ. The first signs of industrialisation were to be seen here: 1,300 hands worked in highly standardised mass production. In the course of the time the site was used as a naval location, machine factory and wharf for steamers and was known as Werkspoor. Later the factory merged with Stork and specialised in diesel engines and rolling stock. Around 1900 Werkspoor commissioned A.L. Gendt, the architect of the Concertgebouw, among other buildings, to design factory sheds. Characteristic features are the Neo-Renaissance brick façade and the fact that different units can be distinguished within a single whole. The elongated factory workshops have a rectangular ground plan and masonry walls. Three of them have long gable roofs with a monitor roof, partly with tiles.

At the moment the 150-metre factory sheds are the only remaining significant part of this industrial complex. In 2001 it was declared a national protected monument. The buildings are now owned by Het Oosten housing corporation in Amsterdam. They are let temporarily to creative entrepreneurs, who are free to do as they choose in the endless spaces. Architect Jo Coenen has been invited to make a design for their reuse. It is intended to make the 12,000 m² of industrial space suitable for flexible business accommodation, catering and parking facilities. The potential above the sheds is being investigated for an upper world of apartments and other services. The Rappange firm of architects has been approached to supervise the restoration process in the reuse of this monument.

INIT (2003)	**Architect**	**Commisioned by**	6.16
Isaac Titsingh-kade 101-111, Jacob Bontiusplaat 9-11, Oostenburgermid-denstraat 200-220	Groosman en Part-ners Architecten	Dienst Binnenstad, Stadsdeel Amster-dam Centrum, IBC Vastgoed, Heijmans	

West of the INIT are two enormous factory sheds that were used in the past for the production of engines. Now they are let for big parties and festivities under the name Amsterdam Convention Factory. Theater Fabriek Amsterdam, a modern theatre with seating capacity for one thousand, is located in one of the sheds.

The INIT building is the first new complex to be implemented in the framework of the redevelopment of the former Stork site. The idea is that various buildings will arise around it in the course of time, each with a character of its own.

The INIT has an impressive matt glass membrane façade that preserves the industrial character of the location in a contemporary way. The awnings between the glass panels not only keep out direct sunlight but are also carriers of information.

The 45,000 m² of office and business space have been filled up in various ways. The ground floor houses the Municipal Sanitation Department. The upper storeys, with a second ground level, include a space for events and a three-layer car park in the core of the building. The idea of the second ground level is that future buildings on this level will be linked with the INIT. Every level can be reached by car via ramps. Above the entrance is an independent conference centre in a shell-shaped construction.

Now that the editorial teams of the dailies *Het Parool, de Volkskrant* and *Trouw* have moved to the island, the Stork site has suddenly become a newspaper island.

6.17	Bouwblok N 41 (2004) Conradstraat 76-88, 124-132, Czaar Peterstraat 107, 111, 155-159, Tweede Leegh-waterstraat 50-64	**Architect** Rudy Uytenhaak	**Commisioned by** Woningbouw-vereniging Eigen Haard, New Deal

Unlike the previously designed complex by Uytenhaak with shallow apartments in two strips, here he decided to translate the deepness of the block directly to the ground plans. This has resulted in apartments with a depth of 24 metres that look a lot like warehouses. The apartments are orientated towards the busy Czaar Peterstraat and the quieter Conradstraat. The original idea was to renovate the location as a whole, but in the end two blocks were built with part of an old building between them and a new link between the two streets. The plinth in the Czaar Peterstraat is for businesses, while

Along Amsterdam's Waterfront

in the Conradstraat homes with studios are situated between the entrances.

The sober style of the original buildings is repeated in the new façades, and the characteristic division into three parts with an open lower section, a middle section with windows in the masonry, and a crown with striking gable windows that determines the silhouette. The expressive bays of the business premises give the design a contemporary character.

Romanof (2004) Czaar Peterstraat 176-196, Blankenstraat 179-189	**Architect** Opbouw Amsterdam	**Commisioned by** Opbouw Amsterdam	**6.18**

This block was originally destined to be demolished, but in the end it was renovated. There have been major changes in the interior. To achieve a greater diversity among the apartments, it was decided to make one new staircase for every three apartments. This makes the apartments on the first and second floor one and a half bays wide. The apartments below them are enlarged with the basement, and those on the third floor with the fourth floor. A roof terrace has been created by recessing the rear wall line on the fourth floor. The apartments on the other floors have been given outdoor space by hanging balconies on the rear wall.

The end of the block consists of four group apartments for senior citizens. This used to be the site of a hostel for mariners with a tavern on the ground floor, which figured in the film *Ciske de Rat*. However, this complex has a longer media history. The TV programme *Het Blok* was filmed here in 2004: four couples were each given little time and little money to do up and completely furnish an apartment here. The resulting apartments were publicly auctioned. Afterwards the new residents had many complaints about the poor quality of the finishing.

6.19 Petersburg (2006)
Blankenstraat 382-384, Frans de Wollantstraat 8-80

Architect
TBE Architecten & Ingenieurs

Commisioned by
Lingotto Vastgoed

This soberly designed business premises, which fits perfectly into the nineteenth-century surroundings, in fact consists of two parts: the ground floor plus the first floor, that occupy the whole of the building plot, and the second and third floors, which form a smaller volume. The ground floor units are for beginning entrepreneurs, while above them is space for 'breeding grounds', i.e. studios for artists, run by the local authority.

It is important that the future exploitation of the building should still service the same target group. That is why the district authority is taking the building over after it has been completed by the developer Lingotto. The unprofitable part of the project is funded with grants from the European Union and the Amsterdam local authority (breeding grounds project and Department of Economic Affairs).

6.20 N40 (1993)
Cruquiusstraat 1, Czaar Peterstraat 51-85, Eerste Leegh-waterstraat 2-12, Conradstraat 12-66

Architect
Rudy Uytenhaak

Commisioned by
Eigen Haard

Unlike the block next door, this block, that was designed later by the same architect, has a plot in two parts. It consists of an elongated block on the Czaar Peterstraat side in which 44 maisonettes have been built because it is so lacking in depth. The vocabulary of the façade follows the uniformity that characterises the architecture of the old buildings in the street. Adjacent at a very short distance is a strip with four tower blocks with access in the Conradstraat and in which 51 apartments have been fitted. The open plot structure enters into a relation with the building strips of an earlier project that Uytenhaak realised on the other side of the Oostenburgervaart. Because of the short distance, the corners in the façades of the tower blocks have been rotated so that from the apartment you do not look at the large block but along it. This can be clearly seen on the sides of the block.

N44 (2008)
Czaar Peterstraat 2-58, Cruquiusstraat 24-32, Blankenstraat 1-53, Eerste Coehoornstraat 3-7

Architect
Tom Frantzen

Commisioned by
Woonstichting De Key

6.21

A building is going up here that replaces a complete city block. The new building is regarded as the coping stone of the large-scale urban development operation that got under way in the 1970s. The 120 apartments are largely intended for senior citizens. A service centre on the ground floor is intended to provide services not only for the residents in the block, but also for the neighbourhood. The three layers in the brick façade are intended to harmonise with the surrounding buildings.

The demolition of the original buildings at this end of the Czaar Peterstraat has caused quite a stir. Built in 1880, they were nicknamed 'ten cent' or 'flop' homes. The idea behind the 'ten cent' homes was revolutionary and the principle has lost none of its topicality. To enable workers to become owners of their own home, the tenant paid ten cents extra a week on top of the rent; twenty-eight years later he became the owner.

| 6.22 | Funen Sporenboog, Cruquiuskade (2005) Cruquiuskade 45-307, Funenpark 1-212 | **Architect** de Architekten Cie. (Frits van Dongen) | **Commisioned by** Heijmans IBC Vastgoedontwikkeling |

The main challenge on this site was the noise from the passing trains. The building has to function as a noise barrier for the urban villas behind it, but the units in the Sporenboog itself had to be inhabitable as well. For this purpose Van Dongen opted for a facing wall integrated in the façade. There is a minimal distance of 20 cm, filled with sound-absorbent ceilings, between the facing wall and the façade. The dynamism of the passing trains is echoed in the scales and coloured façade plates. With the south side orientated towards the Funenpark, there is more emphasis on the city aspect, with the canalside houses as points of reference. The elongated building accommodates a large variety of housing:

penthouses, apartments with studios, as well
as rented apartments in the social sector and
student studios.

6.23 **Syntax, Bodoni, Palatino** (2007) Funenpark

Architect
De Architecten-groep (Bjarne Mastenbroek, Dick van Gameren), DKV Architecten, Van Sambeek & Van Veen Architecten

Commisioned by
Heijmans IBC Vast-goedontwikkeling

Sixteen small-scale housing blocks are planned for the Funenpark. Some of them are already under construction. The maximum number of apartments per block has been fixed at twelve. The blocks – referred to as the hidden delights in the master plan by Frits van Dongen – are designed by different architects and are scattered, as it were, in a park-like setting. The Bodoni block, named after an Italian typographer, stamp-cutter, printer and publisher who lived at the end of the eighteenth century, has been designed by DKV. It stands in the armpit of the Sporenboog building and contains ten apartments and two penthouses. Each apartment has windows from floor to ceiling with French balconies. The façade is masonry in a grid of prefab concrete. Wood has been applied in the entrance, the access to the boxrooms, and the ground-floor terraces. The windows are irregularly distributed to create a chessboard pattern. Palatino in the south corner, named after the sixteenth-century Italian calligrapher Giambattista Palatino, has been designed by Van Sambeek & Van Veen. The block consists of ten ground floor urban villas with three storeys. The façade has a diagonal woven pattern in black and white brick. The building has a central corridor that cuts diagonally through the volume. There are five entrances with boxrooms on either side of this corridor. The Syntax block, which borders on the Funenpark, has been designed by de architectengroep. This name also refers to the jargon of typography. The building has ten large apartments and a studio. The façade is of uniform masonry, interrupted by internal protruding triangular balconies, some of them with a view of the park.

Along Amsterdam's Waterfront

Canal on Java-eiland

HOUSING TYPO-LOGIES

Marinus Oostenbrink

New housing concepts

Housing has always been the raw material of the city. Differentiated housing environments offering a variety of housing cultures are vital to the quality of urban living. In Amsterdam, the reconsideration of housing patterns commenced around 1990 with the development of new housing concepts for new target groups by, among others, the city itself in its *Woonatlas Amsterdam*. In previously inaccessible areas on the east side of the city (Entrepotdok, Abattoirterrein, Kazernes) the shells of former warehouses provided generously sized lofts with an abundance of light and views. Spatial qualities and freedom of choice for residents and market players represented a breakthrough in municipal housing policies.

Social housing

The urban design concept for KNSM island is based on the *genius loci*, the specific quality of the place. Monumental housing complexes by Wintermans, Coenen and Kollhoff, pay homage to the scale of the former industrial area, offering 'affordable mansions' in the tradition of social housing. They opened the eyes of many bureaucrats, housing corporations and developers to a new housing market in a new context and a new age. In terms of programme, the KNSM housing was largely a continuation of policy-driven housing supply, with small, one and two-person units and compact family dwellings with traditional floor plans.

Differentiated housing

On Java Island, the next of the old finger wharves to be redeveloped, lifestyle- and market-oriented development was introduced for the first time. Market parties were challenged to come up with innovative development strategies resulting in an array of dwelling types and price categories. The urban design concept, with small-scale canals and large gardens, supports the high degree of housing differentiation. Each of the spacious, water-facing apartment blocks has a distinct architectural identity. The elegant narrow canal houses are suitable for a combination of work and living. The surface area increased exponentially, with the traditional living room transformed into an imposing living room. Petit bourgeois living standards were cast off and urban living came of age.

Street-access housing

In the masterplan for the Borneo and Sporenburg finger wharves the emphasis is on urban forms of street-access housing. The typical west Netherlands mansion with upstairs and downstairs apartments and internal courtyards was rediscovered and reworked to produce unusual variants within an intelligent 'bar-code layout'. Houses with roof terraces, patios and internal parking together form a tight-knit 'carpet' of housing. On Scheepstimmermanstraat, the individually designed townhouse was reintroduced. Personal living space was amplified with light wells, skylights, long sight-lines to the water and sky. A few big, tall apartment blocks dramatise the contrast between expansive, street-access living and intensive 'air-access' living in the 'vertical city'.

Combination of functions

This high housing density is carried to new levels along Piet Heinkade and Oostelijke Handelskade. The sophisticated, hybrid architecture accommodates generously proportioned loadbearing structures with high-ceilinged storeys suitable for a variety of living and work functions. The floor plans are dominated by large living areas; multiple

use, neutrality, flexibility, freedom of choice
and monumentality are the new watchwords.
The standard of housing is high, with extra
amenities like a caretaker and swimming pool,
while the local presence of cultural and tourist
facilities, restaurants and bars adds to the
quality of the living environment.

Orientation towards the IJ

Water remains a guiding principle and source
of inspiration for the development of the
Western Harbour Area, where two landmark
apartment buildings on Silodam (MVRDV and
J. van Stigt) set the stage for a new housing
landscape. The Westerdokseiland sub-plan, with
its network of semi-public courts, combines
high density with multi-level villas and
penthouses. Long sight-lines and views of both
the IJ and the city centre offer unique amenity
values – the sine qua non for the new housing
culture on the border between inner city and
water plaza.

Along Amsterdam's Waterfront

South-side Java-eiland

7.

OOSTELIJKE HANDELS-KADE, RIET-LANDEN

The Rietlanden area has not really been a part of Amsterdam for a long time. As the name indicates, it was a marshy area in the past and was only attractive to smugglers. Market gardening, vegetable fields, shunting yards and industrial sites came later, until the year 1874 marked a profound change with the construction of the Oostelijke Handelskade.

After the opening of the North Sea Canal in 1876, the Eastern Harbour Area and the Oostelijke Handelskade already in fact came to lie on the wrong side of the city right from the start. With the decline in the number of shipping lines and the use of containers instead of warehouses to store commodities, the Eastern Harbour Area only functioned at full steam for a relatively short period. The 1970s witnessed a transfer of harbour activities to the west side of the city, and artists occupied the empty warehouses.

The urban development plan for the Oostelijke Handelskade drawn up by the Environmental Planning Department (Hans van der Made) is based on a 'train of buildings', with old and new warehouses as carriages and the Muziekgebouw as the locomotive. The limiting conditions for the architects were formulated in such a way that it must be impossible to see from the façade whether the buildings contained apartments or offices. A large combination of functions have settled here, ranging from apartments in every price category and cultural functions to offices and catering.

The design for Rietlanden by the same department (Ton Schaap) is based on the mikado principle: using and accepting the complex form of this zone, where the entrance to the Piet Heintunnel, the tram stop, the railway line and the entrance to the Eastern Harbour Area all converge.

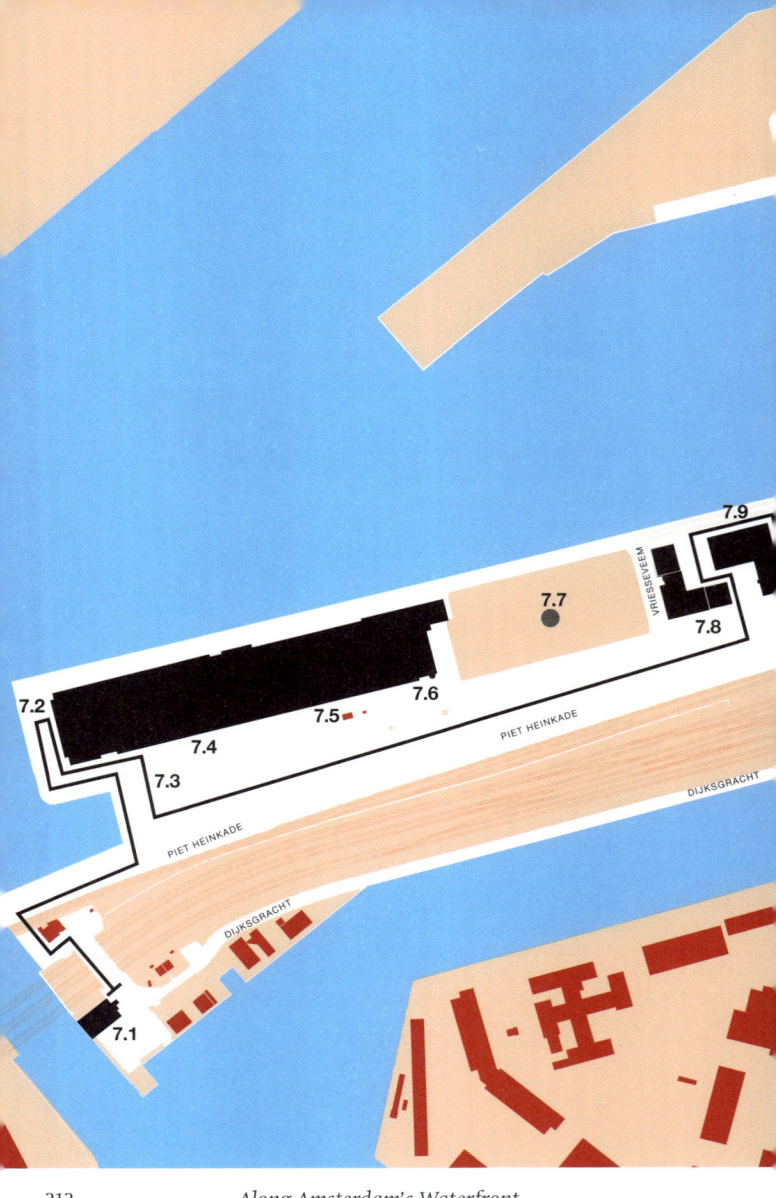

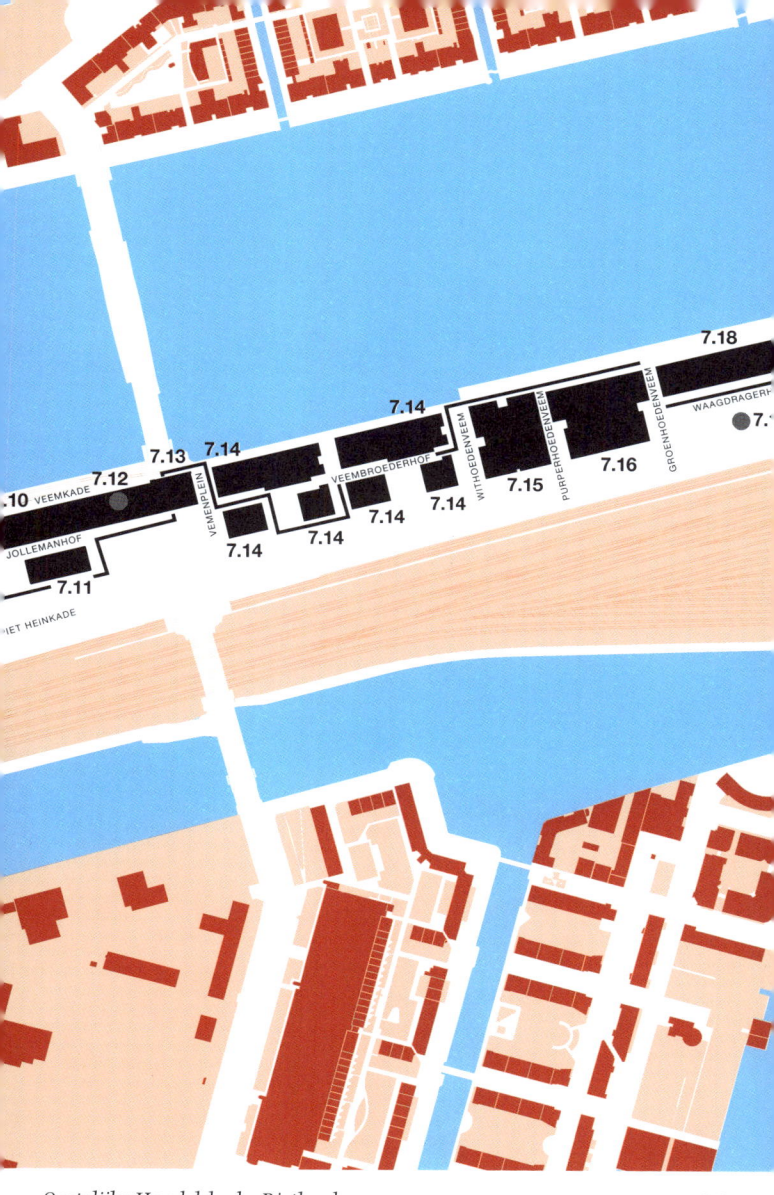

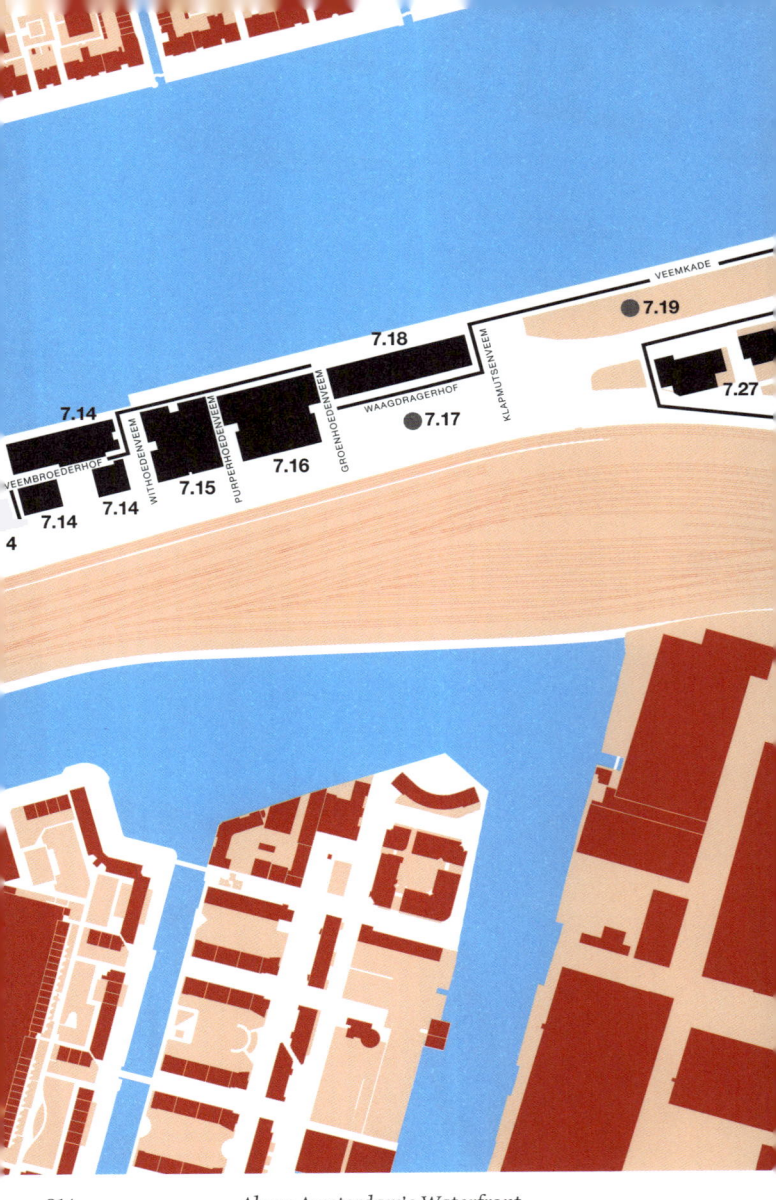

VEEMKADE

7.19

7.18

7.27

7.14

WITHOEDENVEEM

PURPERHOEDENVEEM

GROENHOEDENVEEM

WAAGDRAGERHOF

7.17

KLAPMUTSENVEEM

VEEMBROEDERHOF

7.15

7.16

7.14

7.14

4

Along Amsterdam's Waterfront

| 7.1 | **Centraal climbing wall** (1996)
Dijksgracht 2 | **Architect**
Loof & van Stigt | **Commisioned by**
Rock Steady
Haarlem |

The top of the Dijksgracht will also be developed in the course of the next few years. There is room for a public function of 5,000 m². Work is in progress on an urban development plan in which the function of this location as a link between the Oosterdokseiland and the Piet Heinkade forms the starting point.

The main theme of the Dijksgracht itself is living on the water. The houseboats will remain, but landing stages will be tackled in the same way as beside the Westerdok (3.14). All the boats will be placed at right angles to the quay like a piano keyboard to restore the view of the water.

The function of this climbing hall finds very direct expression in the form and choice of materials. The outer walls of the tilted box, clad with polyester and aluminium-coloured corrugated sheeting, are almost entirely closed, which enables optimal use to be made of the walls sloping forwards and backwards. Climbing routes of different levels of difficulty can thereby be created.

The building was completed in 1996, in the first instance on the side of the railway line facing the water. The Building Inspectorate was strongly opposed at first on the grounds that it would result in 'an unacceptable fragmentation of the public space'. However, a building permit was eventually issued because of the temporary character of the object. It has no foundations and was built in a mere twelve weeks. In 2003 the complete climbing wall was loaded onto a pontoon in a single night and transferred to its present, equally temporary location.

| 7.2 | **Muziekgebouw aan 't IJ/ BIMhuis** (2005)
Piet Heinkade 1 | **Architect**
3xNielsen | **Commisioned by**
Port of Amsterdam
Amsterdam |

The Muziekgebouw can certainly be regarded as the most striking new building on the South Bank of the IJ, not only because of the quality of the design, but above all because of the function (centre for contemporary music) on this location in the city. While in other cities such unique locations are barely able, if at all, to withstand the pressure of commercial

investors, the Amsterdam local authority has implemented a cultural centre here that has given a clear impulse to the image of the South Bank. In the 1990s the undeveloped land at the top of the Piet Heinkade was used by the Traffic Department as a depot for cars that had been towed away and could be reclaimed after a hefty fine had been paid. It was not a pretty sight, on the edge of the city behind the railway line, and it was also used as an illegal prostitution zone. Now the cultural élite of the city use the pedestrian bridge to reach the Muziekgebouw and BIMhuis, which opened in 2005, for a concert or a drink and a bite to eat in the café-restaurant with a large terrace overlooking the water.

After a multiple study assignment, the design by the Danish firm of architects 3xN was chosen as the most suitable for the location. The potential of the site is used to the full by making every side of the building equally important. Moreover, the plan was able to manage with the limited budget of 60 million euros.

Immediately to the left of the pedestrian bridge a black volume like a shoe box sticks out of the façade. This is the BIMhuis, with a small concert hall and bar to cater for an

The Muziekgebouw received several international awards in 2006: Award for Excellence Europe competition of the Urban Land Institute, and the Premio Internazionale Dedalo Minosse alla Committenza di Architettura (for commissioning a building).

After the redevelopment, the stretch of the original Oostelijke Handelskade between the Muziekgebouw and Panama was given a new name: the Piet Heinkade.

audience of around 500. On the inside the hall is like a peep-box, with a large window behind the stage offering a view of the railway line and the historic centre. The hall and bar, the work of the De Vries Bouma firm of architects, have been designed in such a way that the two connecting areas can be divided up in various ways by using partitions that can be left open or closed.

The main concert hall in the Muziekgebouw consists of a functional concrete box with seating capacity of 750. The concrete walls were cast in situ in the work to provide optimal soundproofing from the noise of trains and other traffic. The apparently arbitrary seams were in fact designed beforehand with the aid of a computer.

The walls inside the hall itself are clad with Canadian maple. LED lighting elements have been installed behind the slats which can produce any colour of the rainbow. A genuinely innovative feature of the hall is the moveable ceiling, which makes it possible to create a different volume depending on the type of concert and thereby to influence the length of resonance of the sound waves.

The façade round the concrete box is like a transparent shell. The space between the façade and the concert hall is designed for all public functions, as well as for music company offices. The floors on each level are covered with untreated Brazilian hardwood. The longer the floor is used, the rougher the appearance of the wood will become. Together with the steel, concrete and glass of the façades, it reinforces the apparently uncontrived architecture of the complex. Daylight reaches deep into the building through the glass exterior, and after dark the Muziekgebouw is a beacon on the South Bank of the IJ.

| **Pedestrian bridge over the Zouthaven** (2004) Piet Heinkade 1 | **Architect** Hans van Heeswijk architecten | **Commisioned by** Amsterdam Development Corporation (OGA) | 7.3 |

The bridge over the Zouthaven connects the through tram road and the tram stop with the Muziekgebouw. The bridge spans the Zouthaven, which is to be excavated again, at the top of the Piet Heinkade. The design refers to the pedestrian bridges that used to be a common sight between the ships and the quay, but upside down. It is a suspension bridge made of a fan-like steel tensile construction with 21 cross trusses, whose tension cables extending gracefully under the steep bridge deck. The tension cables run along the sides and underneath the bridge but cannot be seen above the bridge deck. There is therefore nothing to block the view from the bridge. Because it was difficult to predict the vibration with such an elegant construction, tests were conducted after completion to determine whether and where absorbers were required. It is still quite an experience to cross the bridge when it is windy or raining.

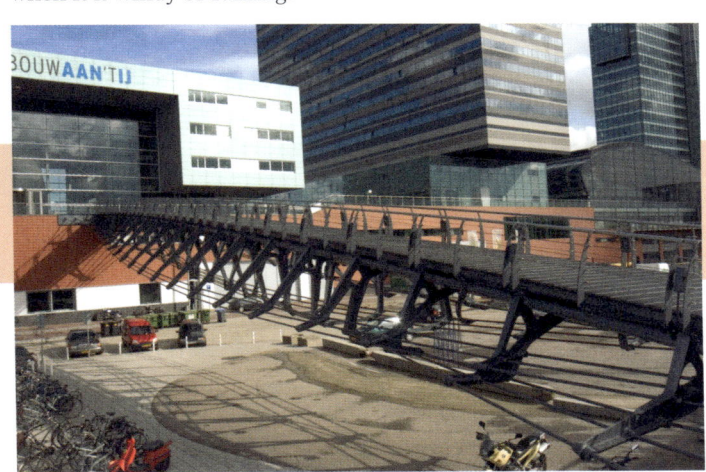

Oostelijke Handelskade, Rietlanden

7.4 **Mövenpick Hotel**
(2006)
Piet Heinkade 11-19

Architect
Claus en Kaan
Architecten

Commisioned by
Mövenpick,
Amplan

The red brown tile used to cover the plinth, devised by the architect of the IJtoren, was later also applied to the neighbouring premises in consultation with the supervisor of the area and the other architects. The idea was to emphasise the elongated shape of the area and to make visible the internal cohesion of the different functions. The separate parts of the Muziekgebouw, the hotel accommodation, the roof construction of the Passenger Terminal and the office tower block are all clearly visible above the plinth they all share.

Between the Muziekgebouw and the IJtoren rises the tall building of Mövenpick Hotels & Resorts, a chain with branches in Europe and the Middle East.
The building was originally planned to be considerably lower than the Dexia Bank office, which would have created a gradual increase in height between the Muziekgebouw, the hotel and the office block. Under pressure from the client, however, the hotel is almost as tall as the tower block, resulting in a more static composition from the Central Station than had been intended in the master plan.
The lower storeys accommodate public functions, including conference halls and the hotel lobby. The upper storeys contain the more than 400 rooms of the four-star hotel. The height of the façade strips, in glass, green granite, white

marble and white concrete, does not correspond to that of the storeys. So this is not a case of form follows function, but one with a Modernist twist.

Passenger Terminal Amsterdam (1999) Piet Heinkade 27	**Architect** HOK	**Commisioned by** Port of Amsterdam, Amsterdam Local Authority, NS Stations	7.5

The Passenger Terminal Amsterdam (PTA), commissioned by the local authority harbour department, was built in 1999, making it one of the first of the new projects on the Piet Heinkade. The main function of the building is the reception of passengers from ocean cruisers in Amsterdam. Between seventy and a hundred cruisers moor at the terminal each year. In addition there are meeting, conference and reception facilities for a maximum of 3,000 persons.

The PTA was designed by Larry Malcic from the US firm of architects Hellmuth, Obata + Kassabaum (HOK). The architect has emphasised the nautical appearance of the building with its pronounced wave-shaped form. That form also indicates that this is a point of intersection between water and land. Since the façade is mainly glass, each of the three decks – Main Deck, Promenade Deck, and Panorama Deck – offers a wide view of the IJ.

Partly in response to terrorist attacks, the security at international ports for cruisers has been tightened up. As a result, since 2005 part of the quay has been closed off during the cruise season. Since other users of the area also have to make use of the quay, it has been widened at that point. Research is going on into the possibility of a raised promenade for pedestrians.

Oostelijke Handelskade, Rietlanden

7.6	**IJtoren Dexia** (2002) Piet Heinkade 55	**Architect** HOK	**Commisioned by** Amplan, ING

The 90-metre IJtoren is the tallest building on the South Bank of the IJ. It was developed by Dexia Bank Nederland and incorporated in the investment portfolio of ING Real Estate via sale and lease back.

The Dexia Bank occupies nine of the nineteen floors. The upper floors, which are also let to third parties, afford a wonderful panoramic view of the city and the river. All the same, this building has suffered from the decline in the office market in the last few years: although it was completed in 2002, not all of the office space has yet been let. The tower was designed by Larry Malcic of HOK, who also designed the adjacent Passenger Terminal. The British architecture periodical Building Design reported in 2006 that HOK (Hellmuth, Obata + Kassabaum) is the biggest firm of architects in the world, with a staff of more than 1,600 operative in different continents. The architecture of the façade and the interior design are in conformity with this international anonymous style.

As in the case of the more recent Mövenpick Hotel, there were serious protests from the Association of Friends of the Amsterdam Inner City because of the obstruction of the historic lines of vision from the centre to the harbour and the IJ.

7.7	**Nieuw Europa** (2009) Piet Heinkade, Veemkade	**Architect** Hans van Heeswijk architecten, de architectengroep (Dick van Gameren)	**Commisioned by** Amplan

The area between the Passenger Terminal and Huys Europe is the site of the projected Nieuw Europa (New Europe) office complex: 28,000 m² with parking facilities and a touring car terminal. The terminal, which can also be used for handling luggage, is on the side facing the waterfront. It is a big, multifunctional hall at ground level with translucent glazed façades designed by Hans van Heeswijk. Above it are four massive office volumes. Different materials have been used for each of these four independent blocks to give it a look of its own. Dick van Gameren designed a block on the east side and one on the waterfront. The façade is of prefab brick elements and refers to the old warehouses that have been preserved on the quay. Van Heeswijk designed the entrance block, an intermediate block, and the rest of the building. The entrance block, on the Piet Heinkade, has a more open glazed façade with vertical strips clad with a robust industrial grey brick.

The interiors of the four office blocks have been designed so that they can be combined to form a whole or kept separate.

A taxi rank and a loop for traffic to turn with a tram stop are planned on the city side. The side facing the quay has a pedestrian bridge leading to the cruiser terminal.

The building project has run into some delays because of the collapse in the office market at the beginning of the decade. However, this has had its positive effects too: the development of the terminal can now respond better to the new insight into its use for cruisers.

Huys Europa	Architect	Commisioned by	7.8
(2005)	de Architekten	IBC/Heijmans,	
Piet Heinkade	Cie. (Branimir	Rodamco	
141-173,	Medić, Pero Puljiz)		
Jollemanhof 1-4			

The robust façade elements of Huys Europa (Europe House) are an attempt to blend with the large-scale maritime atmosphere of the waterfront. The plinth and four floors of office space are let by the Ahold food concern. The upper storeys contain twelve apartments, each with a floor space of almost 200 m². The façades are transparent thanks to the glass window fronts and glass sheeting of the outdoor areas. This is the former site of the Pakhuis Europa (Europe Warehouse), which formed a 200-metre wall together with Pakhuis Azië and Pakhuis Afika. While the latter are now being renovated, the Europe Warehouse was demolished in 1999

after several renovations.

The transfer of the Ahold top management to the South Bank of the IJ and not to the South Axis, for instance, was a deliberate choice, influenced by the combination of housing, business and cultural facilities on the Piet Heinkade. Next to the building is a statue of a woman with shopping bags, presented by supermarket magnate Albert Heijn when he retired, with the text: 'So that we never forget who we work for'.

| 7.9 | **Huys Azië** (2005)
Jollemanhof
5-7 en 8-20 | **Architect**
KCAP Architects
& Planners | **Commisioned by**
IBC/Heijmans,
Rodamco |

Huys Azië (Asia House), not to be confused with Pakhuis Azië (Asia Warehouse, which has been renamed Pakhuis Amsterdam), is the counterpart of Huys Europa in terms of urban design. The complex consists of two buildings. An L-shaped low-rise three-storey block stands on top of two underground levels of parking lots. The heavy dimensions of the steel H-profiles that frame the wall-length rows of windows give the building the appearance of a stripped old warehouse. A brick volume leans against it that looks fairly massive at ground level, but which grows increasingly slender as it rises because of the 'evaluative window articulation', that is, the fact that the windows grow steadily larger storey by storey.

| 7.10 | **Pakhuis Amsterdam** (1999)
Jollemanhof 9-17 | **Architect**
Meyer en Van Schooten Architecten, Urban Office (Madir Shah), Antarctic (Antoine van de Vijver) | **Commisioned by**
Konig & Cie |

Pakhuis Amsterdam (Amsterdam Warehouse) acquired its present name after the thorough renovation of the former Pakhuis Azië in 1999. The design for the renovation is by Meyer en Van Schooten, commissioned by the Nederlands Interieur Collectief. The wooden shutters were replaced with glass; the original holes for the bars are still visible in the window openings. Voids and breaches have been implemented inside to make the warehouse suitable as a modern office space.

After the departure of the Interieur Collectief, the warehouse was let to various parties, including Greenpeace. The ground floor is the site of restaurant Fifteen, where underprivileged youths can be trained as chefs, a scheme based on a project by the English chef Jamie Oliver. The original dark cast-iron columns have been given a central role in the interior, designed by Madir Shah and Antoine van de Vijver. The corrugated cladding sprayed with graffiti is eye-catching.

Gibraltar (2004)	Architect	Commisioned by	7.11
Jollemanhof 22-152	Claus en Kaan Architecten	IBC/Heijmans, Ymere	

The development of the Piet Heinkade was based on the principle of preserving the atmosphere of the huge and solid warehouses as far as possible. This meant that the new building must look like a block that is lived in, but not like domestic apartments. The Gibraltar complex contains 66 rented council flats and 6 owner-occupied business units on the ground floor, but from outside it looks like an office block. The apartments do not have any

balconies or terraces. Three façades have been composed of floor-to-ceiling prefab elements in a sand-coloured concrete. The north wall, where the galleries give access to the apartments, is entirely of glass. This allows a maximum of light to enter, because the five-storey Pakhuis Amsterdam stands right in front of it.

In allocating the council flats, the Ymere housing association has experimented with a new procedure. Although they were eventually allocated in accordance with the standard procedure, that is, on the basis of length of registration, applications were pre-selected by lifestyle on the basis of an extensive questionnaire. The future residents had to appreciate unusual housing typologies, like severe design, and be receptive to fellow residents from different social and ethnic classes. The idea behind this was to avoid problems among the residents. The experiment was not entirely successful and the composition of the residents is fairly one-sided, but there are some successful points: one year after completion, the caretaker had still not received a single complaint about other residents. Though there are some residents with a will of their own: one has ventured to hang bright red geraniums in his window, a cheerful interruption of the minimalist look of the façade.

7.12	Huys Afrika	Architect	Commisioned by
	(1913/2007)	KCAP Architects	Heijmans
	Oostelijke	& Planners,	Vastgoed
	Handelskade 19	Villanova	

Huys Afrika (Africa House), which was built in 1913, has so-called mushroom floors: overhanging concrete columns in the floor – which were very modern at the time – which could carry a lot of weight. That is why the warehouse has been declared a state protected historic building. It functioned as a cold store, but the construction was not ideal. The walls started to rust and there was too little insulation.

In 2003 the warehouse was squatted and in the two following years it became more and more of a breeding ground. The squatters made a name for themselves with the recurrent cultural event 'Damoclash'. In the spring of 2005 the premises were evacuated because of the risk of fire, after which work on the new building could commence. The new Huys Afrika is being built in front of and on top of Pakhuis Afrika. The old building is earmarked for businesses, while the new building will consist of 52 owner-occupied apartments.

The new complex is clad with rust-coloured concrete elements to match the atmosphere of the old warehouses. The raised north wall, which faces the water, is supported by columns that penetrate the old building. They are in the same pattern as the warehouse columns, so that justice has been done to the dimensions of the monument.

Oostelijke Handelskade, Rietlanden

7.13 Pakhuis De Zwijger
(1934/2006)
Piet Heinkade
179-181

Architect
J. de Bie Leuvelink
Tjeenk and K.
Bakker/ Architec-
tenbureau J. van
Stigt

Commisioned by
Maatschappij
Blaauwhoeden-
veem-Vriesseveem,
Stadsherstel
Amsterdam

De Zwijger owes its name to the holding of a competition among the personnel of the Maatschappij Blaauwhoedenveem-Vriesseveem. What motives led to the selection of this particular suggestion are not known. Café-restaurant De Zwijger, which is open all day, is located in the underground corridor of the building. The interior design has been done to preserve the robust character of the building as far as possible. The bar has been folded between the octagonal columns.

Pakhuis De Zwijger (De Zwijger Warehouse) is one of the most striking projects on the Piet Heinkade. The Jan Schaefer bridge leading to the end of the Java Island runs right through it. Moreover, because of its status as a preserved historic building, De Zwijger has managed to hold on to its old silhouette in spite of the hole. The De Zwijger cool store, designed by the architects J. de Bie Leuvelink Tjeenk and K. Bakker and completed in 1934, has a no-nonsense expressionist style and was already a famous example of modern architecture in its day. It was one of the most modern cool stores where perishable foodstuffs such as meat could be kept for longer periods. The supporting construction consists of a skeleton of reinforced concrete with octagonal columns and mushroom floors to carry a lot of weight. The façade is clad with half-brick masonry for extra isolation and to prevent concrete rot. Nine blue mosaic sheets have been attached to the east wide with the names of the places where the Maatschappij Blaauwhoedenveem-

Vriesseveem, the owner of the premises at the time, had its offices.

De Zwijger was squatted in the 1980s, after which it was used primarily as a rehearsal place for bands. Because of the insulating thick walls, musicians like Loïs Lane and Herman Brood could let rip. Underground parties were also regularly organised there.

For a while there was talk of demolishing the complex because the foundations did not seem to be in order after the bridge had been driven through the building. The Cuypers Association asked for the building to be declared a state protected historic monument, and the application was accepted. After intensive feasibility studies by the Stichting de Zwijger and many talks with the local authority, it was decided that the premises would be renovated and be assigned a cultural function in the form of a multimedia centre.

André van Stigt and Stadsherstel Amsterdam carried out the renovation. Openings were made in the façade on the north side to let in daylight. Cultuurfabriek, Waag Society, the Amsterdam Art Fund, Salto Broadcasting Amsterdam and the Mediagilde are the new users.

De Loodsen	Architect	Commisioned by	7.14
(2006)	Köther en Salman	Ymere, Hopman	
Veemkade 232-364,	Architekten,	Interheem Groep	
Veembroederhof	hvdn architecten,		
1- 287, 4-366,	Wingender Hove-		
Piet Heinkade 183,	nier Architecten		
199-201, 211			

The ensemble known as De Loodsen (The Sheds) consists of two buildings like railway carriages on the waterfront, called Cocoa and Cotton. The form, colour and choice of materials of these elongated buildings with roof terraces match the old and new buildings on either side of the complex. Each 'carriage' has a higher section. On the south side are four individual towers, each 35-metres high, called Cinnamon, Coffee,

Tea, and Pepper.

The urban development plan is by Köther en Salman Architekten. They also designed the Cotton 'carriage' and the Tea tower block. The Cocoa 'carriage' and the Coffee tower block, which leans against Cotton from the fifth floor up, are by hvdn architecten. Wingender Hovenier was responsible for the Cinnamon tower and the Pepper tower. In short, it is a real mixture of spices.

Atria with a glass roof facing the water provide access to the entrances of the carriage complexes. The latter have business units on the ground floor and owner-occupied apartments above them as well as in the higher sections. The atria are open to the public and are closed at night – a model imported from the USA. Coffee also consists exclusively of owner-occupied apartments. Cinnamon, Tea and Pepper, situated on the Piet Heinkade, include both council and private apartments to let. The master plan for the entire strip along the former Oostelijke Handelskade opted for austere external walls, which ruled out hanging balconies. Small industrially designed, staggered balconies were possible in the side walls of some of the apartment blocks.

The Kunstplein (Art Square) has been wedged between the buildings on the east side. Bureau KKEP devised Ledwork, a large number of solar-powered lamps that are incorporated in the paving of the square. By day the sun charges the battery, while at dusk and in the night the lamps flicker, though not in sync, resulting in a constantly changing artistic pattern.

Along Amsterdam's Waterfront

Detroit (2006)
Veemkade 366-560,
Purperhoeden-
veem 7-15,
Withoedenveem
8-16

Architect
awg architecten

Commisioned by
Ontwikkelings-
combinatie Nieuw
Amerika (Het Oos-
ten, Ymere, Johan
Matser)

Luxury beside the IJ – this complex offers it. The
Detroit residents have at their disposal a health
club with swimming pool, two saunas and a
fitness area, laundry area and two guest rooms for
the guests of the residents. There is a shopping
and dry cleaning service, and various modern
domestic devices have been incorporated in the
apartments. Vesteda, which lets apartments in
the free market sector, lets these apartments and
has its office on the ground floor.
They are not cheap: the rents start at 1,350
euros and run up to more than 4,600 euros for
apartments between 100 and 150 m². But for
that money you have a space whose interior
design can be exactly as you choose – it can be
divided up in different ways by means of a raised
floor with power points wherever you like. The
access to the apartments, an imposing entrance
hall, also exudes what the residents pay for: the
floors are surfaced with black natural stone, the
wall panelling on each floor has a minimalist
design and is finished with natural stone and
aluminium sheeting. The furniture consists of a
carpet designed by the architect and two black
leather sofas designed by Mies van der Rohe.
The combination of daylight from above, from
the two-storey high entrance on the street side
and the artificial light on every floor, confer a
chic look on the whole. A nice detail is that you
can see exactly who is at home from the light
that shines through the matt glass walls of the
apartments into the atrium.
The volume on the waterfront side follows the
entirety of the long wall of warehouses, while the
building facing the railway line seems to be more
of a self-contained object. That is what Christian
Rapp had in mind in the urban development
plan that was made for the ensemble of three

complexes called Nieuw Amerika. Rapp also devised a rule, following the example of New York, to determine the maximal building volume per storey: 100 per cent on the ground floor, 70 per cent in the middle, and 50 per cent on top. This has been followed by awg architecten by letting the sturdy volume, clad in dark brick with hardly any grouting, effect a transition from a rectangular to a wedge-shaped form to ensure optimal daylight for the apartments. There are roof terraces on the second and sixth floors, while when seen from the city the volume has a slender appearance.

7.16 **Boston** (2005) (Nieuw Australië) Veemkade 562-568, Purperhoeden-veem 2-140, Groen-hoedenveem 1-139, Piet Heinkade 215-225	**Architect** DKV architecten	**Commisioned by** Ontwikkelings-combinatie Nieuw Amerika (Het Oosten, Ymere, Johan Matser)

The old Pakhuis Australië (Australia Warehouse) has a turbulent history. Like the Pakhuis Amerika, it was originally built in 1893–1895 for the Blaauwhoedenveem company. When fire broke out in 1948, the Amerika was completely gutted; Australië was seriously damaged, but

could be restored. DKV, the architects of the new
Boston building, originally planned to wrap up
the old building by erecting the new one over
it. However, during the building stage the old
warehouse caught fire again in 2003, and this
time it was completely destroyed. The planning
stage was so advanced by now that it was
decided to reconstruct the Australia as it had
been before 1948 so that the DKV plans could be
implemented with as few alterations as possible.
The new building has a U-shaped mass which is
connected to the old building by glass volumes.
The plinth is completely filled with business
units. On top of them is a shared garden on a
slope, which yields an unusual perspective. The
apartments in both parts – 90 owner-occupied
and 40 to let in the free market sector – are like
lofts. The clustering of the shafts for piping
and cabling has resulted in ground plans that
can be divided up in all kinds of ways. The
computer floor (various power points) and
moveable wall elements enable residents to
shape their own rooms. The window fronts are
completely foldable so that an internal balcony
can be created.
The project won the Concrete Award 2005,
a competition organised by the Concrete
Association, for its creative and innovative use
of concrete.

Chicago (2006)	**Architect**	**Commisioned by**	7.17
Piet Heinkade	Rapp+Rapp	Ontwikkelings-	
		combinatie Nieuw	
		Amerika (Het Oos-	
		ten, Ymere, Johan	
		Matser)	

The third and last building in the Nieuw
Amerika ensemble is Chicago. This apartment
complex has been built in a U-shape beside and
half over the Pakhuis Wilhelmina (Wilhelmina
Warehouse).
The overhanging volumes caused a good deal of
commotion among the residents of the Pakhuis
Wilhelmina. The artists who have their studios

in that warehouse were seriously worried about fire safety: the old and new buildings would be less than three metres apart, resulting in a chimney effect if fire were to break out. This led to a number of court hearings, after which a temporary cessation of building activity was announced. In the end the parties concerned agreed to the implementation of a package of extra fire safety measures for the Pakhuis Wilhelmina, that the developer would offer a number of studios elsewhere in compensation, and that fire safety measures would be implemented on the access balconies of the apartments in the inner courtyard of Chicago. Building activity could then be resumed. Chicago contains 89 rented apartments in the free market sector and 4 domestic cum business units. There are business units on the lowest two floors. The architects, who also worked on Piraeus on the KNSM Island, linked the two ends of the letter 'U' that hang above Wilhelmina with steel walkways on each of the five floors. Characteristic of the façades is the construction of horizontal floor strips, masonry window piers, and floor-to-ceiling folding casements with closing stile.

| 7.18 | Pakhuis Wilhelmina (2004) Veemkade 570-598, Groen-hoedenveem 2-30 | **Architect** CASA architecten | **Commisioned by** Stichting Wilhelmina, Firma de Ridder |

Along Amsterdam's Waterfront

Built in 1892 by the Vriesseveem company and drastically renovated in 1967, the Pakhuis Wilhelmina (Wilhelmina Warehouse) was squatted in the 1980s by artists, architects and musicians, who formed a close-knit community. A more commercial exploitation had to be found to guarantee the survival of the complex and to pay for the renovation. The Wilhelmina working group has put a lot of effort into this and a large number of the original users still have a space in the complex. There are a venue/bar for pop music, a gamelan house, design and woodwork shops, and a good deal more.

The residents of the Pakhuis Wilhelmina were vigorously opposed to the new Chicago building, which has been constructed in front of and over the warehouse. Not only has this darkened various studios on the south side, but it posed an acute threat to fire safety. After various court hearings, during which building activity ground to a halt, a number of modifications were introduced to guarantee fire safety.

Nieuw Argentinië	Architect	Commisioned by	7.19
(2009)	Rob Krier,	Het Oosten, Kristal	
Oostelijke	Marc Breitman		
Handelskade,			
Veemkade			

Originally a building was designed for this area, one of the last sites on the Piet Heinkade to be built up, by the architect Koen van Velsen. The massive character of this complex and the fact that it only contained owner-occupied apartments in an area that otherwise showed little signs of life at the time were probably the factors which caused such a stagnation in the pre-building sales that it was decided not to go ahead with the plan. It has been replaced by a new plan for this area, commissioned by Het Oosten housing corporation and drawn up by Rob Krier (Luxembourg) and Marc Breitman (France), both of whom had already established a reputation in

Amsterdam with such projects as the Noorderhof and the Westermoskee. The programme now consists for 70 per cent of smaller rented accommodation in the free market sector, and for 30 per cent of rented council flats and a hostel for young drifters.

The plan has three parts: two oblong complexes, each consisting of two blocks separated by a garden; the façade is continuous on the side facing the water, which makes it look like a whole. The third part is a more vertically shaped building that is slightly taller. The style of the design is a mixture of robust nineteenth-century warehouse style with a sort of fin-de-siècle style, with dominant arched shapes in the façade, classicising railings in front of the windows, and overhanging verandas. In this sense the design is not entirely in line with the severe architectural idiom of the new buildings that were planned for this strip.

7.20 **My Side** (1995)	**Architect**	**Commisioned by**
Veemkade 1000-1210	de Architekten Cie. (Frits van Dongen)	Amstelland Vastgoed

The two symmetrical identical parts of the building were already completed in 1995 as one of the first housing developments in what was a fairly desolate looking area at the time. They are thus not included in the master plan for the Oostelijke Handelskade (now Piet Heinkade), in which the appearance of the warehouse architecture has been taken as the starting point. The apartments – 106 owner-occupied units, most of them maisonettes of various types – are distinguished by the large number of smart devices, such as computerised heating, bath and lighting which can also be remotely controlled by telephone, touch screens for leaving messages, and video monitors next to the door bells. In fact these facilities are a precursor of the trend that was to continue in this housing district: a luxurious metropolitan housing environment, orientated towards the city and comfort. The two parts of the building are orientated towards both north and south. The waterfront side has a monumental character. Large elements and hard materials have been used such as corrugated sheeting, glass and plaster. The apartments on the top floor and at the end of the block jut out slightly and frame the whole. The south side, on the Oostelijke Handelskade, is far more differentiated and lively. This effect is achieved by means of terraces, balconies and the staggered wooden façades of the top floor which create a jagged look. The use of so many different kinds of materials in the façade was a trend in the 1990s. Later, starting with Piraeus, a more sober choice of materials came into fashion.

Lloyd Paviljoen (2000) Oostelijke Handelskade 997-999, Veemkade 1212	**Architect** Bekkering Adams Architecten	**Commisioned by** Blauwhoed vastgoed	**7.21**

This free-standing pavilion was designed as two volumes that fit into one another: catering facilities on the ground floor and an office on the first. The space is currently let to a fitness/ health centre, which is a welcome addition to the programme in the neighbourhood. Two patios separate the volume from its

surroundings. The enormous row of windows facing the quay juts slightly out. The façade is in a dark manganese stone in tile bond with zinc frames.

| 7.22 **Winkelcentrum Brazilië** (1998) Veemkade 1224-1286, Oostelijke Handelskade 1001-1063 | **Architect** Neutelings Riedijk Architects | **Commisioned by** Blauwhoed Vastgoed |

Moored near the shopping centre is a replica of a Russian merchant vessel, the Odessa, from the port of the same name. It has been thoroughly renovated and is used as a café-restaurant. Nearby is Lizboa, now a party ship as well, with a terrace on the deck.

At first sight the Brazilië (Brazil) shopping centre seems to be a new construction, but the complex consists of an iron skeleton and the roof trusses of the original Koninklijke Hollandse Lloyd Brazilië coffee and cocoa warehouse dating from 1915. After the local authority had organised a competition, which was won by the Neutelings Riedijk firm of architects and developer Blauwhoed, the warehouse was razed to the ground and the material used as the basis for this new shopping centre slightly west of the original site. The shopping centre has not been designed very practically. Although there are two roofed patios, some shops are only accessible from the outside.

IJtoren (1998)
Veemkade 1288-1312, Oostelijke Handelskade 1065-1213

Architect
Neutelings Riedijk Architects

Commisioned by
Blauwhoed Vastgoed Euro-woningen

This tower block on the corner of the connecting dam and the Piet Heinkade is an important landmark in the Eastern Harbour Area. The 60-metre tower has twenty storeys and stands on a three-tier plinth. Bites have been taken out of the façade at different points, so that each floor is different from the others. In accordance with the fashion of the late 1990s, there are 20 different types of apartment out of a total of 68. They are all owner-occupied. The façades are clad with wide vertical elements of fibre cement sheeting, accentuated by aluminium connecting profiles. The recessed parts of the façade are given extra emphasis through the different choice of materials. A noteworthy feature is that the windows are not placed in vertical rows, but are staggered.

Oostelijke Handelskade, Rietlanden

| 7.24 | **Harbour officers' homes** (1915) Oostelijke Handelskade 44-66 | **Architect** J.H.W. Leliman | **Commisioned by** Koninklijke Nederlandsche Stoomboot Maatschappij |

Among the original buildings of the former docklands are the ones that the KNSM had built for its personnel and their families. The designer was the architect and writer J.H.W. Leliman, who was responsible for several housing complexes in the Indonesian quarter and in North Amsterdam, including De Meeuwenlaan, as well as the Noord-Zuid Hollandsch Koffiehuis opposite the Central Station. But his best-known design is the Dutch Royal Touring Club mushroom-shaped signpost from 1918, which can still be seen all over the Netherlands. The complex contains twenty-one apartments in the Oostelijke Handelskade. The façade forms a symmetrical whole, with a recessed central part and dormer windows that are reminiscent of a house in the country.

| 7.25 | **Koffiehuis Lloyd** (1917/2003) Oostelijke Handelskade 44 | **Architect** Evert Breeman/ CASA architecten | **Commisioned by** Woningstichting Zomers Buiten |

Koffiehuis Lloyd (Lloyd Coffee House) was built in 1917 by Evert Breeman, who also designed

Along Amsterdam's Waterfront

the Lloyd Hotel. The building was divided by social class: the front room was the decorous domain of the higher-ranking personnel, while the dockhands and day labourers ate their sandwiches and pea soup in the back room. Unemployed labourers also came here to apply for work and could drink a cup of coffee there for ten cents. The coffee house disappeared when the company did. After the war the premises housed a grocer's shop and a souvenir wholesaler. The front part of the building was taken into use as a coffee house again in 2003. Faithful to its history, the coffee house still offers good food at a reasonable price. The back room is used as a meeting place for the neighbourhood, a conference room, and as a rehearsal room for stage and other productions.

Lloyd Hotel	**Architect**	**Commisioned by**	**7.26**
(1918/2004)	Evert Breeman/	Woonstichting	
Oostelijke Han-	MVRDV	De Key	
delskade 34			

Few buildings on the banks of the IJ have such a turbulent history behind them as the Lloyd Hotel, now one of the cultural hot spots of the city. As part of a complex including offices, accommodation for personnel and a delousing building, it was taken into use in 1921 as a hotel for migrants: Jewish refugees and peasants from Eastern Europe spent the night here waiting for the Koninklijke Lloyd ships that sailed for South America once every three weeks. Because they were not allowed to leave the premises during that period, the building could provide everything they needed: shops, a small hospital, restaurants, and even a kosher kitchen.

After the Lloyd shipping company went into liquidation in 1935 – one of the reasons for the bankruptcy was the high expense of building this hotel – the building passed into the hands of the local authority. Because of its isolated position at the time, it was used as a prison for resistance fighters during World War Two, and later as a detention centre and remand home until 1989. When the building no longer met the criteria of the prison service, it was used by artists as a studio. Although the surroundings were renovated on a large scale, the building declined more and more. A round of new plans for it began in 1997, which resulted in its renovation as a hotel with a catering function and a so-called Cultural Embassy in 2005.

The MVRDV firm of architects had to abide by strict regulations because by now the Lloyd Hotel had been put on the list of preserved historic monuments. It retained its classical, dark exterior with decorative masonry in a mixed style of Art Déco and Dutch Neo-Renaissance elements. But inside there have been major changes. The introduction of a large, central void brought in much more light. An unusual feature is that each of the 116 hotel rooms is different, not only in comfort but also in design. Different designers, including the artist Joep van Lieshout, devised the design of each room. There are one-star rooms with a shared shower in the corridor, and highly individualised five-star suites: a room with an eight-person bed, a very high room with a grand piano to suit a travelling musician, a room with an open bathroom, or an entirely wood-panelled *Twin Peaks* room.

Along Amsterdam's Waterfront

Panama
(1885/2001)
Oostelijke Han-
delskade 4

Architect
B. de Greef,
W. Springer/ VASD
ontwerpers and
Ruud van Empel

The building in which Club Panama is now
housed was built in 1885 as a hydraulic power
station to supply steam for the cranes on the
dockside. It was converted into an electric
power station in 1899, when an extra wing was
added to accommodate the boilers. In 1951 the
whole complex was transformed into a rectifier,
the so-called Eastern Docklands Power Station.
The style of this industrial monument, which
was declared a state protected building in 2001,
is characterised by eclectic and Neo-Gothic
influences, which can be seen in the arched
friezes and the decorative masonry in red brick
alternating with bands in natural stone. The
interior, which is still visible in the main hall,
has an open roof construction with Polonceau
gable roof trusses. These are thin iron trusses
that hang from the ceiling, named after the
engineer Camille Polonceau, who first used this
type of truss in the construction of the Paris-
Versailles railway in 1839.
The building has been in use under the name
Panama since 2001 as a theatre, dance hall, café-
restaurant with terrace, concert hall, and TV
studio for talk shows.

7.28 **School and office block De Schijf**
(2003)
Oostelijke
Handelskade 6-10

Architect
Hans van Heeswijk
architecten

Commisioned by
Amplan Vastgoed,
Stadsdeel Zeeburg

From the severe, no-nonsense, simple façade
composition of this school and office block,
in dark grey brick with striking white window
frames and cames, it almost looks like a
renovated office block from the 1960s, left over
from the commercial activities of the past. It is in
fact the new building for the Piet Hein primary
school, which had to put up with temporary
accommodation on the waterfront for years.
Next to the school, the building also contains
space for offices and business units.
The structure of the building has been kept
as clean as possible. This means that a sharp
distinction has been made in the architecture
between the skeleton, the functional division
into spaces, and the finishing. This has been
done so that in the event of a change of function,

the building can remain an architectural whole and no structural interventions will be required. This anticipates the possibility of a different function in the future, because the primary schools in the Eastern Harbour Area are expected to shrink again within ten to twenty years once the children of the present young families have grown up.

A so-called learning street has been developed for the interior of the school. This is a spacious corridor adjoining the classrooms. It contains toilet and cloakroom units, in a different colour for each classroom, as well as space for joint activities.

Rietlanden Park Towers (2001) Rietlandpark 1-255, 275-357	Architect VenhoevenCS, Hans van Heeswijk architecten	Commisioned by Woningstichting Zomers Buiten, Gemeentelijk Grondbedrijf Amsterdam, Amplan Vastgoed	7.29

There are a total of nine tower blocks in the Rietlandpark, built on top of a joint underground car park. The four on the east side, with a total of 120 owner-occupied apartments and business units on the ground and first floor, were designed by Ton Venhoeven, who also designed the Jan Schaefer bridge. The façades are clad with vertical aluminium sheeting. Because of their colour and location next to the Piet Heinkade, they are also known as The Silver Fleet (after the conquest of the Spanish silver fleet by the Dutch admiral Piet Hein in 1628). On one side they lean over the lower two floors, while the other side slopes downwards. Roof terraces have been made on this side so that the apartments will get more sun.

On the west side of the area between the IJ tram and the rear of the Oostelijke Handelskade there is a carpet of grass on which stand five office tower blocks, designed by Hans van Heeswijk, clad with black and aluminium-coloured metal. Each of them has a slightly different shape.

A large, striking window section has been introduced at a different point each time, so that a different view is framed from each one. The façades of the buildings are interrupted by the flights of emergency stairs, which combine with the concrete core to provide stability.

7.30 IJ tram (2005) Central Station to IJburg	**Architect** Hans van Heeswijk architecten, npk industrial design	**Commisioned by** Dienst Infrastruc- tuur, Verkeer en Vervoer

Because of the proximity of the Piet Heintunnel, the IJ tram stop in the Rietlandpark is about 6 metres below street level. The sunken stop is a water-tight basin with walls of anchored steel sheet pile planks and a concrete floor. All of the civil works, such as fixed and moveable bridges, viaducts, tunnels and platform constructions and buildings have been designed by the Van Heeswijk firm of architects in collaboration with npk industrial design. Because of the scale of the project, that includes 6 kilometres of fencing, it was possible to develop special fences with cast steel balusters. Achieving a good, clear and logistical structure was the most important part of the design.

'For the bees'
(2004)
Fred Petterspoor,
Piet Heintunnel

Artist
Frank
Mandersloot

Commisioned by   7.31
Amsterdam
Development
Corporation
(OGA), Stadsdeel
Zeeburg

Next to the sunken Panama junction, where the IJ tram and tram number 10 intersect, is a work of art consisting of three huge tables, stacked and skewed on top of one another. Beehives, which are supervised by beekeepers, have been placed on the table in the middle. The huge sculpture is a symbol of the immediate surroundings, where pedestrians, cyclists, trams, cars and trains intersect on three different levels. The bees fly in the air as a virtually invisible layer of traffic above the other three.

The tables refer to the text 'Notes on a Table' (1988) by the New York conceptual artist Lawrence Weiner, in which he writes the following about Amsterdam: 'This city. This Amsterdam built on poles sunk in the mud and the mire. This city built on poles that stand on sand is thus a table. A table for the presentation of the work.'

The bees feed on the wild flowers that have been planted on the embankment, or swarm to the flower pots on the balconies of the new residents of the Eastern Harbour Area.

Tram stop Rietlanden

IJ
DIKES

Yttje Feddes

Defence against water

The new residential districts in Amsterdam's former docklands (IJburg, Eastern Harbour Area, Oostelijke Handelskade, Westerdokseiland and Houthavens) stand on areas of landfill along the foreshores of the dikes that were built to contain the waters of the IJ inlet. It is here that the city has for centuries defended itself against the sea while at the same time benefiting from its accessibility by water. From 1200 onwards, an unbroken system of sea dikes ('zeedijken') was built between Het Gooi and the dunes in order to protect the nascent city of Amsterdam and the newly drained peat polders against the waters of Zuiderzee. From Diemerzeedijk on the eastern edge of Amsterdam, the mediaeval sea dike continued over Zeeburgerdijk, diagonally across the site now occupied by Artis Zoo, to St. Anthoniedijk (now St. Anthoniesbreestraat), via Zeedijk, curving back along the mouth of the River Amstel, which became a natural harbour, over Warmoesstraat, Dam, Nieuwendijk and Haarlemmerdijk to Spaarndammerdijk.

New dikes

In subsequent centuries, sections of the route were repeatedly shifted in response to land reclamation on the water side of the dikes and the evolution of the harbour. Now, in the twenty-first century, the lines of the old and new IJ dikes are still discernible in the city and the landscape. For those prepared to listen, they tell the history of water management in Amsterdam.

Emphasis on linear structure

But the significance of the IJ dikes extends beyond that historical narrative. In a consolidating urban area, the presence of water defences, which by definition form continuous lines, is a gift that must be carefully cherished. The IJ dikes can help to anchor Amsterdam firmly in the landscape, both as a 'lobe city' and as a waterfront city.

To achieve this, green routes need to be created, running from the centre outwards over the dikes and creating the illusion of rusticity and freedom within a stone's throw of the city. Long stretches already exist. For example, the quiet beaches at Muiderberg, the green world of allotment gardens along the foot of the dike, the meadow landscape saved from developers at Spaarndam. But the idyl is vulnerable and in the western section in particular, where the construction of the harbour rendered the dike obsolete and turned it into 'interior', the continuity of the green line needs to be emphasised.

Characteristic differences

In the eastern section, along the IJ dike, the Amsterdam-on-Sea feeling has been better preserved, thanks to the pattern of islands, which has been picked up in the new urban expansions (IJburg, Eastern Harbour Area, Houthavens), and to the multifarious nautical use of open waters and harbour basins.

In the city centre, the old IJ dikes became narrow, winding, mixed-use city streets with characteristic differences in height which are best appreciated when you approach from a side street. Which dikes are still 'primary barriers' can be deduced from the presence of locks.

The task for the future is to preserve that whole diversity of IJ dikes as striking, somewhat contrary lines in the urban fabric and to develop them further.

Along Amsterdam's Waterfront

Azartplein Java-eiland

8.
ENTREPOT-WEST, BORNEO AND SPOREN-BURG

The suburbanisation of Amsterdam began to take off in the 1970s and 1980s. For years the emphasis had been on inexpensive housing, but it now became clear that something had to be done to keep the more well-to-do residents within the municipality. While in the 1980s the local authority was still building exclusively rented council housing in strips on the former site of the abattoir, in the 1990s the Entrepot-West project of Atelier Pro experimented with unusual architecture and urban design which engages with the water. After the success of this project, this method was also applied in the rest of the Eastern Harbour Area.

The urban development plan for Borneo and Sporenburg was strongly influenced by the requirement to build many ground-level buildings with a density of one hundred per hectare. After a competition had been organised, the design by Adriaan Geuze of West 8 was selected. He designed 'a sea of houses struck by meteorites'. Amid narrow streets with more than 1,500 low-rise homes, three superblocks, each containing 600 apartments, would be constructed on unusual locations. Pacman and The Whale have already been built, although the plans for The Fountainhead have not yet been completed.

To achieve the high density, the streets are narrow and most parking is on the private lots. The homes have been built back-to-back, all with a roof terrace or patio, and often with a separate room that can be used as an office or studio. To compensate the lack of public space, the principle of 'blue for green' has been applied: the water between Borneo and Sporenburg is conceived as a 'square' of water which links instead of separates. This is reinforced by the spectacular red bridges.

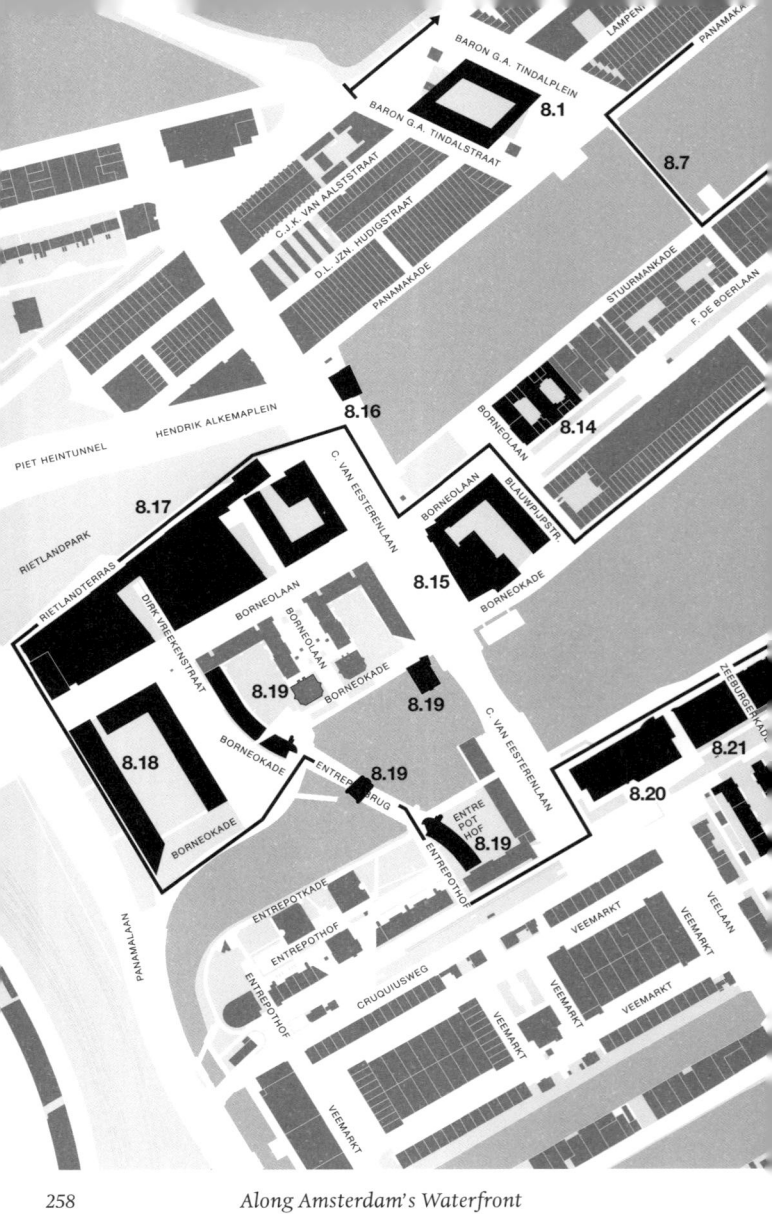

Along Amsterdam's Waterfront

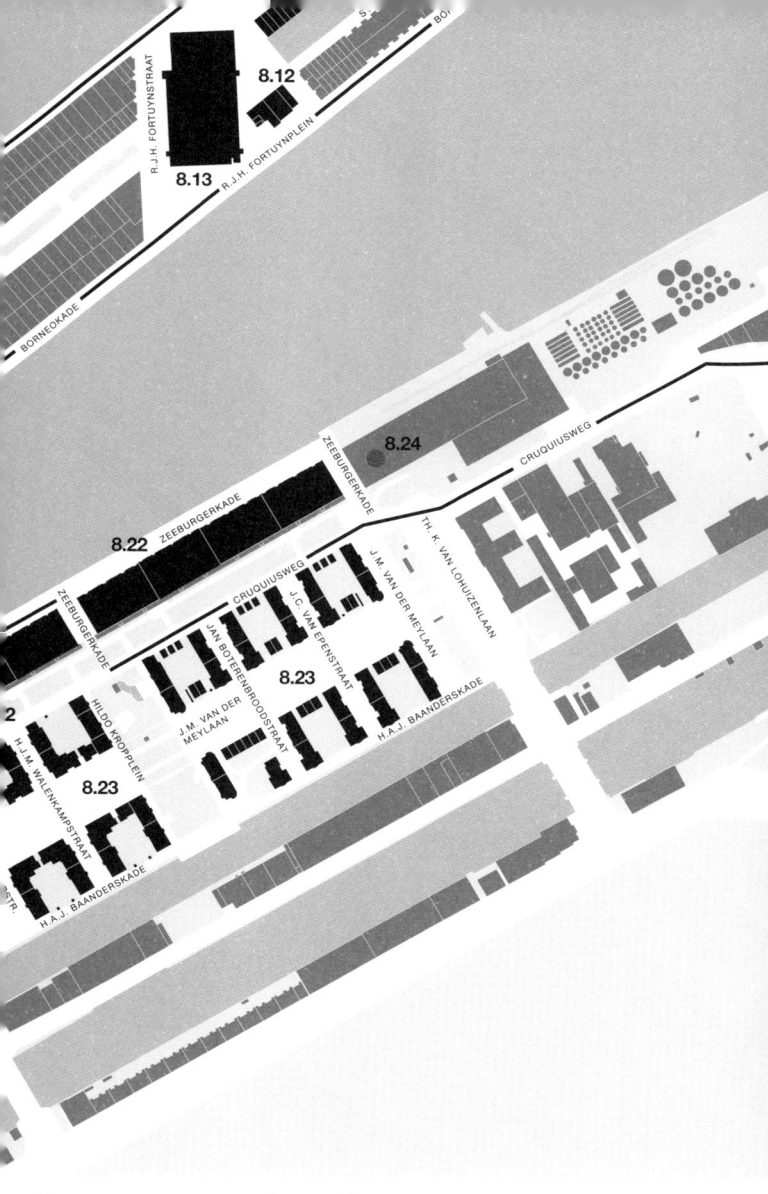

R.J.H. FORTUYNSTRAAT

8.12

8.13

R.J.H. FORTUYNPLEIN

BORNEOKADE

8.24

ZEEBURGERKADE

CRUQUIUSWEG

ZEEBURGERKADE

8.22 ZEEBURGERKADE

TH. K. VAN LOHUIZENLAAN

ZEEBURGERKADE

CRUQUIUSWEG

J.M. VAN DER MEYLAAN

J.C. VAN EPENSTRAAT

JAN BOTEREMBROODSTRAAT

8.23

2

H.J.M. WALENKAMPSTRAAT

HILDO KROPPLEIN

J.M. VAN DER MEYLAAN

H.A.J. BAANDERSKADE

8.23

STR.

H.A.J. BAANDERSKADE

H.A.J. BAANDERSKADE

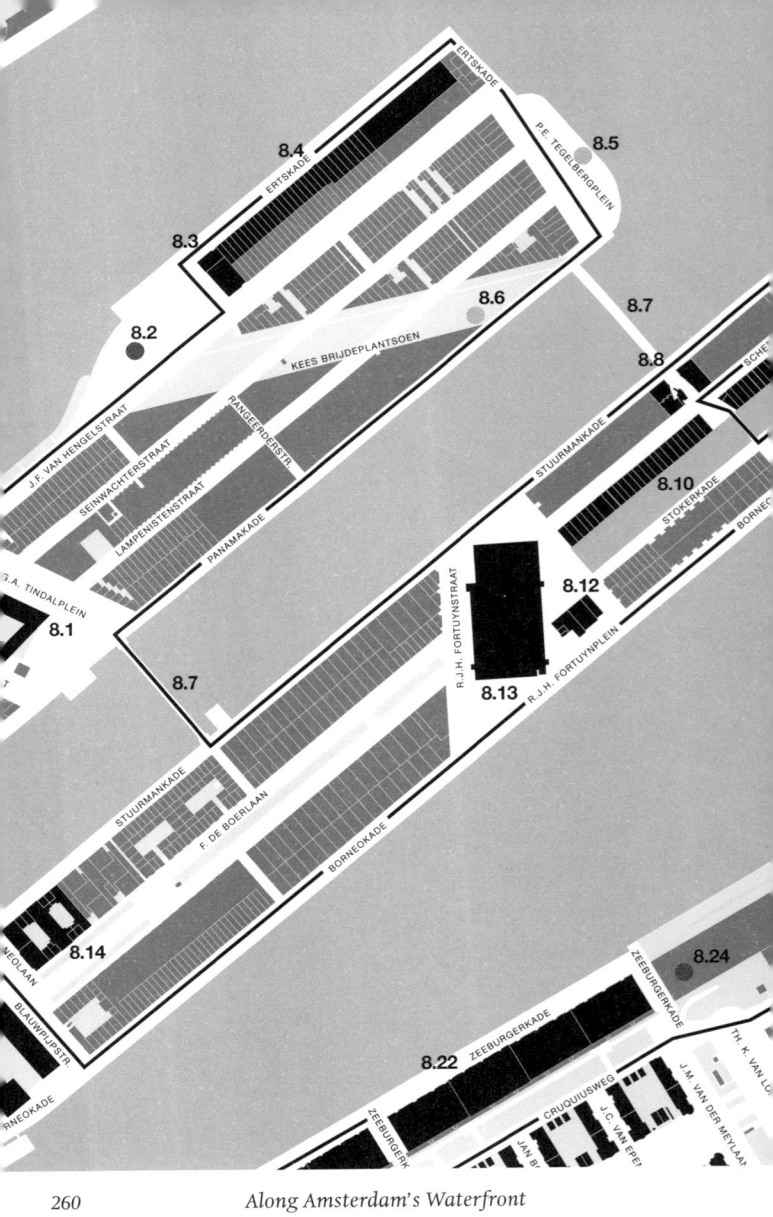

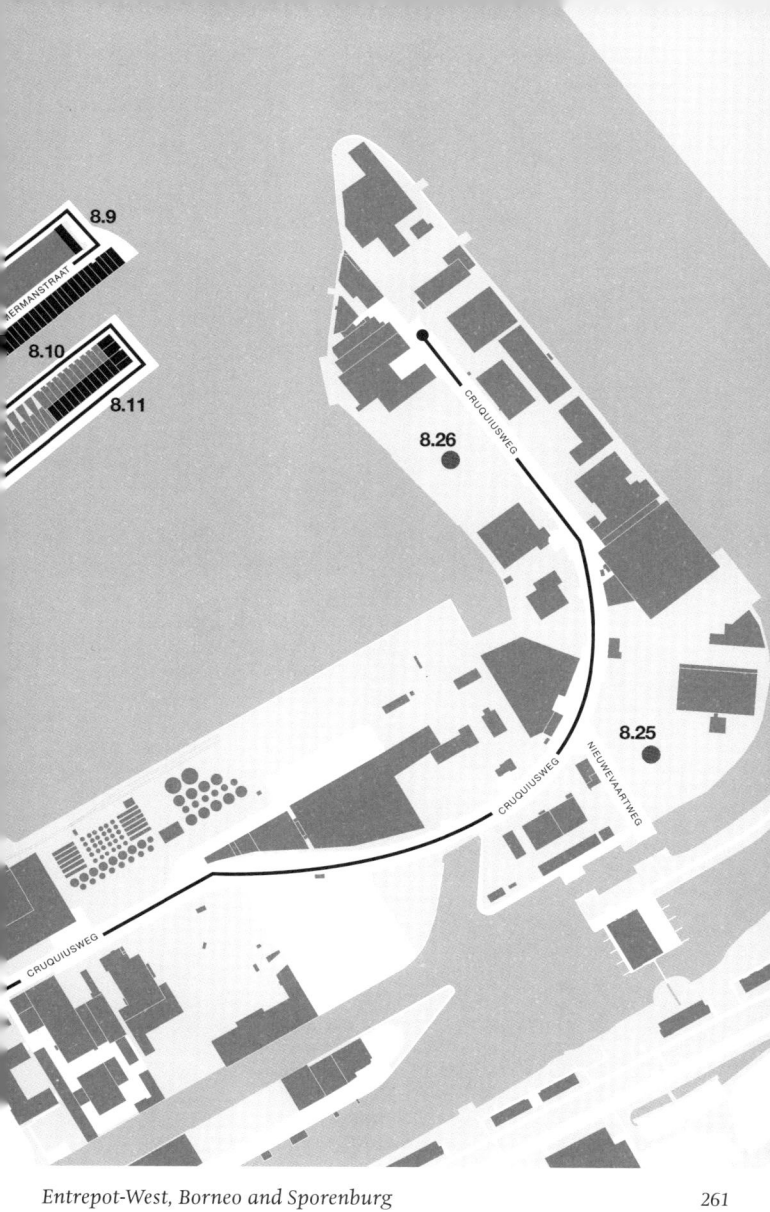

8.1 The Whale (2001)
Baron G.A. Tindalstraat 2-240, Baron G.A. Tindalplein 1-149

Architect
de Architekten Cie. (Frits van Dongen)

Commisioned by
Ontwikkelings-maatschappij New Deal

The design of the inner courtyard, which can be seen from the street, is the work of West 8. It contains six zinc vases, each 5.5 metres tall, on a Norwegian slate base. Gingko trees have been planted among the sober vegetation, giving a surrealist look to the whole. The garden is enclosed by a fence made of steel sheets to which the pattern of gingko leaves has been applied.

The Whale, one of the three meteorites of Borneo Sporenburg, continuates in the line of the Verbindingsbrug. The building owes its name to the image it conjures up of a beached whale because of its enormous size, the unusual folded form, and the uniform silver façade material. The ends of the building have been raised to create a gradual transition from the public space to the closed block and to ensure that the water of the harbour can be seen from the inner courtyard. The sloping roof lines are based on studies of sunlight and allow optimal penetration of light.

There are more than 200 apartments in The Whale, most of them three-room or four-room apartments. The access system of the building is a variant of the regular gallery: the apartments grouped around the courtyard are accessed at every other floor by galleries which are interconnected by stairs. The staircases and lifts are situated in the raised corners of the building.

Along Amsterdam's Waterfront

The Fountain-head (2009)
Ertskade

Architect
KCAP Architects &
Planners

Commisioned by   8.2
Fountainhead
Enterprise (De
Key, Eigen Haard,
BAM Vastgoed en
Heijmans)

The Fountainhead is planned as the third
meteorite – mega-building – between the sea of
low-rise houses, in accordance with the urban
development plan that Adriaan Geuze drew up
for Borneo Sporenburg. Initially a futuristic
block of apartments in the shape of a chair was
to be built there, based on a proposal by the
US architect Steven Holl and fellow designer
Kees Christiaanse, but at that time there were
not enough buyers for apartments – which
numbered less than a 100 – with prices of
700,000 euros or more. The newly developed
plan consists of an envelope of more than 60
by 60 by 60 metres and has three towers which
combine to form a U-shape. It is built half in
the water and half on land, and is situated at an
angle to the quay. The complex has been divided
into twenty storeys with a total of 238 owner-
occupied apartments at an average price of
300,000 euros, as well as eight classrooms for the
Achthoek primary school, and business units on
the ground floor. The complex also has a three-
level car park above ground level.
The façade is clad with panels in nine different

The name The Fountain-
head is taken from the
book of the same name
by Ayn Rand from 1943
about the Modernist
architect Howard Roark.
Above all his statement
that function and
position determine the
construction and form of
a building inspired the
architects at the design
stage. The architect's
struggle to defend his
design philosophy and the
conflicts with the outside
world are some of the
themes that are discussed
in the philosophical novel.
It was certainly not the
intention that the Amster-
dam Fountainhead should
also refer to this line of
the narrative, but the
difficulties surrounding
its implementation are
certainly beginning to
show very many parallels
with the book.

patterns that look like fragments. From a distance the building will be a landmark, as high as the Skydome and the IJtoren near the Verbindingsdam. At the same time the scale level of the individual apartments will remain visible everywhere, because the façade will be articulated with prefab concrete elements that afford space for bays, winter gardens and loggias.

Because the location has been left empty for so long, the locals, many of them large families by now, have grown very attached to the open strip of land between the dense buildings. There is a lot of opposition to the building of this last monolith, also because the density of the project is much higher than was originally planned.

8.3	Gym and office (2000) Ertskade 105-111	**Architect** Hans van Heeswijk architecten	**Commisioned by** Ontwikkellings- maatschappij New Deal

There was a blank spot in the urban development plan for Sporenburg: a site of 17 by 34 metres, where the gym for a school nearby was to be built. The proposed envelope offered more cubic metres than were strictly necessary for the gym, and so there was room to build an office above it, which is now the office of the architect who designed the building.

The gym has been built of brick to match the façades of the housing in the rest of the area. The office has a glass façade consisting of a wooden frame in which alternating transparent and matt sheets of glass have been placed. The building is a beacon for the surroundings in the evening.

| One-family homes (1998) Ertskade 1-103 | Architect Claus en Kaan Architecten (85-103), Köther en Salman (61-83), Ruth Visser (45-59), Neutelings Riedijk Architecten (1-43) | Commisioned by Ontwikkelings- maatschappij New Deal | 8.4 |

Several firms of architects have come up with their own individual designs for the one-family homes with an extremely high density of one 100 units per hectare on the Borneo and Sporenburg islands. Some built projects on a number of plots, often employing variations on the same theme.

This row of homes on the Ertskade, the first to be built, are a good example of how the concept of back-to-back patio homes with a width of 4.2 metres on a narrow and long plot of land has been elaborated and which variations are possible within a fixed grid of guidelines. Homes designed by four different firms of architects stand here side by side in the same way as the rest of the low-rise housing: situated within the building line, a simple choice of materials in predominantly reddish-brown brick, a lot of private parking lots, and a closed outdoor space that turns its back on the street.

Claus & Kaan opted for a closed façade above the carport with a large window and French balcony. As in most of the homes of this type, the living room with open kitchen is on the first floor, bedrooms on second, and the room adjoining the patio on the ground floor can be used flexibly as a working space or an extra bedroom. The rooms have been designed around the patio and as a result have unexpected cross-vistas and good access for daylight.

Köther & Salman were pioneers in the development of the patio home model in this area. They were the first to start building. The patio is situated in the middle of the home on the ground floor and provides light for all the rooms. Small variations have been introduced in

The population of the Eastern Harbour Area has far more children than was originally supposed. Many residents look for ways to extend their home. Many box rooms and patios have been converted into extra rooms in the last few years. Since a number of owners often entrusted this to the same architect, the aspect of the façade has remained reasonably uniform.

the arrangement of the tall narrow windows and French balconies on the level of the living room. According to the concept of the patio home, you live in what is virtually a traditional one-family home that has been turned inside out, with the private outdoor area on the inside.

Visser solved the parking problem by placing an underground garage partly beneath the homes and partly beneath the street behind them. As a result, there is one room directly adjoining the quay, which stands out for the choice of materials: orange stained multiplex in a steel window front. It is easy to remove the partitions between the rooms if required, so that the home can be adapted to changes in the family situation.

Neutelings Riedijk situated the living room with kitchen diner over the width of two plots to make optimal use of the view over the water. A striking verandah has been created on the double-width first floor. On the ground floor, work spaces belonging to the houses at the rear on the street side alternate with the homes with verandahs.

| 8.5 | 'Fragment of a living room reduced to 88%' (2001) P.E. Tegelbergplein | **Artist** Mark Manders | **Commisioned by** Amsterdams Fonds voor de Kunst |

There is a striking work of art by Mark Manders on the rugged, cobbled square at the end of Sporenburg. It was created within the framework of the programme for art in public space of the Amsterdam Art Fund. The architect did not intend to add an architectural element to the square, but opted for a work that would behave like a visitor. It is a fragment of a living room, a project on which Manders had previously worked. The work consists of a workbench and chair, with a bucket of water in front of them. There are two figures on the table who at first sight seem identical, but closer inspection shows that they are two successive moments of the same figure, with

a minuscule difference in facial expression
and posture.

**Keesje Brijde
Plantsoen**
(1944/2000)

In his scruffy threadbare clothes
With nothing to eat
Little Amsterdam kid
Little rascal of the street

This is a verse from the poem next to the
white cross, a monument to Keesje Brijde that
stands on the Panamakade. It was written by
J. Schagen while the war was still in progress.
It refers to the sad story of the twelve-year-old
Keesje, one of a family of thirteen children.
During the Hunger Winter of 1944, he and
other children searched the shunting yard for
coal that had fallen from the trains, sometimes
three times a day. Everyone at home was
suffering from the cold and there was nothing
to eat. The shunting yard was patrolled and was
forbidden territory. When the children were
caught, they were shut up in a special wagon.
A German security guard threatened: 'If I catch
you again, I'll shoot you dead!'. He was true to
his word. Keesje was shot in the neck and died
in hospital soon afterwards.
The space that has been left as a diagonal
strip between the three slat-shaped apartment
blocks of Sporenburg is the only greenery on
Borneo Sporenburg. It is intensively used by
children as a play area.

Adriaan Geuze from West 8 designed the master plan for Borneo Sporenburg and acted as supervisor. In addition, the firm designed two striking red bridges to connect the Borneo Island and Sporenburg with one another. The westernmost bridge is low and is suitable for cyclists and wheelchair users. The eastern pedestrian bridge rises in an arch to a height of 12 metres. The top offers a view of the roof landscape of the low-rise housing with the numerous patios. Pleasure boats can pass beneath the bridge and children use the spectacular height in the summer as a diving board to plunge into the water.

Both bridges are made of steel T-profiles with a red industrial paint that lights up at night. The profiles combine to form a membrane that gives the bridges their sculptural form. The deck and railing are of untreated wood. The lighting consists of cast aluminium fittings in the form of gull's heads.

Borneo 4 and 5
(1999)
Pompmanstraat 2-
4, Stuurmankade

Architect
Miralles Tagliabue
Arquitectos

Commisioned by
Smit's Bouw-
bedrijf

On both side of the alley that ends at the eastern bridge to Sporenburg are homes designed by the Barcelona firm of Miralles Tagliabue Arquitectes. Enric Miralles made a name for himself with his abstract organic style with attention for the human dimension. Another of his works in the Netherlands was the large-scale renovation of the town hall in Utrecht, which was completed just before his premature death.

The homes on Borneo deviate from the rigid pattern that was imposed on the buildings. Two of the six homes are more or less detached from the block and also rise above it. They mark the connection with Sporenburg through the curves in the façades on either side of the alley. The three apartments which extend over the whole depth of the block fan out towards the quay, where the front doors are situated. Unlike most of the buildings in the vicinity, the façades are colourful thanks to the alternation of blocks and strips of brick in reddish brown, red, yellow, blue, green and orange.

**Three apart-
ments** (1999)
P. Dijkstraplein 2

Architect
de architecten-
groep (Masten-
broek & Van
Gameren)

Commisioned by
Smit's Bouw-
bedrijf

8.9

This striking façade wall of one of the two spits of Borneo Island is part of a complex of 57 apartments that extend from the Stuurmankade to the Scheepstimmermanstraat. Three apartments have been placed at the tip that are 24 metres wide and 5 metres deep, each of which has one floor that extends over the entire width of the plot. They have a wall-to-wall balcony and a protruding verandah on the upper floors which stands out for its light green

and turquoise glass. By placing both the living room and the kitchen diner at the corners and arranging the intervening rooms along a corridor, long communication lines are created inside the apartments.

| 8.10 | Free building plots (1999) Scheepstimmer-manstraat | Architect various | Commissioned by private parties |

One of the main architectural attractions of recent Amsterdam architecture is the row of homes in the Scheepstimmermanstraat. Though that was not the prior intention, this section of the street presents a sample card of the architectural taste of the late twentieth century.

Prompted by the national policy of encouraging individual building initiatives, the local authority conducted an experiment on Borneo Island by issuing sixty plots of building land to private builders. After registration, private individuals who were selected by lot could build their dream home here. The future residents and their architects were coached in workshops to direct this unique building project in the city through the right channels.

There was nevertheless strict supervision by Adriaan Geuze, who was responsible for the master plan of the area, to ensure some measure of consistency in the buildings. The limiting conditions included a minimal ground floor height of 3.5 metres, the same condition that applies to all of the low-rise buildings on Borneo Island and Sporenburg. The façades must combine to form a closed street wall. Brick, untreated wood and little or no colour were prescribed, but in the course of the building process other façade materials were eventually accepted. As for parking, the idea was that it would be done on the owner's own land, which led to ingenious solutions. All the same, a number of homes were built without a garage. The owners nevertheless obtained a parking permit for the street, which led to great commotion in the neighbourhood.

The design and interior of most of the houses have been made to measure. From both the street side and the water side – there is a view from the bridge to and from the Stokerkade – it is easy to see that each of the designs is unique and that the whole is easy to place in a particular period. What follows is a selection of the different design solutions.

Number 126 was designed by Studio

Hertzberger. Only half of the 6-metre wide plot has been used for building, leaving a sort of alleyway with a large void which is used as a parking lot. The rooms are divided over three floors. The living room on the first floor has been extended over the alleyway, ending with a riverside terrace. The house is a timber-frame construction.

Koen van Velsen centred the design for number 120 around a tree. It rises grandly in a partly pierced void past all the floors to the roof. The rooms are situated on the waterfront side. The façade is made of large, stacked black concrete elements which fill the entire width of the plot.

At number 80-82, designed by the sub-contractor and developer Piet Vertelman with Heren 5 Architecten, a façade of rusted Corten steel sheets conceals two apartments, one on top of the other. The sheets have been perforated in such a way that it is impossible to look inside, while it is possible to look out from inside without being seen. Two apartments have been built on one plot. Sections of the façade can be opened by means of horizontal and vertical sliding systems. The door handle betrays the entrance, and behind the left-hand part there is parking space for two cars.

Along Amsterdam's Waterfront

At number 72-74 resident Marianne Elbers has also constructed two apartments, one on top of the other, on one plot. Each of them has its own entrance. The design pattern, based on a modular dimension of 0.9 by 0.9 metres combined to form squares and cubes, has affinities with the architecture of Gerrit Rietveld. Number 62 was designed by the Höhne & Rapp firm of architects. The volume of the building has been divided up by cutting out two sections lengthwise, resulting in an H-shaped façade. On the ground floor this cavity forms an alleyway where the entrance to the flat is situated and which ends in a staircase to the water. On the second floor the cavity forms an elongated terrace which can become a part of the apartment by opening the sliding window frames. The façade is clad with thick Belgian hardstone blocks, the frames are of untreated wood.

| **One-family homes** (1999) Borneokade 327-347 | **Architect** MAP Arquitectos (Josep Lluís Mateo) | **Commisioned by** Bouwbedrijf M.J. de Nijs & Zn | 8.11 |

Like his fellow countryman Enric Miralles, the Spanish architect Josep Lluís Mateo has tried to distance himself as much as possible from the building criteria laid down. The project of 26 apartments that extends over the entire tip of this spit at the eastern end of Borneo Island appears as an apartment block with clear horizontal lines of continuous façade surfaces and window strips. On the Stokerkade facing north this has been done in regular brick, but at the tip and on the Borneokade facing south the façade is mainly clad with untreated Western cedar slats. The front doors are on this side, on a raised verandah four steps above ground level and stretching over the entire width of the apartment, with a store room below. Each apartment has a roof terrace overlooking the water and a patio on the first floor.

8.12 De Oceaan (1951/1999)
R.J.H. Fortuyn-
plein 11-29

Architect
CASA architecten

Commisioned by
Stoomvaart-
maatschappij
De Oceaan/
De Principaal

The only tangible memory of the dockland past of Borneo Island and Sporenburg is the building called De Oceaan (The Ocean). It was built as a canteen and office building for the steamshipping company of the same name. The sheds that stood around it have been demolished. De Principaal took the initiative of converting it into three owner-occupied apartments, five council rented apartments with studios, and a restaurant.
A lot of attention has been paid to restoring the original style of the façades. The rusted steel frames with stool profiles have been replaced by elegantly detailed aluminium frames with thermal separation. To avoid visible duct silencers and ventilation grills in the façade, balanced ventilation with heat recovery was adopted.

8.13 Pacman (1998)
R.J.H. Fortuynplein
2-214, R.J.H. For-
tuynstraat 1-209

Architect
Koen van Velsen

Commisioned by
SFB BPF Bouw

The name Pacman refers to one of the first computer games from 1980, in which the player manipulates a 'mouth', Pacman, that is supposed to eat all the coins in the field of play. That field is dangerous because of the spooks that can eliminate Pacman. The labyrinthine façade bears a resemblance to the field of this computer game.

The Pacman building, which accommodates 207 apartments with two, three or four rooms, is one of the three superblocks or 'meteorites' on Borneo Island and Sporenburg which give the suburban area a metropolitan allure. The building breaks up the pattern of long parallel streets on the island. It has been deliberately placed at an angle in the continuation of the Oranjesluizen, even though they are a long way away when you are on the spot.

The architect's design emphasises the building as a utility and expresses this in its appearance. The complex makes a large and ponderous impression because of the use of dark brick, steel and wood. At the same time, however, the façade is very varied with different types of apartment, shops and business units. Part of the ground floor is occupied by apartments with their front door opening onto the street, and above them are apartments that are accessed by means of the entrances at the four corners. A wooden 'curtain' has been adopted for the façade, behind which the different functions remain in view. It is noteworthy that the three-level car park above ground level is clearly visible. The word 'Borneo' has been stamped into the grid on the Borneokade side.

Housing complex	Architect	Commisioned by	8.14
Borneo 1 (1997) Feike de Boerlaan 3-83, Stuurman-kade 2-100, Borneolaan 511-517	CASA architecten	Stichting Bo-1	

A typical procedure of Hein de Haan's CASA architecten is to develop and implement building plans in consultation with the residents: cooperative project development. The future buyers enter the planning process at an earlier stage than usual and also assume obligations at this stage: they contribute to the initial expenses in return for the right to an apartment and/or business unit.

In 1993 CASA sent a letter to the councillor for housing, Genet, with the request to make a piece of land available for this type of development. It met with a positive response. A foundation was set up together with the interested parties which placed the commissions through different working committees.

The block, which measures about 40 by 100 metres, has three storeys with roof terraces and rooftop constructions. The apartments are grouped around four courtyards. There are also business units and collective areas, including a kindergarten and a restaurant. In spatial terms it is an exciting project, but the architecture is sober. Because commitments had already been made by the local authority, the project deviates from the master plan for Borneo Island and Sporenburg, which was premised on individual homes. The project was selected by the local authority in 1997 as a Housing Quality Model Plan in the category of Customised Building.

8.15 School and apartments Borneokade (1994) C. van Eesterenlaan 301-313, Borneo-laan 392-528, Blauwpijpstraat 2-38, Borneokade 103	Architect Groos de Jong, Atelier Z	Commisioned by De Doelen

This block, which is closed on three sides, is a combination of a Montessori school, 88 rented council apartments, and business units. It was jointly designed by two firms of architects. They were given the commission after winning the first and second prizes respectively in a national competition for schools in an urban context. The project was the first new building to be built on Borneo Sporenburg.

The school is fully integrated in the block: the classrooms are in two layers along the Van Eesterenlaan. In combination with the auxiliary rooms, a flexible space has been created that can be used in a variety of ways. The gym on the inner courtyard has a roof that slopes down to the water and is covered with moss and sedum. This provides good insulation and at the same time gives the complex a green appearance amid the stony surroundings.

The apartments above the school are accessed by means of galleries in the inner courtyard. The other two parts of the block are accessed through doorways.

| **Piet Hein Tunnel Service Building** (1997) C. van Eesterenlaan 41 | **Architect** UN Studio | **Commisioned by** Amsterdam Local Authority | **8.16** |

The 1900-metre long Piet Hein tunnel, the longest in the Netherlands, has two tunnel corridors for cars and one for the tram to IJburg. The tunnel, which passes underneath the Amsterdam Rhine Canal and the Spoorwegbassin, connects the A10 motorway with the eastern side of the city centre.

The construction of the tunnel made it possible to exploit the spatial qualities of the Eastern Harbour Area with long strips of land surrounded by water. Earlier plans for a bridge were therefore dropped and a low-noise housing district could be created. There is even a schoolyard on the roof of the extension of the tunnel entrance.

The tunnel consists of different tubing elements that are connected to one another by rubber profiles. These are pressed together so tightly by the water pressure that they make the tunnel waterproof. The concrete service buildings at the east and west entrances were designed by UN Studio. They are almost entirely encased in sheets of perforated steel.

Their shape is based on that of a box that has been distorted by torsion and twisting at the corners, resulting in a closed asymmetrical object that expresses the inaccessibility of this service building. The inside is illuminated at night.

UN Studio also designed the aluminium-clad tunnel drives with crossed steel girders.

Entrepot-West, Borneo and Sporenburg

| 8.17 | Hope, Love, Fortune (2002) Rietlandterras 2-54, Borneolaan 1-327 | **Architect** Rudy Uytenhaak Architectenbureau | **Commisioned by** Woningbedrijf Amsterdam, Bouwfonds Woningbouw |

Hope, Love and Fortune, named after three wind-powered sawmills that used to stand here, has 369 apartments; more than half of them are council rented property and the rest are owner-occupied. The complex consists of three blocks and an elongated sloping section beside the entrance to the Piet Hein tunnel that connects the various parts. The ensemble has been deployed in urban development terms to function as a connective tissue between the three neighbourhoods that come together at this point: Borneo Sporenburg, Entrepot-West, and the Rietlanden.

The block on the Van Eesterenlaan contains apartments for senior citizens with collective access. The two other blocks on the Borneolaan contain rented apartments in the form of town houses, each with four apartments with their own front doors. The plinth and one of the façades on the inner street are articulated with black masonry in a scale motif.

The part of the building overlooking the park is accessed through four large entrance halls which can only be reached on foot. Access to the apartments from a car is via the underground car park.

This example shows that the current trend to avoid making residential buildings look like housing was already anticipated by Uytenhaak a few years ago. The monumental relief façade that leans forwards is in Norwegian marble that turns as white as chalk when it oxidises. It forms a skin that conceals the fact that different apartments with a diversity of curtains are hidden behind the façade. The sculptural form determines the identity of the surroundings. The design received the Zuiderkerk Award of the Amsterdam Local Authority in 1999 for the best housing plan.

Along Amsterdam's Waterfront

Batavia (2000)
Panamalaan
10-186, Borneolaan
8-18, Dirk Vreeken-
straat 1-163

Architect
de Architekten
Cie. (Frits van
Dongen)

Commisioned by   8.18
De Principaal

This large U-shaped block designed by Frits van
Dongen contains 167 apartments and 1,100
m² of commercial space. The volume of traffic
noise made it necessary to build noise buffers
on the side of the Panamalaan. These function
as verandahs in the winter, but if weather
permits the residents can open the folding
window frames and use them as a balcony. A
poem by Gerrit Kouwenaar has been written in
the bricks of the wall.
The side facing away from the traffic is closed
in character. The terraces of the ground floor
apartments are on the roof of the half-sunken
garage. The rest of the fenced off area serves as
a garden for the residents in the upper storeys
to look at. Trees, planted in the ground, poke
through the roof of the garage. The façades are
clad with transparently finished wood, which
gives the complex a natural character.

8.19 Entrepotbrug and Watertoren Entrepot-West
(1993/1997)
Entrepotbrug 55-218, C. van Eesterenlaan 308-424

Architect
Atelier PRO

Commisioned by
Muwi Vastgoed
Rotterdam

In the second half of the 1980s, after the housing on the site of the former abattoir had been completed, the Environmental Planning Department placed a multiple commission for the Entrepot-West planning zone with five firms of architects. The jury voted unanimously for the plan submitted by Atelier PRO for being in tune with the high ambitions. The plan for 600 homes included U-shaped semi-closed blocks, freestanding urban villas, and a five-storey apartment block which winds its serpentine way diagonally over the Entrepothaven. To cover the high costs of building such a complicated ensemble, it was decided that in addition to the council rented apartments there would be owner-occupied apartments, a phenomenon which was still novel at the time.

In spite of the uniform choice of materials – light grey masonry and plaster – the Entrepotbrug has a varied façade thanks to the alternation of balconies, galleries, rectangular and circular windows.

Hides were worked and tanned on the Veemarkt in the past. The pollution was not very serious, but the ground smelt so bad that it had to be cleaned before anything could be built on it. A few characteristic buildings have been preserved. The rest is intended as a small-scale business park for enterprises that have had to leave the nineteenth-century residential neighbourhoods within the framework of urban renewal.

The size of the complex and the way in which its robust columns stand in the water make it the first in the development of the former docklands to engage with the scale of the surroundings, in which the harbour basins and railway are so characteristic.

The 60-metre tall apartment tower block, the coping stone of the PRO plan, was built later in the 1990s. The tower is lighter and more slender than in the original design, which required a heavy foundation 60 metres deep. The Watertoren has twenty-two floors, with three apartments on each floor. The volume hangs over the existing quay wall so that most of it stands in the water.

Two spacious penthouses spread over three floors are situated in the ziggurat-like top. From the bays which have been placed on the side walls it is possible to look along the façade. The entrance hall, like a box of glass bricks, extends beyond the building line two storeys high. Landing stages have been placed on top of the box rooms just above the water level to blend with the atmosphere of the harbour. The entire skyscraper has been plastered in white with dark grey horizontal stripes which decrease with the height of the building.

Entrepot-West, Borneo and Sporenburg

8.20 International Institute for Social History (IISG) (1961/1989) Cruquiusweg 31

Architect
Wegener Slees-wijk/ Atelier PRO

The former warehouse Willem II, which was built in 1961, now houses the Press Museum and the International Institute for Social History, the largest archive in the world for social history, containing the archives of such politicians as Troelstra and Den Uyl, but also documents of Karl Marx and Friedrich Engels, the Chinese student opposition and the squatter movement.

The reuse of the former warehouse for this function was only natural in this case. Willem II has a concrete construction and rests on columns 120 centimetres thick. The heavy load of more than 30,000 metres of archival material thus did not raise any problems at all for the construction.

Atelier PRO renovated the building, adding a number of openings to improve organisation and to allow light to enter, including a large void on the side facing the water, as well as cladding the façade in insulation plaster.

8.21 Warehouse Sunday (1992) Zeeburgerkade 30-148

Architect
Pieter Weeda

Commisioned by
Bouwfonds Neder-landse Gemeenten

Warehouse Sunday was built a few years after the series of warehouses named after the other days of the week and was specially designed for highly aromatic goods such as spices and tea. A new tablet in the wall overlooking the quay with a steaming teapot is a memorial of that past. The complex was converted into sixty owner-occupied apartments in the early 1990s. To ensure that daylight would penetrate the deep plot, it was decided to create a big inner courtyard and to group the apartments around

Along Amsterdam's Waterfront

it. There are access galleries to them there.
The openings through which the bales of tea
were hoisted in the past are now bays. The
entrance with access to the lift in the northwest
corner of the building will presently be
renovated and the hall will be reorganised so
that it is only accessible for residents.

Warehouses Monday to Saturday (1900/1991) Zeeburgerkade 152-826	**Architect** Chris Smit	**Commisioned by** Bouwfonds Neder-landse Gemeenten	8.22

The 300-metre long row of warehouses Monday
to Saturday, to which Warehouse Sunday was
added a few years later, was built at the turn
of the century for the storage of transit goods
which were exempt from import duty. It was an
ideal location for that purpose: easily accessible
by rail and water, and on the outskirts of the
city. To prevent the goods from being smuggled
into the country, high walls were built around
the warehouses and a customs police station
was established nearby (in what is now the
Boulevard Café). During the war the warehouses
were used as storage depots for the Germans.
With the shift of the docks from the east to the
west, the warehouses lost their function, but
not for long: the development of the Eastern
Harbour Area as a residential district started
with the renovation of the warehouses Monday
to Saturday in the late 1980s. Although there
was a lot of scepticism at first with regard to the
feasibility of building housing in this area, the
local authority eventually decided to go ahead.
Architect Chris Smit converted the complex
into 330 owner-occupied apartments, 110 of
them with special subsidies. To allow daylight
to enter, glass roofed inner streets have
been made four storeys high which provide
access to most of the apartments. Most of the
characteristic features of the old façades were
removed, such as the steel galleries on each

floor. They were replaced by triangular bays on the side overlooking the quay and French balconies alternating with loggias on the side facing the land. All the same, it is clear that attempts were made to retain some of the dockland past of the buildings, as in the protruding towers which used to house the hoisting installations and now accommodate the balconies.

| 8.23 **Housing complex Abattoir site** (1987/1989) Hildo Kropplein, J.M. van der Meylaan | **Architect** Van Dillen & Ogier/ Lafour & Wijk | **Commisioned by** Stichting Onze Woning |

The Hildo Kropplein has a work of art by the Danish artist Per Kirkeby, which was specially commissioned for this site in 1990 by the Eastern Harbour Area Art Committee of the local authority. Kirkeby's work combines architectural elements with a clear autonomous form. He often uses masonry, which is just as common in Copenhagen as in Amsterdam. This object, in which the forms of a stall can be recognised, refers to the former brick buildings of the abattoir. The vertical walls frame the view between the Indische Buurt and the docklands.

The moving of the municipal abattoir to another site left the Abattoir site open for development. A total of 550 council rented apartments were built, designed in two blocks by two firms of architects. The distribution of the building plots was still entirely based on the conventional approach to urban renewal. Apart from the entrance on the Veelaan, all of the abattoir buildings were demolished and a completely new layout was designed. The apartments are grouped in four-storey blocks, in a U-shape or in short strips, and the surroundings have been designed as a residential area. The dimensions of the plan engage with the Indische Buurt on the other side of the Nieuwe Vaart, but have nothing

Along Amsterdam's Waterfront

to with the water and the dockland architecture on the north side of the area. The streets have been named after architects of the Amsterdam School, which has earned the district the name of Architects Quarter.

The first, western part to be built by Van Dillen is rather monotonous and block-like because of the use of grey-brown brick. In contrast, the apricot coloured plastered façades with curving balconies by Lafour & Wijk have a fresh look about them. Both parts of the complex seem rather dated today, but they nevertheless bear witness to the concern for design and the well-conceived ground plans of high-quality council housing which were characteristic of the late 1980s.

| Kopgebouw (2009) Zeeburgerkade | Architect Bik + Mulder architecten | Commisioned by HBB/Amplan | 8.24 |

According to the district authority, the Cruquius Island should function as a link between the four neighbourhoods of Zeeburg: IJburg, Zeeburgereiland, the Eastern Harbour Area, and the Indische Buurt. This is not yet the case; a policy memorandum refers to it as an 'undefined centre', 'lacking in public spaces for pedestrians', and 'a confusion of industrial and business estates, urban renewal architecture and converted warehouses'. One of the solutions that the district authority has proposed is the construction of a jetty and

The Albeton company with its subsidiary MSA have been established on the Entrepothaven waterfront since 1977. The shiny silver silos are a striking landmark. The company supplies concrete mortar, anhydrite and other cement-related products from this central point. The raw materials are delivered by boat. Sand and gravel are also sold via the funnels. On a working day it is a hive of activity with cement mixers coming and going.

a building (the Kopgebouw) to accommodate harbour services, a hotel, café, conference and meeting rooms, a fitness centre and business units.

The Zeeburg district authority organised a competition for a design on the site where a brick shed still stands. The winning submission by Bik + Mulder architecten is a striking building with two lines of vision carved out of it so as not to disturb the view over the water. For the same reason the ground level has been kept as empty as possible. By placing the building at an angle to the quay, it refers to the meteorites on Borneo Island and Sporenburg.

The residents, organised in the action group 'Save the Blue', are putting up a lot of opposition to the building and the jetty. They are afraid that the peace will be disturbed and protest against the expected large scale of the recreation on the water.

8.25	De Nieuwe Vaart business centre (2007) Cruquiusweg	Architect Borski, Noordhoek, Bleichrodt architecten	Commisioned by Sikking Vastgoed bv

The last piece of undeveloped industrial land in the Eastern Harbour Area will be redeveloped in 2007. The district authority has organised a closed competition for the redevelopment of the former Hoogovens site. The winning submission came from Borski/Noordhoek/Bleichrodt architecten.

The assignment was a business centre of about 16,500 m² with intensive land use. The solution that has been adopted is a single building with 65 business and office units on four floors. A second ground surface is created roughly eight metres above the first which is accessible by ramps. This means that every unit can be reached by car and that there is parking space in front of the door. The second ground surface is a fully-fledged high-quality outdoor area. The units can be linked vertically or horizontally, which results in a highly flexible complex. There are plans for showrooms beside the road, industrial workshops on the second ground surface by the waterfront, starters units, combined work and domestic units, and storage spaces.

| **Het Cruquius Kwartier** (2007) Cruquiusweg 111 | **Architect** Dedato ontwerpers en architecten | **Commisioned by** HVBM Vastgoed, PFC2 Vastgoed | 8.26 |

Like the buildings that Dedato designed in the Minervahaven, this business complex takes on a robust industrial look through the use of rough concrete and glass. The first of a series of four building has already been completed.
The four units are twenty metres high, and the interiors have a ceiling four metres high. The visible installations and the partly unfinished concrete elements on the inside wall give the impression of a studio. The loft-like spaces are very light thanks to the voids in the heart of the building and the enormous glass façades in the side walls.
The rented units, which are of different sizes, can be linked vertically or horizontally, as the client chooses. Four penthouses are planned for the topmost storey with a surface area of between 200 and 300 m². Because housing is not allowed in this business park, they are intended as offices with a large roof terrace overlooking the Eastern Harbour Area.

Muziekgebouw aan 't IJ

OUT AND ABOUT ON THE IJ

Daphna Beerdsen

New part of the city

One weekday, I take a stroll along the Oostelijke Handelskade, enjoying the view over the IJ on one side and the new warehouse-style apartment buildings on the other. Along the way I pass the Fifteen restaurant, a little later the Panama terrace, and a bit further along again the café boats *Lizboa* and *Odessa* are moored. I can't help remembering the first time we went to the Panama. What was then quite a long trek seems to have become progressively shorter over the years. I got to know the area better, and there was more going on there, so that the long, barren, windy trip to a wasteland in which the Panama was the only oasis, turned into a pleasant bike ride through a new part of the city. Nowadays no one is surprised when you have a night out on Oosterdokseiland, suggest a day at the Houthavens beach, or dine at the Lloyd Hotel.

Squatters' spirit

Who would ever have thought it would become such a hot spot? Ten, fifteen years ago I would probably never have taken this stroll. The bit of Amsterdam behind the railway line was the domain of artists and squatters, prostitutes and vagrants. They found their niche among the abandoned warehouses, rusty rail tracks and empty sheds. Most of them have since decamped to the new fringes of the city. Fortunately something of the squatters' spirit has remained so that we young ones, who were still in nappies in the 1980s, can also sample something of that atmosphere.

Experiment

The *Einde van de Wereld* ('end of the world'), a boat diagonally across from the *Odessa* and *Lizboa*, is a good example. Begun as a squatters' canteen, this eatery was set up along quasi socialist lines: the macrobiotic food was offered at low prices and anyone who couldn't even afford that was allowed to eat the leftovers for free. The restaurant moved to a boat in the 1990s and no longer gives food away but, staffed by volunteers who serve up affordable organic food, it is still imbued with the same atmosphere. This spirit lives on in other establishments, too: in addition to its delicious food and a fantastic view, 11 on Oosterdokseiland holds experimental club evenings. And once, seated on a beanbag with a cocktail in my hand, after a day sunbathing on Amsterdam Plage, I was surprised by a conjuring show.

Personal stamp

Little by little my own generation is putting its stamp on the area along the IJ. Affluent twenty- and thirty-somethings have discovered it for their leisure activities. The clientele of Onassis on Westerdoksdijk is sometimes described as 'slicked-back hair and sunglasses'; Strand West and the Oceano restaurant target the same yuppie group. The occasional drink on the Muziekgebouw's big terrace is about all the student population can afford. Paviljoen aan 't IJ, between the container houses, is becoming increasingly popular with this target group; since more and more of them live in such containers, the night life is also slowly moving in that direction. And for the 'days after', when the overindulgence needs to be sweated out, there are several possibilities: Klimmuur Centraal (climbing wall), Squash City or, slightly more extreme, bungee jumping at Westerdokseiland.

District with variation

So, on a walk like this it is not just the local inhabitants I meet; a cross section of the Amsterdam population comes here to relax, from old-time Jordaan residents to newcomers to Amsterdam. Gradually, almost imperceptibly, more and more cafes, restaurants and clubs are opening up here, helping to give the area a distinctive character. The resulting new piece of city is varied, attractive and innovative, but with just a dash of anarchism added to the mix it will unquestionably also become a genuine piece of Amsterdam.

Along Amsterdam's Waterfront

Head of the Oostelijke Handelskade

9.
JAVA-EILAND, KNSM-EILAND

The histories of the Java and KNSM Islands proceeded in parallel until twenty years ago. Originally constructed as a breaker to protect the Oostelijke Handelskade, the embankment was widened at the end of the nineteenth century to accommodate the Royal Netherlands Steamship Company (KNSM) and other shipping companies. After the transfer of the harbour to the west in the 1970s, the area was occupied by urban nomads and artists.

The first area that could be redeveloped was the KNSM Island, but not without controversy. Plans with many cars and plans for blocks at right angles to the water were turned down in favour of a master plan by Jo Coenen: a real waterfront that paid a lot of attention to the contrast between land and water. The monumental, robust superblocks form façade walls with a high level of coherence. Memories of the docklands past are kept alive by preserving as many old buildings as possible. About 1,500 apartments have been built on each of the two islands.

The Java Island was developed a few years later. The plan by Sjoerd Soeters is in many respects a reaction to Coenen's plan. The island is divided by four canals into five 'rooms'. The easternmost of these does not have a south wall, so that the inner area is a public park. The maximum height for the buildings on the virtually traffic-free Javakade, facing south, is seven storeys, while it is ten storeys on the northern Sumatrakade where through traffic passes.

The building principle of the Java Island is based on 'stamps': different architects each designed an apartment block 27 metres wide. They are distributed over the five 'rooms' in different combinations, resulting in a façade that displays variety.

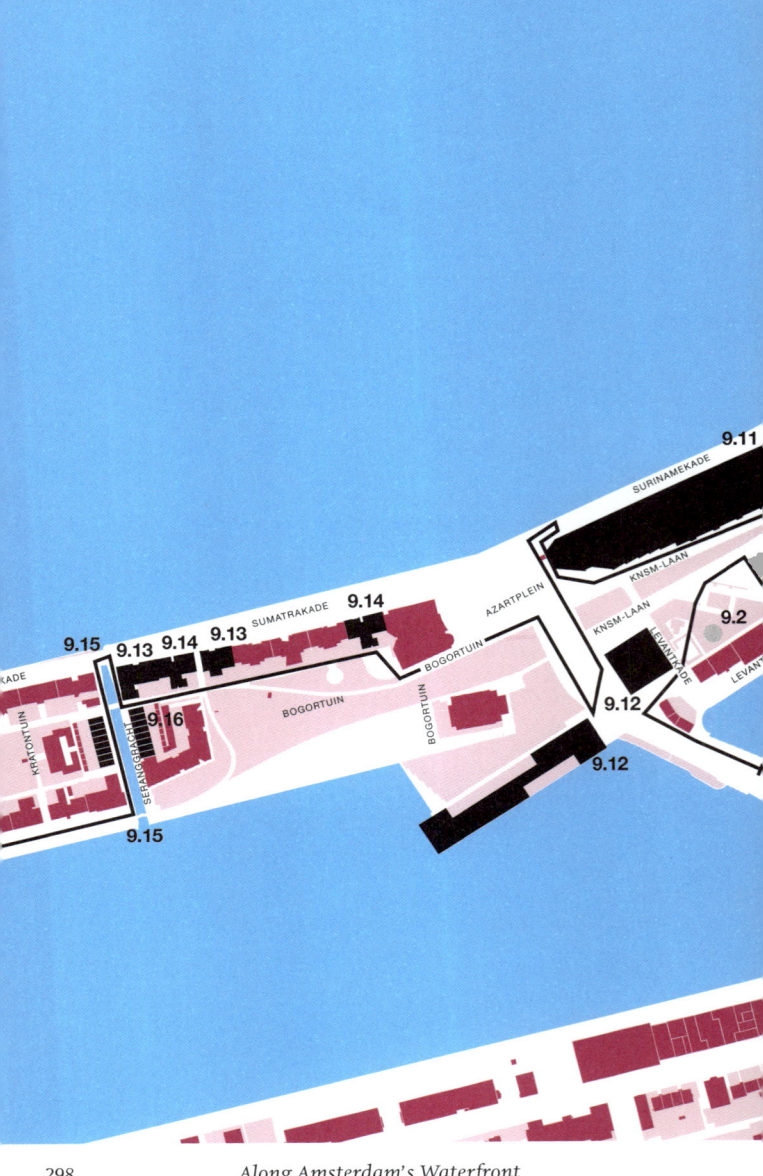

Along Amsterdam's Waterfront

Java-eiland, KNSM-eiland

9.18 9.15 SUMA
9.18 9.14
TOSARITUIN
9.17 BRANTASGRACHT
TOSARISTRAAT 9.14
9.13 9.13
JAVAKADE 9.15
SUMATRAKADE 9.13
9.19

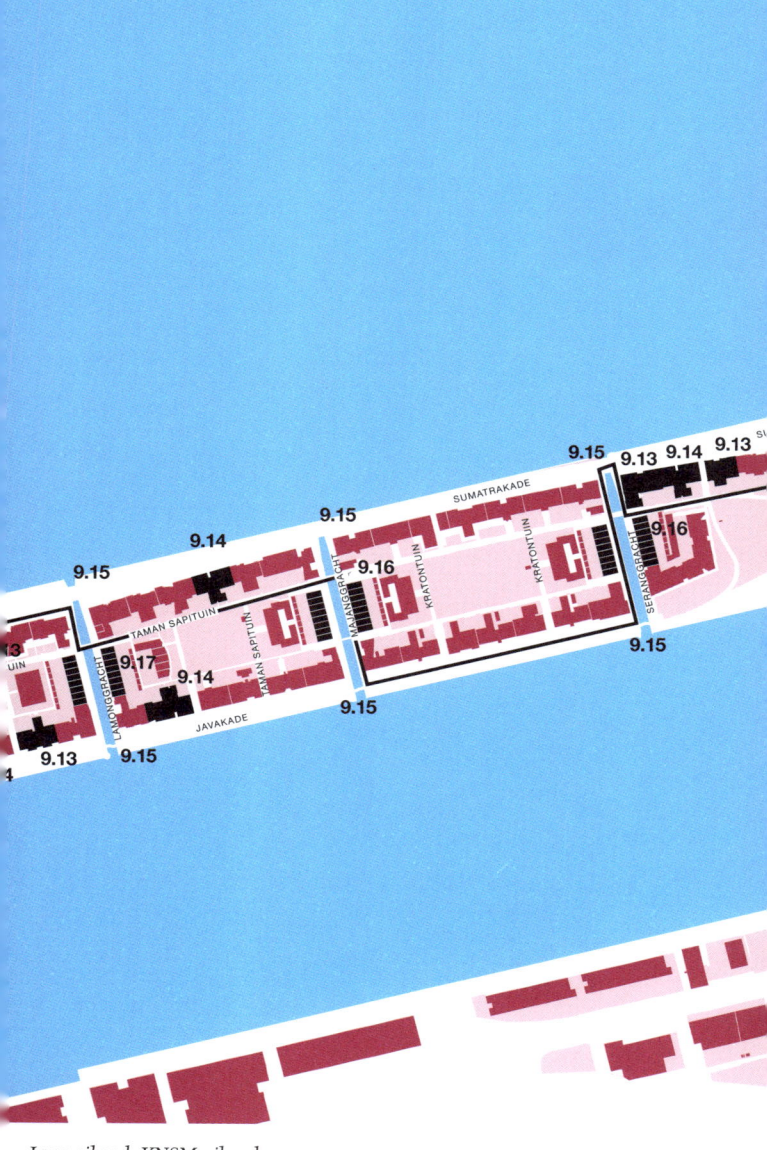

9.15

9.13 9.14 9.13 SU

9.15

SUMATRAKADE

9.15

9.14

9.16

KRATONTUIN

KRATONTUIN

9.16

9.15

TAMAN SAPITUIN

TAMAN SAPITUIN

MANGGRACHT

SERANGGRACHT

9.15

9.17

9.14

LAMONGGRACHT

9.15

JAVAKADE

9.13

9.15

Java-eiland, KNSM-eiland

9.1	Verbindingsdam (1997)	**Architect** Hans van Heeswijk architecten	**Commisioned by** Dienst IVV

The name Verbindingsdam (connecting dam) goes back to when the link between the KNSM Island and the Java Island was still a dam with a goods train line that connected the islands with the mainland. The old bridge that interrupted the dam had to be replaced to increase the traffic capacity in connection with the development of the former docklands into a commercial and residential area and to make the bridge suitable for trams. The oblique angle of the dam and bridge in relation to the river banks is a result of its previous use: the trains that travelled from Sporenburg to the Java Island were unable to negotiate a sharp bend. The possibility of straightening the connection from the Panamalaan was considered to facilitate the flow of traffic, but was turned down in the face of local protest.

The bridge, designed by Hans van Heeswijk, is very wide in relation to the span. That would have given it a relatively heavy appearance. That is why the surface of the bridge was divided into three separate, parallel sections to allow light to enter in between. The construction of the bridge is located in these voids and consists of two pairs of steel arches supported by seven transverse beams.

9.2	Mien Ruys-plantsoen (1956/1995)	**Architect** Mien Ruys	**Commisioned by** KNSM

The landscape architect Mien Ruys designed an elongated park on the south side of the peninsula for the KNSM in the 1950s. It was a park where personnel and passengers who were saying farewell could take a stroll. The design is characterised by a diagonal play of lines that broke up the elongated shapes of the buildings, and is typical of Ruys' work of the period. She often worked with architects from the New Building movement at the time and tried to find an answer to the rectangular plots that were so common in the architecture of the postwar reconstruction period. Her nickname then was Schuine Mien (Diagonal Mien).

With the development of the KNSM Island in the 1990s, only a small part of the park was left. Mien Ruys, who had reached the age of 89 by then, was invited by the supervisor to come up with a new design. Only the diagonal pond could be preserved, and that determined the line of the new design. A few of the large trees from the original design could be incorporated in the new one. Diagonal pedestrian routes connect roads and paths logically with one another. The park is connected with the enclosed garden of the Piraeus block by means of an opening with a colonnade.

Arno van der Mark has put a work of art, Passages, in the colonnade on the west wide of the Piraeus building. In consultation with the architect, the artist added twelve columns to the existing twelve supporting columns. Pentagonal corbels were applied to the joins between the column sections, and silk screen prints of photographs combined with fragments of the ground plan of Paris were attached to them. Just as Kollhoff respects the past of the site by leaving the KNSM office and waterfront park of Mien Ruys as they were, so Van der Mark refers to the history of a location, though an arbitrary one in this case. He has chosen the medium of photography as a symbol for looking back on the past.

9.3 Piraeus (1994)

KNSM-laan 204-610,
Levantkade 51-149,
Piraeusplein 2-32,
1-75

Architect
Hans Kollhoff,
with
Christian Rapp

Commisioned by
De Doelen

The Piraeus block by the Berlin architect Hans
Kollhoff is the most eye-catching of all the projects
on the KNSM Island. The sculptural form clad with
dark-brown brick towers above the waterfront.
This was the first building to be completed on the
KNSM Island and has had a strong influence on
the architectural debate on large-scale housing.
More than 300 apartments have been distributed
among the four to eight storeys. Most of them
are rented council flats, while a couple of large
patio apartments have been placed under the
roof. Because the former KNSM administration
and mustering building had been rescued thanks
to the dedication of the squatters, the Piraeus
has been folded around the old building, as it
were. The tips enclose two inner courtyards.
This unusual shape serves to temper the large
dimensions.
The south side is characterised by the steel frames
that have been placed between the brickwork
without any recessing, giving the façade a flat
and sober look. The folding windows can be

completely opened so that the verandah can be used both as a winter garden and as a balcony. The actual façade of the apartment is thus some distance behind it.

The sloping roof of the complex is covered entirely with aluminium, as can be clearly seen from a distance.

KNSM Canteen	**Architect**	**Commisioned by**	9.4
(1962/1991)	CASA achitecten	Stichting Edelweis	
Levantplein 1-15			

The former canteen building, which rests on columns, was built for the KNSM dockers. Soon after it fell into disuse in the 1980s it was squatted by artists. In consultation with the local authority, the building changed hands for the symbolic price of one guilder, and agreement was reached on the renovation, which left the interiors of the studio apartments as the occupants had arranged them intact. However, the building application was turned down because the building was only accessible on one side and therefore failed to comply with fire safety regulations. The entire initiative was on the point of being dropped when at the last moment ship's staircases found on a demolition site happened to become available and provided each apartment with its own access. The artists were not allowed to sell their homes for ten years. By now a number of the very spacious apartments have been put on the market and sold for astronomical sums.

The organisation of the public space was specially designed for the KNSM Island by the Environmental Planning Department. On the sunny Levantkade, where the landing stages for the boats are situated, the quay has been paved with yellow cobbles, while Stelcon plates have been recycled for the Sumatrakade on the north. The same rust-brown material has been used around the Piraeus as an allusion to its maritime past. The KNSM-laan has a more elegant character because of the row of trees on either side of the street. The paving is of Belgian hard stone. In front of the Canteen is the Waterstoep, a square that slopes down to the water and is primarily a place for children to play.

9.5 **Barcelonaplein**
(1993)
Levantkade 169-
263, Barcelona-
plein 1-177, 2-180,
KNSM-laan 612-754

Architect
Bruno Albert

Commisioned by
Het Oosten

The greatest stylistic differences in the choice
of the architects for the KNSM Island can
be seen if the Piraeus is compared with the
Barcelonaplein. In spite of the fact that they
are both housing blocks of large proportions,
the project of the Belgian architect Bruno
Albert has a clear Neo-Classical look about it.
Two seven-storey semicircles encircle a public
square. Two five-storey U-shaped sections meet
the convex sides of the semicircles, with which
they enclose two private inner courtyards.
A total of 321 apartments of various types
have been distributed over the whole block.
They are rented council flats, ranging from
one-room to six-room apartments, group
apartments, and apartments for wheelchair
users.
The small semicircular balconies in front of all
the windows overlooking the square and the

layered alternation of dark and white brick
also bring about a distortion of scale. On the
level of the square the palazzo seems at first
sight to be very spacious, but the height of the
balcony fencing betrays the low ceilings of the
apartments. In this respect the complex recalls
the architecture of the Barcelona architect
Ricardo Bofill, who made a name for himself
with his Neo-Classical council flat complexes
in the suburbs of Paris at the beginning of
the 1980s. The name of the square is an
allusion to the line that the KNSM ran to the
Catalonian capital.

Fence (1993)	**Artist**	**Commisioned by**	**9.6**
Barcelonaplein	Narcisse Tordoir	Eastern Harbour Area Art Committee	

The Belgian artist Narcisse Tordoir has placed
a work of art at the southern entrance to the
circular Barcelonaplein. It has the form of a
monumental fence that follows the curve of
the building.
Tordoir combines small, usually painted
little panels in his work to form ensembles.
His idiom is one of simple forms: geometric
figures, pictograms and the contours of
figurative motifs. Each form is shown on its
own pictorial surface or panel next to the
others. The fence on the Barcelonaplein follows
the same procedure. It is subdivided into
squares of 3.3 by 3.3 metres; the steel contours
in each square can be read as scenes from
a crudely drawn figurative comic strip. The
rectangular grid, the artist states, is at the same
time a reaction to the rhythmic architecture of
Bruno Albert.

9.7	**Emerald Empire** (1996) Venetiëhof 1-224	**Architect** Jo Coenen & Co Architekten	**Commisioned by** Verwelius

While Jo Coenen drew up the master plan for the KNSM Island and supervised the architecture, he himself designed a superblock on the most striking location at the eastern tip of the island as a monumental conclusion to the KNSM-laan. The contrast between the spaciousness of the surroundings and use of inner courtyards to create a sense of being closed, which runs through the whole of the master plan, finds very literal expression here in this cylindrical block with ground plans that fan out.

The 206 three-room apartments and 18 four-room apartments, distributed over eight storeys and available to owner occupiers, are almost all of the same type. Each apartment has a balcony over the whole width of the apartment with a view of the water. The deeply framed balconies in a varied rhythm give the façade a lot of expression. Access to apartments from the protected inner courtyard is via a gallery.

9.8	**Villas** (1998) Venetiëstraat 26-78	**Architect** Jo Coenen & Co Architekten	**Commisioned by** Eurowoningen

'Like a pearl necklace' around the Emerald Empire, Jo Coenen designed seven semi-detached homes and, on a lower level, thirteen riverside homes. In fact this row of villas with private ground for parking is in complete contrast to the master plan, which is based on medium-height superblocks. The villas are designed in a rectangular functionalist style and are plastered in light grey. Access to the riverside homes is on the street side. They have a narrow terrace directly beside the water.

Socrates, Pericles, Archimedes and Diogenes (1994) KNSM-laan 527-891

Architect
Frank and Paul Wintermans

Commisioned by
Eurowoningen

9.9

The tricky part about designing on this shallow and elongated plot was that the best view is to the north, while the sun is in the south. This is reflected in the external appearance of the four apartment blocks in a flat façade facing the windy Surinamekade, three of them in light concrete. The horizontally articulated red brick façade on the KNSM-laan side shows more differentiation, with internal balconies, a recessed top floor with roof terraces, and overhanging balconies on the side blocks. The orientation problem has been solved in the ground plans by opting for maisonettes with one and a half floors. The living area extends from the front to the back wall, while the bedroom and other rooms are situated on a (higher or lower) half floor.

9.10 Skydome (1996)
KNSM-laan 327-525

Architect
Wiel Arets
Architects

Commisioned by
Wilma Bouw

The sixty-metre Skydome tower block is one of the tallest blocks of apartments in Amsterdam. The façade consists of dark-grey concrete elements with a relief, giving it the appearance of natural stone. The building has a rather monotonous look because of the regular distribution of the windows and balconies and the fact that only one colour has been used. It functions as a landmark for the island when seen from a distance and it is not for nothing that it has earned the nickname The Black Madonna. The 100 owner occupied three-room and four-room apartments are distributed over twenty-one floors. The apartments on the north side have a side balcony so that all of the residents can enjoy the sun.

9.11 Loods 6
(1900/1956/1997)
KNSM-laan 311

Architect
Jan Tienhoven/
Villanova
architecten

Commisioned by
KNSM/ Stichting
Kunstwerk Loods 6

Loods 6 (Shed 6), which is now a business complex, was built at the beginning of 1900 by the Koninklijke Nederlandsche Stoomboot Maatschappij as a transshipment and customs shed. In the mid-1950s the shipping architect Jan Tienhoven was commissioned to turn part of the building into a passenger terminal. The Baggage Hall is situated on the ground floor, but the most striking is the authentic Compass Hall on the first floor with a wide balcony overlooking the IJ. This was used at the time as the departure hall for first-class passengers with the KNSM. A number of artists worked on the decoration of the hall and entrance. The interior contains a mural by Cuno van den Steene and a glass wall by Lex Horn. There are two mosaics by Dick ten Hoedt, representing 'The Leave-taking' and 'The Family' in the vestibule on the ground floor.

At the moment the Compass Hall is a café-restaurant which can be hired for special occasions. A.H.O.Y., an information centre on the history and new buildings of the Eastern Harbour Area, is located on the ground floor. The complex was renovated for a second time in 1997, when Villanova architecten wrapped the entire façade in insulating plaster. The identity of the original waterfront shed has been preserved by leaving the grid of columns and beams visible. A new verandah-like extension has been added on the west side to improve the presentation of the side of the building facing the Java Island.

The interior was left without any internal divisions, leaving the concrete columns to determine the layout. A galvanised steel staircase determines the look of the main entrance. The office spaces are let to firms of architects, advertising agencies, and other professions in the creative sector. The ground floor is mainly occupied by interior and fashion shops.

There is an original red dockside crane from 1957, a Figee crane, on the Sumatrakade behind Loods 6. There are plans to create a one-person hotel in it with a hotel 'suite' on three levels. The crane itself is being restored, and the additional function will affect the appearance of the crane as little as possible.

Java-eiland, KNSM-eiland

9.12 Hoogwerf and Hoogkade (2001)
Azartplein 2-16,
KNSM-laan 2-98,
Bogortuin 3-255

Architect
Diener & Diener
Architekten

Commisioned by
Amstelland Vast-
goed

*Unlike the KNSM Island,
hardly any of the original
buildings have been
preserved on the Java
Island. The only one left
is the Samenwerkende
Havenbedrijven building
from 1918 on what is now
Azartplein 1-47. Squat-
ters and the De Doelen
housing corporation have
elaborated a plan to turn
it into 21 housing units
(some with studio) and
business units.
Another existing building
that was integrated in the
planning was the canteen*

The two large monotonous apartment blocks
– one elongated, the other square – in red-brown
brick with identical windows, that stand on either
side of the Verbindingsdam, form the transition
from the KNSM Island to the Java Island. The idea
for a transitional block of this kind was already
fixed at an early stage of the planning. In 1995
the local authority commissioned a couple of
big firms of architects with an international
reputation to carry out a multiple investigation
of the possibilities, and the design by Diener &
Diener Architekten was the successful one.
The Hoogkade block on the side of the Java Island
is an elongated block of 127 apartments. It stands
partly in the water on newly raised ground in the
angle between the island and the dam. There is
a large parking facility in the basement that also
caters for the residents of the other block. The

Along Amsterdam's Waterfront

entrance is behind a long wall to protect it from the cold north side adjoining the Azartplein. The Hoogwerf block has 45 apartments and business units. It borders on the Mien Ruysplantsoen. Access to the apartment is by means of a gallery around a closed inner courtyard, which can be reached by two lifts. An unusual feature of the ground plans of Hoogwerf is that the rooms, usually three, are of the same size. This means that the apartment can be divided up in a variety of ways, for example for duo housing, or a combination of private and work space.

of the Cornelder stevedores company further along the Javakade, better known as the squatters' restaurant Einde van de Wereld, serving cheap and healthy fixed menus on long tables. Although it is not common for buildings to have to be completely demolished because of the polluted ground beneath them, the Einde van de Wereld could not be saved and the plot has been thoroughly cleansed.

Apartment blocks	Architect	Commisioned by	9.13
(1997) Sumatrakade 195-237, 285-325, 1157-1191, Javakade 516-542, 580-618 and 700-728	Sjoerd Soeters	BPF Bouw	

The most colourful blocks on the Java Island were designed by Sjoerd Soeters, author of the master plan and supervisor. The flat façades on the Sumatrakade catch the eye with their green, pink, yellow, purple, orange, blue, turquoise and red corrugated spandrels.

On the Javakade the blocks are different in character: a steel grid affords a view of the façade in white plastic panels. Large entrances clad with red sheeting give access to and a view of the inner courtyards, or even from one side of the island to the other. Soeters himself designed another block of apartments on the Java Island, on the corner of the Sumatrakade and the Lamonggracht, but that is relatively inconspicuously finished with prefab concrete panels clad with red-brown tiles.

9.14 Apartment blocks
(1997)
Sumatrakade
13-51, 241-279, 853-
891, 1249-1293
Imogirituin 1-55,
Javakade 364-398,
544-578, 664-698

Architect
Cruz y Ortiz

Commisioned by
SFB, BPF Bouw

Huibert Groenendijk, whose designs include the Maxi-Cosi, designed the transformer houses that stand in the five courtyards. He described the buildings clad with black and white ribbed material as 'Roman Catholic chapels from which the blessings of modern technology are distributed'.

The firm of the Spanish architects Antonio Cruz and Antonio Ortiz is responsible for the current renovation and extension of the Rijksmuseum in Amsterdam, but they have worked in Amsterdam before. On the Java Island they designed two free-standing buildings with one-family homes on the central area and six blocks with different types of apartment on the waterfronts, distributed among the five courtyards into which the island has been divided.

The basic design for all the blocks consists of prefab façade elements of yellow-orange brick with a minimal width of joint, interrupted by windows with cream-coloured wooden panels on either side. The window openings and loggias are cut out of the façade as continuous horizontal strips. The blocks designed by the Spanish duo are the most sober in appearance among the multi-coloured buildings of the Java Island.

9.15 Bridges
(2000)
Java-eiland

Architect
Paul Wintermans,
G. Rombouts,
M. Droste

Commisioned by
Gemeentelijk
Grondbedrijf
Amsterdam

The whimsical and amusing black ironwork bridges for pedestrians and cyclists over the canals and along the south waterfront are all different. They were designed by the Belgian artistic duo Rombouts-Droste. They devised an alphabet of their own consisting of words with an emotional association that they incorporated in the bridge, although it is not really possible

Along Amsterdam's Waterfront

for the unsuspecting visitor to recognise them. The bridge covered with curved arches is a reference to the word 'idea', and the steep bridge with steps represents the word 'light'. Other words with associations that they have applied are 'art', 'society', 'image', and 'science'. The opposite of these light-hearted bridges are the much more sober ones clad in brick for motorised traffic on the north side of the canals, designed by Paul Wintermans.

| **Java canal houses** (2000) Seranggracht 1-15, 4-18, Majanggracht 3-18 | **Architect** Babet Gakis, Bjarne Mastenbroek, Dick van Gameren, D. de Meijer, R. Onsia, W.H. Schenk, ROW Architectuur, Marx & Steketee architecten, Onix Architekten | **Commissioned by** Moes Bouwbedrijf | **9.16** |

9.17 Java canal houses
(1998–2000)
Lamonggracht 3-17,
6-20,
Brantasgracht 7-21,
2-16

Architect
John Bosch,
Dana Ponec,
Architectenbureau
Marlies Rohmer,
Architectenbureau
Art Zaaijer, Jos van
Eldonk, C. Heuff,
René van Zuuk
Architekten,
M. De Maeseneer,
G. Kruunenberg

Commisioned by
SFB, BPF Bouw

Various young architects, and in some cases the younger partners of large firms of architects, were invited to design the canal houses beside the four newly created canals. Each of them designed a house that is repeated several times in a different sequence each time. As a result, no canal is exactly the same as another. The width of the building plot is only 4.5 metres, but the architects were free to use their imagination on it.

The canalside buildings appeared in two stages. The first batch, beside the Brantasgracht and Lamonggracht, is more extravagant in design than the second batch, beside the Majanggracht and the Seranggracht, where the façades are somewhat stricter and have less protruding elements. Eye-catchers from the first batch are the verandahs framed with planks and set at an angle by Dana Ponec, the sloping zinc façade clad with slate by Jos van Eldonk, and the wide concrete frames of the windows in the houses designed by Marlies Rohmer. The façades by Art Zaaijer are high tech with glass, aluminium and iron.

The outstanding designs from the second batch are the severe details of the windows by Bjarne Mastenbroek, ROW Architectuur and Dick van Gameren. Onix designed façades with wide black planks on the level of the topmost storeys which refer to the wooden façades of houses in the polders of North Holland. Marx & Steketee used copper and zinc as façade cladding to

reinforce the diversity in the façades of the
canal even more.

The ground plans also betray the search for
innovative solutions, for example in the way
in which the staircase is placed in front, in the
middle or at the rear of the apartment. Almost
all of the apartments have a balcony, roof
terrace or small patio.

There is no comparison with the canals in the
historic city centre, because some of the houses
there were built centuries before others. But
the variegated whole of the buildings alongside
the canals of the Java Island gives a good
impression of the Postmodern architectural
idiom of the late 1990s.

Amicitia, Concor-
dia, Hollandia,
Olympia (1997)
Sumatrakade 1297-
1341, 1391-1433,
1483-1537,
Tosaristraat 5-31

Architect
Karelse van der
Meer Architecten

Commisioned by
Moes Bouwbedrijf

9.18

The idea of the master plan was for the Java Island
to evoke an image reminiscent of the canals in
the historic centre of Amsterdam: each building
resembles its neighbours in terms of size, details
and colour, but if you look closely you can see
that the details are different. Karelse van der Meer
Architecten tackled their assignment in the same
spirit. Setting out from the same basic principle,
they gave the four nine-storey blocks a character
of their own through differences in orientation,
use of colour, and the design of the entrances.
The façades facing the waterfront refer to old
warehouses with high windows and French
balconies in a masonry façade. The south façade
facing the inner courtyard has been kept as open
as possible and is characterised by large balconies
and wide window strips. Most of the apartments
have a view of both the water and the inner
courtyard, so that the two different atmospheres
can be clearly distinguished. There are business
units on the ground floor.

Java-eiland, KNSM-eiland

The Batavia and Hispania blocks in the same row and commissioned by the same client also have nine storeys. Batavia (Sumatrakade 1343-1389) was designed by Cees Nagelkerke; Hispania (Sumatrakade 1435-1481) was designed by baneke, van der hoeven architekten. Nagelkerke's façade emphasises the vertical dimension by making the brick window piers stand out sharply between the large window strips, alternating with light-beige sheeting. baneke, van der hoeven designed a large window strip that protrudes slightly from the façade. The topmost storeys consist of apartments with a glass skylight over two floors on the side facing the IJ. These apartments also have a roof terrace with a view of the city on the south side.

Tip of Java Island

At the tip of the Java Island stands the monument *Mariner on the Lookout*. The labrador granite statue, made by Pieter Starreveld in 1950, symbolises the mariner who, dressed in oilskins and sou'wester with his hand above his eyes, peers in the direction of the North Sea Canal as he awaits the arrival of those on board one of the Stoomvaart Maatschappij Nederland steamers.

Otherwise the site has not yet been built up. This western tip was deliberately left indeterminate in the master plan. There were plenty of wild plans, but it was decided to leave this spectacular location for a while until an appropriate metropolitan function should arrive. In the meantime the empty site is used as a site for festivals, a skating alley, and a parking place for buses. On the site which was once reserved for a hotel there is now a colourful temporary school: the primary school de Kleine Kapitein (The Little Captain). The district authority has given the school permission for more permanent premises on the same site, provisionally for fifteen years. Architectenbureau SeARCH has been approached for the design.

Along Amsterdam's Waterfront

The Jan Schaeferbrug has been constructed to optimise access to and from the 1,200 metre long Java Island. The position of the bridge was determined by the circulation of traffic on the city side. That it why it was decided to make the link over the water connect with the Kattenburgerstraat. As a result, the bridge had to go right through the De Zwijger warehouse. Contrary to what was originally supposed, the foundations of the warehouse were not too weak for the construction.

The local authority held a closed competition among three firms of architects for the definitive design of a bridge which would occupy such a prominent place in its surroundings. The winning design was by Ton Venhoeven. The bridge had to have components that could be dismantled to allow large sailing vessels to pass during the SAIL festival, which is held once every five years. Each of the two removable parts weighs 200 tons. Pedestrians, cyclists and motorised traffic enter the bridge from separate access ramps, but meet one another on the bridge. The construction is very flat and almost without vertical elements. High tech materials were used, and the Jan Schaefer bridge has earned itself the nickname The Lizard.

The Jan Schaefer bridge is named after the leader of the Partij van de Arbeid (PvdA) in Amsterdam, who was a councillor (including Urban Renewal) from 1978 to 1982. Building activity had more or less come to a standstill just before his period of office, and only a few hundred homes were still built. Four years later more than 8,000 had been built in one year. He is famous for the immortal words: 'You can't live in bullshit'.

Along Amsterdam's Waterfront

Construction on the Oosterdokseiland

THE IJ: MOTORWAY FOR SHIP- PING AND TRADE

Aart Hiemstra

Building on the banks of the main waterway

People are instinctively drawn to water and have a strong desire to build as close as possible to – and preferably in – water. Amsterdam has in fact rediscovered the IJ as a nice place to be. So building is going on beside the IJ: the South Bank project extends along a large stretch of a main waterway through Amsterdam. Residents and users enjoy a view of the dynamism that the shipping and trade of a busy harbour bring with them, because that is what the IJ is: the motorway of our harbour.

Transport versus housing

Without exception, developments on the bank of the IJ have had a direct influence on the waterway, and vice versa shipping entails certain risks for the use of the bank. In short, there is a conflict on the waterline.
The water of the IJ and the adjacent harbour basins as a motorway is not the same thing as the water that estate agents try to sell in brochures which always have a beautiful yacht in the background. The water that flows through Amsterdam is also of great economic importance in the world of distribution and transport. Of the more than 75 million tonnes of goods that enter the port of Amsterdam by sea, 60 per cent find their way via the IJ to the hinterland, and vice versa. The IJ is part of the corridor that runs from the North Sea Canal via the IJ and Amsterdam to the Rhine Canal, an important artery to the hinterland of the Netherlands and Germany for Amsterdam, IJmuiden, Beverwijk and Zaanstad.

Pressure on the IJ

As a motorway, the water that flows through
Amsterdam – the fourth largest port in North-
West Europe – is of crucial importance for
the capital. Harbour trade is growing, the
ships are increasing in number and size. More
than 7,000 vessels entered the region of the
Amsterdam maritime docks in 2005. This calls
for appropriate quayside facilities and for more
space, supervision and assistance on the water.
More and more tourists are visiting Amsterdam
by cruiser. Not only the almost one hundred
ocean-going castles that moor at the impressive
Passenger Terminal Amsterdam, but also the
more than one thousand reservations for river
cruisers ensure a tremendous result and a great
added value for the city.

Safe nautical zone

If the IJ is a motorway, how can we organise
the hard shoulders and roadside safely? With
their ideas for the development of the river
banks, the planners are torn between the use
of the IJ for navigation – which calls for quays,
for instance – and the IJ as an attractive, robust
centre for housing, work and recreation. The
mayor and aldermen of Amsterdam already
drew up a zoning scheme for the South Bank
of the IJ in 1992. This Nautical Zone is a zone
on and beside the IJ and the North Sea Canal
within which dangerous materials can be
transported and outside which building can
take place. The Ministry of Transport and
Public Works is now engaged in constructing
a basic national network for the transport
of dangerous materials, so the mayor and
aldermen were a long way ahead of their time
in 1992.
The tip of the Java Island, for example, lies
directly on the transport axis and the risk zones
for the transport of dangerous materials run
partly over the river bank at this point, so that

the construction of housing there is ruled out. The Silodam apartments are further away from the route over the water, just outside the zone for dangerous materials, but there is still the risk of collisions, so an anti-collision barrier has been constructed in front of the Silodam.

Development

The plans for the South Bank strengthen the connection between the city and the water, a traditional link that distinguishes Amsterdam from other metropolises. It goes without saying that a choice between harbour and other activities has to be made all the time.
As Port of Amsterdam, we join in planning and developing the banks of the IJ on both sides of the water.
Whenever it comes to a choice between harbour and other activities, the principle is always that we want to do justice to the growth of the harbour and the importance of that for Amsterdam and the region. At the same time, we realise that everyone should be able to enjoy the panoramic view, the smell of the water, and the ships that continue to pass by.

References

- Abrahamse, Jaap Evert, et al. (2003), *Eastern Harbour District Amsterdam; Urbanism and Architecture*. Rotterdam: NAi Publishers
- Brunt, Lodewijk, et al (2002), *11ha; Het Stork-terrein in Amsterdam verkend door kunstenaars en onderzoekers*. Amsterdam: De Balie
- Exel, Irene van & Eireen Schreurs (2003), *Wonen in de Wolken; handboek woontorens in Amsterdam*. Amsterdam: Ontwikkelingsbedrijf Gemeente Amsterdam/Dienst Ruimtelijke Ordening (Amsterdam Development Corporation/ Spatial Planning Department)
- Haeck, Eveline (2006), *Inventarisatie bouwplannen zuidelijke ventweg De Ruijterkade*. Amsterdam: Projectbureau Zuidelijke IJoever (South Bank Development Corporation)
- Heijdra, Ton (1999), *Een roerig volkje; de geschiedenis van de Oostelijke Eilanden, Kadijken en Czaar Peterbuurt*. Alkmaar: René de Milliano
- Ibelings, Hans (1995), *20th Century Urban Design in the Netherlands*. Rotterdam: NAi Publishers
- Ibelings, Hans, Johanna Günther & Marieke van Giersbergen (2005), *Hans van Heeswijk: architectuur 1995–2005*. Tübingen/Berlin: Ernst Wasmuth Verlag
- Ibelings, Hans & Ton Verstegen (1998), *Westerpark; Architectuur in een Amsterdams stadsdeel 1990–1998*. Rotterdam: NAi Publishers
- Inbo Adviseurs Stedenbouwkundigen Architecten (2004), *Vitaal werkgebied aan het IJ*. Amsterdam: Gemeentelijk Havenbedrijf Amsterdam (Port of Amsterdam)
- Jansen, Ton, et al. (1999), *Wonen in een huis naar eigen ontwerp op Borneo-eiland*. Amsterdam: Stedelijke Woningdienst Amsterdam (Amsterdam Municipal Housing Agency), ProjectManagementBureau, dienst Ruimtelijke Ordening (Spatial Planning Department), Grondbedrijf van de Gemeente Amsterdam (Amsterdam Local Authority Development Department)
- Lebesque, Sabine & Leo Platvoet (2001), *Stappen door de Nieuwe Stad; Tochten langs de jongste woningbouw in de Binnenstad van Amsterdam*. Amsterdam: De Balie
- Lubbers, Annette (2004), *Lloyd Hotel*. Amsterdam: Bas Lubberhuizen

- Mak, Geert (1992), *De engel van Amsterdam*. Amsterdam/ Antwerpen: Atlas
- Mak, Geert (1995), *Een kleine geschiedenis van Amsterdam*. Amsterdam/Antwerpen: Atlas.
- OKRA Landschapsarchitecten bv (2006), *Beeldkwaliteitsplan Amsterdam Minerva Waterfront*. Utrecht: Port of Amsterdam, Projectgroep Minervahaven (Project Group Minervahaven)
- Ontwikkelingsbedrijf Gemeente Amsterdam (Voorheen Stedelijke Woningdienst Amsterdam en Bouw- en Woningdienst Amsterdam) (Amsterdam Development Corporation (formerly the Amsterdam Municipal Housing Agency and Amsterdam Development and Housing Department) (1990–2005), *Projectdocumentatie*. Amsterdam: Gemeente Amsterdam (Amsterdam Local Authority)
- Platvoet, Leo (2003), *Stappen door de Nieuwe Stad; Tochten langs de jongste woningbouw in het Oostelijk Havengebied van Amsterdam*. Amsterdam: De Balie
- Projectbureau Zuidelijke IJoever (2005), *In Uitvoering*. Amsterdam: Projectbureau Zuidelijke IJoever (South Bank Development Corporation)
- Projectgroep Oostelijke Binnenstad (Project Group Eastern City Centre) & Woningbouwvereniging Eigen Haard(Eigen Haard Housing Corporation) (1991), *Nieuwbouw op Wittenburg-Noord*. Amsterdam: Bouw- en Woningdienst Amsterdam, afdeling Binnenstad (Amsterdam Development and Housing Department, City Centre Department)
- Vermaas, Ine (2006), *Tot ziens op Kattenburg*. Amsterdam: Wijkcentrum Oostelijke Binnenstad
- Vermeer, Gerrit & Ben Rebel (1992), *d'Ailly's Historische Gids van Amsterdam*. The Hague: Sdu Uitgeverij
- Vermeer, Gerrit & Ben Rebel (2004), *Historische gids van Amsterdam; de 17de-eeuwse stadsuitleg*. Amsterdam: Amsterdam Publishers

Websites

- Amsterdam 'Breeding Ground':
  www.broedplaatsamsterdam.nl
- Amsterdam Centre for Architecture:
  www.arcam.nl
- Amsterdam Federation of Housing
  Associations: *www.afwc.nl*
- Amsterdam Local Authority: *www.amsterdam.nl*
- Architects Web: *www.architectenweb.nl*
- Archive of the Squatters' and Activists'
  Movement in the Netherlands:
  http://iisg.nl/~staatsarchief/
- Building Regulations Committee:
  www.welstand.amsterdam.nl
- Eastern Harbour Area:
  www.oostelijkhavengebied.nl
- Friends of the Amsterdam City Centre:
  www.amsterdamsebinnenstad.nl
- Funenpark: *www.funen-park.nl*
- Het Funen: *www.funen.nl*
- Het Stenen Hoofd Foundation:
  www.stenenhoofd.nl
- IJ side Stationseiland: *www.ijsei.amsterdam.nl*
- La Grande Cour: *www.lagrandecour.nl*
- De Loodsen: *www.deloodsen.nl*
- Ministry of Transport, Public Works and
  Watermanagement: *www.verkeerenwaterstaat.nl*
- Municipal Department for the Preservation
  and Restoration of Monuments and Sites:
  www.bma.amsterdam.nl
- Netherlands Architecture Institute: *www.nai.nl*
- Oosterdokseiland: *www.oosterdokseiland.nl*
- Port of Amsterdam: *www.portofamsterdam.nl*
- Het Parool: *www.parool.nl*
- Passenger Terminal Amsterdam: *www.pta.nl*
- Silodam Home Owners Association:
  www.silodam.org
- Skyscraper City: *www.skyscrapercity.com*
- Spatial Planning Department:
  www.dro.amsterdam.nl
- Stadsdeel Centrum: *www.centrum.amsterdam.nl*

- Stadsdeel Westerpark:
  www.westerpark.amsterdam.nl
- Stadsdeel Zeeburg: *www.zeeburg.amsterdam.nl*
- Stationseiland: *www.stationseiland.amsterdam.nl*
- Het Veem: *www.veem.nl*
- Vierwindenhuis: *www.vierwindenhuis.nl*
- Website IJ Banks: *www.ijoevers.nl*
- Website NRC Handelsblad: *www.nrc.nl*
- Westerdokseiland: *www.westerdokseiland.nl*
- Wikipedia: *www.nl.wikipedia.org*

On the authors

Yolanda Backer (Paramaribo, 1955) graduated in art history (specialising in the history of architecture) from the University of Amsterdam in 1989. Since 1990 she has been working for the ProjectManagementBureau (PMB) of Amsterdam Local Authority. The projects on which she has worked during that period include the North-South Line, IJburg, and the South Bank of the IJ.

Daphna Beerdsen (Alkmaar, 1983) obtained her bachelor's degree in Planning Studies from the University of Amsterdam and is currently studying Comparative Urban Studies at the University of Urbino, Italy. She helped to edit Project Documentation 2004–2005 on the housing plans of the Amsterdam Local Authority.

Yttje Feddes (Amsterdam, 1953) is a landscape architect and partner in the firm of Feddes/Olthof landscape architects. In the Amsterdam region she recently worked on plans for the Defence of Amsterdam and the Sloterplas area, as well as carrying out research on the spatial significance of the southern dykes of the IJ (with the historical geographer Marinus Kooiman) for the Environmental Planning department of the Amsterdam Local Authority.

Aart Hiemstra (Bussum, 1955) completed his training at the Higher School of Navigation and went on to sail for the Amsterdam shipping company Vinke & Co and others. Since 1982 he has been working in the Dangerous Materials department of the Amsterdam Municipal Harbour Authority. As deputy harbour master of the Port of Amsterdam, he is currently concerned with all nautical developments and is in this capacity is involved with the formulation of plans for the banks of the IJ.

Maarten Kloos (Haarlem, 1947) is co-founder and director of ARCAM (Architecture Centre

Amsterdam), where he has organised many debates and exhibitions on developments in the Amsterdam region. He has taught in various institutions, including the Technical University Delft and the Amsterdam Academy of Architecture, and has written many articles in Dutch and foreign periodicals, such as *wonen-TA/BK, Archis, L'Architecture d'Aujourd'hui, Werk and Bauen + Wohnen*. His books include *Le paradis terrestre de Picassiette* (1979), *Alexander Bodon, architect* (Rotterdam, 1990), *Schiphol Architecture* (1996) and *Godin van de Zuidas. De Minervalaan – as in tijd en ruimte* (1999).

Ernest Kurpershoek (The Hague, 1951) is a historian of art and architecture and has (co-)written many publications on Amsterdam, including *Het Grachtenboek* (1991/1992), *De Amsterdamse Haven 1275–2005* (2005) and *Amsterdam Verdedigd* (Open Monument Day 2004).

Sabine Lebesque (Amsterdam, 1965) is a historian of architecture and consultant for the Amsterdam Development Corporation (OGA). In this capacity she has worked on Project Documentation and the Zuiderkerk Award, the series *Stappen door de nieuwe stad, tochten langs de jonste woningbouw* (2001), excursions abroad, the building inspectorate, and the TV programme *Aanbouw* (AT5). From 1991 to 2000 she worked at the Netherlands Architecture Institute in Rotterdam, where she was responsible for several projects, including the publication and exhibition *Yona Friedman, structures serving the unpredictable* (1998).

Merel Ligtelijn (Vlaardingen, 1958) studied social geography at the University of Amsterdam and now works as a freelance writer, editor and researcher. She wrote *De Parken van Amsterdam* (2001) and *Het Beatrixpark. Kroniek van een Amsterdams stadspark* (2005) with Ernest Kurpershoek. She is currently working on the publication *Gebouw Felix Meritis, Spiegel* *van Amsterdam* and the project 'Amsterdam Ondergronds/Bovengronds'.

Marinus Oostenbrink (Amsterdam, 1943) has an independent consultancy as an architect and urban designer, with research and design in the spatial sector as the core of his activities. Oostenbrink has implemented projects in such fields as housing, education, urban design, the building inspectorate and architecture policy in Amsterdam, Utrecht, and Nieuwegein. He has contributed to the following publications: *Woonconcepten Amsterdam* (1991), *Kansen voor stad en markt* (1994), *De Schoonheid van Amsterdam* (1997), *Op Blote Voeten door het Huis* (1997), *Beeldbank Woonbeleving* (1998), *Atlas Gordel 20–40* (2000), *Actuele Architectuurstromingen* (2003) and *Woning + Stad* (2005).

Ingrid Oosterheerd (Marknesse, 1964) is a historian of architecture and works as an image editor, author, exhibition curator and producer for various architecture institutions and architects. She has contributed to the following publications: *The Artificial Landscape* (2000) and *Eastern Harbour District Amsterdam* (2003), and to the exhibitions 'Stadsplan Amsterdam' (2003), 'Stad aan het water' (2005) and 'Amsterdam Nieuw West' (2006) in the Zuiderkerk in Amsterdam. From 1992 to 2000 she was associated with the Netherlands Architecture Institute in Rotterdam.

Evert Verhagen (Veldhoven, 1955) is a project manager, whose fields of activity include urban renewal in Amsterdam. He was involved with the transformation of the Westergasfabriek, a project that won the Golden Pyramid Award 2004. He recently began his own company Creative Cities. Besides many articles on the Westergasfabriek project, he has also published *Van Bijlmermeer tot Amsterdam Zuidoost* (1988) and more recently *Creativity and the City* (with Simon Franke, 2005) and *Noorderpark Amsterdam* (with Aafke Post et al., 2005).

Index of persons and architects

Index of street names

Illustration credits

- **1.1, 1.3, 1.4, 1.5, 1.6, 1.8** Dedato Architecten
- **2.4 De Nieuwe Prins** – Zaanse Ontwikkelings-maatschappij BV
- **3.2 Kop van Diemenstraat** – Lumica 2006
- **3.9 Westerkaap I** – Hofmakerij VOF
- **3.10 Westerkaap II** – Hofmakerij VOF
- **3.11 VOC Cour** – Wodan CV
- **3.12 La Grande Cour** – City Cour Combination
- **3.14 Han Lammers bridge** – Jeroen Musch
- **3.16 Railway bridge 19S/Restaurant Open** – de Architekten Cie.
- **4.1 Central Station** – Benthem Crouwel Architekten
- **4.6 IJ hall** – Benthem Crouwel Architekten
- **4.7 Naco building** – Zwarts & Jansma Architecten
- **below 4.13 Haringpakkerstoren** – Paul van Well/Stadsherstel
- **5.1 Business premises underneath bridge 485** – Hans van Heeswijk Architecten
- **5.2 De Ruyter** – Bouwfonds MAB
- **5.6 Chocoladefabriek** – De Chocoladefabriek 2006
- **5.15 Oosterdokseiland car park** – Zwarts & Jansma Architecten
- **5.16 Post CS** – CIIID, commisioned by MAB Bouwfonds
- **5.17 The Blub** – CIIID, commisioned by MAB Bouwfonds
- **5.18 Amsterdam Conservatory** – CIIID, com-misioned by MAB Bouwfonds
- **5.19 OBA** – CIIID, commisioned by MAB Bouw-fonds
- **5.20 Housing ODE** – CIIID, commisioned by MAB Bouwfonds
- **5.21 Hotel and conference centre ODE** – CIIID, commisioned by MAB Bouwfonds
- **6.6 Royal Military Police District Building** – Wansleben-Architekten, Köln
- **6.21 N44** – Frantzen et al architecten

- **6.23 Syntax, Palatino, Bodoni** – Direct Wonen Nieuwbouw
- **7.7 Nieuw Europa** – Hans van Heeswijk architecten
- **7.12 Huys Afrika** – Heijmans Vastgoedontwikkeling BV
- **7.17 Chicago** – Ontwikkelingscombinatie Nieuw Amerika
- **7.19 Nieuw Argentinië** – Het Oosten Kristal
- **8.2 The Fountainhead** – DPI
- **8.24 Kopgebouw** – Bik + Mulder Architecten
- **8.25 De Nieuwe Vaart** – Borski Noordhoek Bleichrodt Architectuur
- **8.26 Cruquiuskwartier** – Dedato Architecten

With thanks to all the architects and clients for providing information and visual material

It was not possible to find all the copyright holders of the illustrations used. Interested parties are requested to contact the Amsterdam Development Corporation (OGA): www.oga.amsterdam.nl

Along Amsterdam's Waterfront

About this book

This architectural guide presents about 200
projects on the South Bank of the IJ. The
select-ed projects offer a cross-section in time
of the buildings related to the history of port
activities in Amsterdam and the reuse of the former docklands. The routes proceed from the
Minervahaven, where the transformation
recently began, via the Westelijke Eilanden
with the Westerdok, the Stationseiland, the
Oosterdok, the Oostelijke Eilanden and the Piet
Heinkade, to the almost completed Eastern
Harbour Area.
Of course, this is not a complete guide. Projects
that are characteristic of each area have been
chosen, with a mixture of housing, offices,
business units, catering, works of art, parks
and infrastructure. The emphasis is on the area
around the Central Station, where a large-
scale restructuring is going on which will give
this part of the city centre a completely new
function.

All of the illustrations which are underlined are
artist's impressions, sketches or photographs of
models of current or planned projects.

● Symbol for a future project

● Symbol for an artwork, boat, etc.

Colophon

Compilation: Sabine Lebesque, Amsterdam Development Corporation (OGA)
Co-compiler: Yolanda Backer, Project-ManagementBureau Amsterdam (PMB)
Assistant: Daphna Beerdsen
Authors: Sabine Lebesque, Daphna Beerdsen, Yttje Feddes, Aart Hiemstra, Maarten Kloos, Ernest Kurpershoek, Merel Ligtelijn, Marinus Oostenbrink, Ingrid Oosterheerd, Evert Verhagen
Copy editing: Els Brinkman, Marianne Lahr
Translation Dutch-English: Peter Mason
Film DVD: Jord den Hollander
Photography: Johan Olsthoorn, except page 20-21, 38-39, 44-45, 66-67, 72-73, 96-97, 102-103, 128-129, 134-135, 164-165, 170-171, 202-203, 208-209, 248-249, 254-255, 288-289, 294-295, 320-321, 333, 348: Lard Buurman
Production photography Johan Olsthoorn and DVD: Abdel Kwyasse, Amsterdam Development Corporation (OGA)
Cartography: Wibold Jongsma, Alfons Wezenberg, Amsterdam Development Corporation, De Designpolitie
Graphic design: De Designpolitie, Amsterdam
Production: Ingrid Oosterheerd, Astrid Vorstermans
Lithography and printing: Die Keure, Bruges
Publisher: Valiz, Amsterdam

With thanks to all the architects and clients for
providing information and visual material.

*Available in the Netherlands, Belgium and Luxemburg
through Centraal Boekhuis, Culemborg; Scholtens,
Sittard and Coen Sligting Bookimport, Amsterdam, NL,
sligting@xs4all.nl, fax +31-(0)20-6640047
Available in Europe (except Benelux, UK and Ireland),
Asia and Australia through Idea Books, Amsterdam,
NL, idea@ideabooks.nl, fax +31-20-6209299,
www.ideabooks.nl
Available in the United Kingdom and Ireland through
Art Data, London, UK, orders@artdata.co.uk,
fax +44-208-742 2319, www.artdata.co.uk
Available in the USA: DAP, New York, dap@dapinc.com,
fax (+1) 212-6279484, www.artbook.com
All other questions: please contact Valiz: astrid@valiz.nl*

Along Amsterdam's Waterfront:
ISBN-10: 90-78088-10-9
ISBN-13: 978-90-78088-10-3

Also available in Dutch: Langs het IJ:
ISBN-10: 90-78088-09-5
ISBN-13: 978-90-78088-09-7

NUR 648   *Printed and bound in Belgium*

www.valiz.nl
www.oga.amsterdam.nl
www.pmb.nl

**This publication was made possible through
the generous support of:**
Amsterdam Development Corporation (OGA)
ProjectManagementbureauAmsterdam (PMB)
Port of Amsterdam
Netherlands Architecture Fund